The Fleet that Jack Built

Nine Men who Made a Modern Navy

BY

WILLIAM JAMESON

REAR-ADMIRAL, KBE, CB

RUPERT HART-DAVIS
SOHO SQUARE LONDON
1962

Printed in Great Britain by Richard Clay and Company, Ltd.,
Bungay, Suffolk

To the memory of a great man

ADMIRAL OF THE FLEET

LORD FISHER OF KILVERSTONE

CONTENTS

ILLUSTRATIONS

MAPS

Drawn by K. C. Jordan

viii

ACKNOWLEDGMENTS

I AM most grateful to the following who have given me permission to quote from previously published work: Messrs John Murray for the *Memoirs of Sir Henry Keppel* by Sir Algernon West, the *Life of Admiral of the Fleet Sir Arthur Wilson* by Admiral Sir Edward Bradford and Admiral Sir Percy Scott's autobiography *Fifty Years in the Royal Navy*; Messrs Methuen & Co. Ltd for Admiral Lord Charles Beresford's *Memoirs*; Messrs Jonathan Cape, Ltd and Professor A. J. Marder for *Fear God and Dread Nought*, in which the letters of Admiral of the Fleet Lord Fisher are collected; Messrs Hodder and Stoughton, Ltd and the executors of Admiral Sir Reginald Bacon for the latter's biography *Lord Fisher of Kilverstone*; Messrs Cassell & Co. Ltd for the biography of Earl Jellicoe by the same author; Messrs Hodder and Stoughton, Ltd and Rear-Admiral W. S. Chalmers for the *Life and Letters of David Beatty*; Messrs Eyre and Spottiswoode, Ltd for *Naval Memoirs*; the University Press, Cambridge for *Amphibious Warfare and Combined Operations*, and Messrs George G. Harrap & Co. Ltd for *Adventures Ashore and Afloat*, all by Admiral of the Fleet Lord Keyes; and Odham's Press, Ltd for extracts from *The World Crisis* by the Rt Hon. Sir Winston S. Churchill.

Admiral Sir St John Tyrwhitt, C.B., D.S.O., D.S.C. lent me his father's letters and papers which were exceedingly valuable, and both he and his sisters Dame Mary Tyrwhitt D.B.E. and Mrs Lacey helped me with their recollections.

Admiral the Hon. Sir Reginald Plunkett-Ernle-Erle-Drax, K.C.B., D.S.O. gave me the idea for the book and he and a very large number of naval officers have searched their memories and papers on my behalf. The list would be such a long one that I hope they will accept these collective thanks for all they have done.

The excellent library of the Imperial War Museum was a mine of information and I am particularly grateful to the librarian, Miss R. E. Coombs and to Mr V. Rigby. I am also grateful to the Historical Section of the Admiralty, the Admiralty Library, the Admiralty Archivist, Lieut-Commander P. K. Kemp and Miss V. S. Heath. I have made considerable use of the resources of the London Library and of the Library and Documents Section of the National Maritime Museum, Greenwich, including the diaries of Admiral of the Fleet Sir Henry Keppel.

For permission to reproduce illustrations I am indebted to the late Sir St John Tyrwhitt, Bart., for the photograph of his father; to the Imperial War Museum for those facing pages 40, 41, 64, 168, 169, 208, 209 and 289; to the National Maritime Museum for those facing pages 18 and 19; to the National Portrait Gallery for those facing pages 92 and 144; and to the National Magazine Company for that facing page 144. De Laszlo's portrait of Lord Keyes is reproduced by kind permission of his son.

I want to express public thanks to my wife and daughter for their help and for checking manuscript and proofs and to Miss Margaret Dyson who did most of the typing.

Last, but certainly not least, I acknowledge the help and advice of Mr Richard Garnett of Rupert Hart-Davis Ltd. Writing a book is certainly a combined operation.

William Jameson

Ham
Wiltshire
1961

FOREWORD

THE intense naval activity of the Napoleonic Wars was followed by a long period of naval neglect. In 1820 only fourteen of our 105 ships of the line were in commission, and but two of them first-raters (104 to 120 guns). Even in frigates the position was little better, with thirty-two in commission out of 115. Britain's only substantial force was in so-called cruisers, mostly small vessels of less than 400 tons. With no other country threatening our command of the sea such a drastic reduction in naval strength was perhaps natural. A long period of colonial expansion was beginning which was sometimes upheld by warlike operations, but for many years there was little question of the Navy being called upon to fight a major action against a hostile fleet.

It was not until 1858 that the launching of the French battleship *La Gloire* sounded the alarm. The world's first ironclad, she was almost as revolutionary in her day as the atomic bomb in 1945. A Parliamentary Committee was instructed to report on the relative strength of the British and French Navies and the long process of changing from wood to iron and from sail to steam was reluctantly begun. But politicians were apathetic, the public uninformed; the Navy, reared in a splendid but partly out-of-date tradition, went on living on the glories of the past with too little thought of the future. A few officers pleaded for a stronger Fleet, but the Treasury was niggardly; what money was available was not always wisely allocated. In 1876 more was spent on hemp and canvas than on coal, and even the Russian war scare of 1872 caused but a ripple in the calm waters of neglect. Oscar Parkes has called the decade 1872–82 the "Dark Ages of the Victorian Navy." Naval starvation continued, but public opinion, aroused at last by the relative weakness of the Fleet, was beginning to stir. In 1884 a series of articles by W. T. Stead in the *Pall Mall Gazette* entitled

"The Truth about the Navy" caused so much alarm that a number of reforms—re-organisation of the Dockyards, partial mobilisations for annual manoeuvres and the setting up of a Naval Intelligence Department in the Admiralty to work out the effective strength of our own and opposing Navies—preceded the passing of the Naval Defence Act of 1889 which laid down a five-year programme for greatly enlarging the Fleet. It was the beginning of a naval renaissance which, with many setbacks, eventually produced the Grand Fleet of 1914.

For over a hundred years the British Navy fought no major battle at sea. It saw plenty of active service, fighting alone or with the Army in China, the Baltic, the Crimea, Egypt, the Sudan and South Africa, and in other minor wars. But it was fighting of a special kind—in which the personal qualities of officers and men, their courage, initiative and good discipline, were tested rather than the quality of ships and weapons or the ability of their crews to handle them against other ships of their kind. British command of the sea was never seriously challenged and many successful nineteenth-century naval officers went through life without giving much thought to the fundamental realities of the profession or troubling their heads about such matters as the design of their ships as *warships*, their fighting efficiency and their tactical employment in battle. The Navy had plenty of splendid seamen; capable, full of initiative and perfectly prepared to lay down their lives for their country. What it lacked was men of vision, looking to the future rather than the past.

For war is a serious business in which even the most zealous and courageous cannot succeed unless their weapons are up-to-date and properly used. Seamen are by nature conservative. The great majority are averse to change, particularly as they grow older and reach the positions of greatest power. Proper use was not being made of the very rapid technical advances which revolutionised material in the last half of the nineteenth century—long range, quick-firing guns, the torpedo; propelling machinery which made ships much faster and almost independent of the weather.

The lot of the reformer in a highly disciplined force is a hard one, requiring very unusual gifts backed by exceptional moral courage. Wilson, Scott, Beresford and, above all, Fisher were leaders of the men who shook and shocked the Navy out of its part-worn and sometimes even dangerous traditions and formed the Fleet with which men like Jellicoe, Beatty, Tyrwhitt and Keyes fought the 1914–18 war.

SOME IMPORTANT DATES

1868   Naval scare following launching of French ironclad *La Gloire*.

1878   Russian war scare.

1882   Bombardment of Alexandria.

1884   Murder of Gordon at Khartoum.

1884   Public uneasiness about Britain's naval strength. "The Truth about the Navy" articles appear.

1889   Naval Defence Act passed.

1896–1898   The River War (Battle of Omdurman 1898).

1898   First German Navy Act passed.

1899   Boer War. Big German naval building programme instituted.

1900   Boxer Rising.

1914   The Outbreak of the First World War.

1918   Surrender of the German Fleet.

PART ONE

The Forerunners

HARRY KEPPEL
1809-1904

The Mid-Nineteenth-Century Sailor

"If I want a thing done well in a distant part of the world, if I require a man with a good head, a good heart, lots of pluck, and plenty of common sense, I always send for a Captain in the Royal Navy."

Lord Palmerston

FROM 1650 to 1850 the ships and guns used for fighting at sea remained virtually unchanged. True, the line-of-battleship *Victoria*, launched in 1859, had a steam engine of 4,293 h.p. (which would scarcely ever be used) tucked away below her triple-tiered, broadside gun-decks, and two slender funnels which could be raised between her masts. With the funnels lowered she was just a bigger edition of Nelson's *Victory*, laid down in 1759, as the *Victory* had been a slightly larger edition of the ships-of-the-line which formed the backbone of the fleet in the reign of King Charles II. Improvements to armament had been on the same modest scale, and the dumpy, smooth-bore, muzzle-loading guns of 1850 on their wooden carriages were almost indistinguishable from those in use two hundred years before. A late-seventeenth-century sailor, waking from a Rip van Winkle sleep of a hundred and fifty years, would very soon have been perfectly at home in the latest men-of-war of young Queen Victoria's fleet. With the tools of sea warfare more or less standardised (it took an expert eye to distinguish British from foreign warships) everything depended on how they were used—on strategy and tactics, on the seamanlike qualities which brought ships into the most favourable position for fighting at point-blank range and on the courage and initiative of their crews.

B
17

After such a long period of technical stagnation it was natural that sailors should take their ships and their weapons very much for granted. Great changes were afoot, rapidly altering the shape and texture of life ashore, but the Navy, whose officers and men spent most of their time on foreign stations where the Industrial Revolution had not yet penetrated, was excusably backward in appreciating what the technical advances of the nineteenth century might mean. Busy with their own affairs, proudly following the ancient traditions of their calling, Harry Keppel and his kind were not material-minded. Men and not machines were their stock-in-trade.

Harry Keppel was born on 14 June 1809. Three weeks later his puny little body was laid in a footpan whilst a grave was being dug in the garden at the back of the house. But an old nurse noticed that a spark of life still remained. The funeral of Admiral of the Fleet Sir Henry Keppel took place in 1904. He had served his country in four reigns and was the oldest officer in the Royal Navy.

At the age of twelve and a half he joined the Royal Naval College at Portsmouth. Though little more than waist-high to the Captain and other officers he was a well-built, vigorous lad. The uniform was a blue tail-coat with a stand-up collar and gilt buttons, white pantaloons and black buckled shoes. On his red head he wore a round stove-pipe hat with a gold lace loop and cockade. No doubt he thought himself no end of a warrior.

The instruction, part theoretical, part practical, lasted two years: school, visits to the Dockyard where ships were building and fitting out, boatwork in the pulling and sailing cutters and drill on the parade ground under a sergeant of artillery. French, drawing, dancing and fencing gave a polish to the cadets, who in any case were boys of good family. It was an era of dawning prosperity and comparative peace. With much the strongest Navy in the world, Britannia ruled the waves, though only 139 of her 604 ships were in full commission.[1]

Keppel, like most of his contemporaries, was country bred.

[1] 91 of 105 ships-of-the-line and 83 of 115 frigates were paid off in reserve.

Admiral of the Fleet the Hon. Sir Henry Keppel, GCB, OM,
as a Rear-Admiral. From an engraving after H. Weigall (1858)

H.M.S. *Dido* casting off from Spithead, 1841. From a lithograph after Lieutenant Inglefield

Though not so directly connected with the Navy as such lads as Suckling, Pasco, Hallowell and Blackwood whose fathers had served with Nelson, he had a great-uncle Keppel, later Lord Albemarle, who had been with Anson in the *Centurion* on her famous voyage round the world. Norfolk, where he lived, had a strong naval connection. The Cokes of Holkham Hall were lifelong friends of his family and young Harry had already sat in the very chair which Nelson had often used when he was living on half-pay at nearby Burnham Thorpe.

Harry Keppel's first ship was the frigate *Tweed*. His school, after those two years on shore, was the sea. Such book-work as he was given after going afloat was almost entirely practical —mathematics and algebra applied to navigation. There was a great deal to learn. The sailing vessel of those days was an intricate mechanism. The crew took over their ship as a mastless hull, fitted and refitted her. Very little outside assistance was called for or given. Rigging, sails and small spars could be made on board from the rope, canvas and wood which were the raw materials of the trade. With no power but the wind and their own strength they sailed thousands of miles.

Much of the work was hard, difficult and dangerous, calling for teamwork and discipline properly blended with initiative, courage and personal skill. "Able" seaman was no idle term. At sea or in harbour there was plenty to do. In the words of some lower-deck wag:

> Six days you work as hard as you are able
> On the seventh, holystone decks and black the chain cable.

It was an era of rapid commercial expansion. Trade was following the flag to strange and beautiful places. Sailors had to deal with foreign people in far-off lands. Without radio or even the telegraph they were out of touch with any form of higher authority for weeks or even months at a time. If a crisis arose it had to be handled by those on the spot. Captains of small ships on detached service were sometimes confronted with political problems which would nowadays be referred to the Council of the United Nations.

The mid-nineteenth-century sailor, unlike many of his present-day successors, lived an entirely different life from his contemporaries ashore. In forty-five years at sea Keppel only served four years in ships in home waters. For over twenty-six years he was far away from England in China, Malaya and Borneo, South America, Australia, India and Ceylon. Long commissions abroad were often followed by long periods unemployed ashore.

The life produced an easily recognisable type—self-reliant, independent, accustomed to responsibility from an early age—but very varied individually. Eccentrics were common and behaviour sometimes odd.

At the age of seventeen Keppel wrote in his diary:

Had to attend on my Captain at a court-martial which caused an unusual sensation. The prisoner was the Captain of the *Ariadne*. He was tried for having purchased a slave negress at Zanzibar and taken her to sea. She mysteriously disappeared off the coast of Africa.

At twenty-two Keppel, now a lieutenant, was serving in the *Magicienne*, a frigate originally designed to carry 42 guns, but "razeed" by removal of the top deck to a 24.[1] *Magicienne* sailed from England in November 1831, touched at Rio and arrived at Trincomalee in March 1832 after a passage south of the Cape in which the only land sighted in two months was the desolate St Paul's Island, half-way between Australia and Africa in the Southern Ocean. In May *Magicienne* was sent from Madras to Malacca where a recalcitrant native chief was causing much trouble to the all-powerful John Company. Indeed the Rajah of Nanning was in open rebellion, supported by a number of neighbouring chieftains. His territory lay far inland, but he was dependent on the rivers for supplies of arms, ammunition and other necessities. *Magicienne* was ordered to blockade the sixty miles of coast where the rivers from Nanning flowed into the sea.

The frigate could not navigate the rivers or even approach

1 Masts and yards were left as before, giving increased area to the lower sails.

close inshore. Boats must be used. Keppel was given charge of one such force and instructed to close the mouth of the Moowar River.

His flagship was the schooner *Diamond* mounting four brass guns. A pinnace and seven other man-of-war boats, each in charge of a midshipman, and a number of native-manned small craft, completed his flotilla. With Keppel in the *Diamond* were six sailors, three Royal Marines and a Corporal who "did officer." A native interpreter "who likewise played the fiddle" and a native cook, good at making curries, completed the flagship's crew.

Keppel's first duty was to pay a ceremonial call on the chief whose lands bordered the mouth of the river. The Rajah of Moowar was believed to be loyal. Though too weak to defy his much more powerful neighbours inland his co-operation was desired; he must first be convinced of the might and majesty of the British Raj. Keppel appointed the senior midshipman as master of ceremonies being, in his own words, "of too great importance to do more than I could help."

The palace was built in the native style, partly on piles driven into the water's edge. Young Keppel was rowed to it direct, bearing an official letter and a presentation sword. A palaver followed; salutes were fired by the brass guns of the *Diamond*, the men of the "fleet" gave three cheers and coffee and sweetmeats were served by ladies of the harem.

From 10 June to 23 August the blockade continued, to such good effect that the rebellious Rajah of Nanning was eventually brought to heel. Musical comedy, perhaps—but not an easy assignment: quarters were cramped, comforts few; constant vigilance was necessary.

It was grilling hot by day. When darkness fell with tropical suddenness there was nothing for twelve long hours but the silently flowing river and the dense jungle on either bank noisy with night-hunting beasts.

The young lieutenant and the Rajah were drawn together by a common interest in sport. A brass gun landed from the flotilla brought down an elephant which Keppel finished off with a musket. Before the boats finally withdrew the ruler of Moowar had formally offered Keppel the hand of his daughter, if he would agree to be heir to the throne.

At twenty-five Keppel, now a Commander, had his own ship, the brig *Childers*, 16 guns. Advancement was rapid for those with connections in high places. Others might remain lieutenants for forty or forty-five years. (As he wrote at the end of his career: "I never got a step that was not a job.")

In accordance with the custom of the time only the officers and warrant officers were permanent Navy men. Most of the crew were engaged by Keppel himself. Leaflets calling for volunteers for a commission in the Mediterranean were put out: "Wanted, Petty Officers and Able Seamen . . . None but the RIGHT SORT need apply." As soon as the men came forward the *Childers*, with only a modicum of assistance from the Dockyard, fitted herself out. Masts were stepped and rigged, spars hoisted into place, rigging rove, sails bent, ammunition and stores taken aboard. Her young Commanding Officer had her painted white inside, with green rails to the hammock nettings and black ports. On the bows of her boats was a representation of a horse winning the Derby. Four days after she was ready for sea *Childers* sailed for Malta.

For some months she was in company with the great ships-of-the-line commanded by men whose commissions dated from before Keppel was born. He enjoyed the sailing exercises in which he more than held his own. *Childers* was fast and handy. He had a good crew with an old shipmate from the *Tweed* as Master; one Jonas Croaker, "a finer seaman never broke a biscuit." But he often wished himself away on some independent assignment or ashore with his gun where he "knew there was scarcely a bush that did not hold a woodcock."

Keppel was a keen shot, but riding was his greatest joy. Being small, wiry and light (about eight stone) and completely fearless, he was a good man on a horse. In England he never missed the chance of a hunt, and abroad he would ride anything and everything that was offered. "He du ride just like a fule," said an old Norfolk countryman of him when he was a

lad. When he came to grief, as happened pretty frequently, it
was due to over-daring, not lack of skill. Often down, sometimes carried from the field, he always came up smiling and
ready for more; risks were meat and drink to him.

In the *Childers* he had his first introduction to the bestiali-
ties of civil war, when his ship was ordered to Spanish ports to
protect British interests during the latest uprising. Though
described by reckless men as "the bravest man they ever knew"
he was no lover of violence for its own sake. Writing some
years later of his only duel (with a brother officer, as stubborn
and impetuous as himself) he described it as "an event in my
life which I would fain leave out." Too realistic not to recog-
nise that death and wounds were sometimes inevitable and
careless of his own safety, he hated seeing others suffer.

From Spain the *Childers* went to West Africa, patrolling the
coast for the slavers who still did a flourishing business at that
time. After four years abroad he returned to England, and a
period of half-pay.

Keppel was not rich, but he was very well-connected, with
friends and relations in London and the great country houses.
He hunted, shot, attended balls and other functions and was
in the Abbey for the coronation of Queen Victoria. With
other young bloods of his age he sometimes painted the town
rather red, spending a night in Marlborough Street Police
Station after a brawl in Conduit Street. "Ruffianism in High
Places" stormed the press.

He was popular with women; the attraction, as is clear from
his diary, was mutual. Though rarely failing to note a pretty
face, he had only been lightly involved until December 1838
when he wrote: "Spent the next fortnight in London like a
man about to do something desperate." He was about to ask
Miss Kate Crosbie to marry him, and two months later there
was a wedding at St George's, Hanover Square.

His next ship was the corvette *Dido*, 18 guns, 734 tons.
Though only 120 feet long she had three tall masts and carried
a good press of sail. Broad in the beam, but with perfect
underwater lines by the great designer Symonds, she needed

little ballast. Of all Keppel's ships his "lovely *Dido*" was the favourite. Passing south of the Cape into the Roaring Forties on his way to the Far East, Keppel, who liked carrying sail and was never the man to lose a minute on passage, did a run of 286 nautical miles in twenty-four hours and averaged 275 for six consecutive days—good going for such a little ship. *Dido* made Java Head, Ceylon, three months out from Plymouth, but reached China just too late to assist in the capture of Woosung. She joined a great fleet of seventy-three sail which now proceeded up the Yangtse-Kiang to take Nanking. Keppel, with his eye for the beautiful, describes the scene. How on a signal from the Flag "you could see a white cloud, three miles in extent, moving up the river," to be succeeded, when the wind became contrary, by a "forest of masts" as the fleet anchored and furled its sails.

After Nanking had fallen fever raged through the fleet and *Dido* with 97 of her 195 men on the sick list ran aground when returning down river. No outside assistance was available, and the situation was serious, though after Keppel's heart. "When I get into a scrape I like to get out of it without help." Seizing two junks he transferred into them *Dido*'s guns and movable stores, laid out anchors and pulled his lightened ship off the mud by manpower. The men still on their feet were sickly and it was heavy work. "But my Didos were equal to the occasion."

For Keppel, as always, had a willing crew. In days when discipline was often harsh, he preferred to lead by example and affection rather than fear. He could be strict, but was strong and self-confident enough to be lenient. Next day he "harangued and forgave all culprits."

Some months later *Dido* was off on her own. Pirates from Borneo were harassing the trade in and out of Singapore. Keppel, as senior naval officer of the Straits Settlements, "determined on his own responsibility to put some check on these outrages."

This was altogether a more serious matter than the boat blockade of Moowar. The pirate strongholds which must be destroyed were far from the open sea. *Dido* could go part of the way, but most of the journey would have to be in boats.

From Kuching the frigate's gig, pinnace and cutters, a yacht manned by Didos and a number of native auxiliary craft set out for the difficult journey upstream. Keppel's six-oared gig had been covered with a "roof" of matting against the sun and rain; oars and masts were left behind and the crew, facing forward, propelled her with paddles. Each man had a carbine at his side, and the master of the *Dido*'s band, with a bugle, sat in the bow. With Keppel in the gig was "Datu Brooke," the famous English Rajah of Sarawak.

The objective was Padi, seventy miles up the Seribas River. It was hot, hard work. Sometimes Keppel in his gig would pass from end to end of the mosquito fleet, with as much pride as if they had been a squadron of line-of-battleships. After three days a sharp turn brought them into a straight reach. At its end was a hill, cleared of trees and surmounted by a battery of cannon. Between this fortress and the advancing boats was a formidable barrier of tree-trunks supported on stakes driven into the bed of the river. Thousand of Dyaks, in the woods beside the river and in the fort, were yelling and beating gongs. Under a hot fire from the battery the boats swept forward, cut their way through, landed men at the foot of the hill and stormed the guns. The Didos were outnumbered thirty to one; the Dyaks were brave men, but so determined was the onslaught that the natives broke and fled.

After dealing with another pirate stronghold in a similar manner Keppel made a triumphal return to Kuching. Few of his men had been killed outright, though wounds often proved fatal, for medical facilities were rudimentary (Keppel describes how one poor fellow had his arm amputated in the gig).

Rajah Brooke was delighted. He and Keppel, both men of action, had suited each other admirably. "By his measures on this coast," wrote Brooke, "Keppel has done much to strike at the root of piracy."

A long spell ashore followed his commision in the *Dido*. All the larger ships were now fitted with steam engines, though still fully rigged with masts and yards. Keppel was sent to Woolwich for a course of instruction in machinery, where he visited the *Terrible*, "an enormous ship, 1847 tons, 800 horsepower."

Technical matters never greatly interested him. He liked to sail a ship, particularly in heavy weather. He enjoyed leading his men and he loved a fight. When nothing much was afoot he spent his time in pursuit of sport or in the company of amusing people. Although he gave his life to the Navy it was a means to an end, not an end in itself. He found the course at Woolwich rather tedious—"Do not learn much and getting tired of it"—and he was frequently away visiting friends, hunting, shooting and racing. He was to become a well-known and popular figure on the turf, unlike his elder brother Lord Albemarle, who never could see how an intelligent man could spend so much time watching "a fool in yellow ride after a rogue in red." Life, though amusing, was expensive. "Lots of duns," he wrote in his diary, telling later with relief how he had insured his life for £1,500 to raise money to pay his debts. He was glad to get another ship, the *Mæander*, and to be off abroad again, though having "a dear wife it is painful to separate from."

The Navy was changing in other ways. As Keppel was engaging his crew direct in the usual manner a draft of men arrived from the Admiral at Sheerness. Keppel promptly sent them back again. The Admiral was annoyed, but as all the men he needed were "entering well" Keppel shrugged off Their Lordships' reprimand.

The system of promotion by influence, which still ruled, might be unjust, but the favoured few were able to speak and act as they thought best without too much fear of the consequences. Keppel was never unduly awed by the powers-that-be. Sometimes he ran risks which were great even for those rather unruly days. When he brought his "lovely *Dido*" to Spithead after four years abroad the Admiralty ordered him to Sheerness before he could so much as greet his wife, who was living a few miles from Portsmouth. This was too much for Keppel, who rigged his Master in his cocked hat and epau-

lettes, donned the latter's pea-jacket and oilskins, touched his
hat, said "Goodbye, Sir" and landed in a wherry. Posting to
Sheerness ahead of his ship he went off in the pilot boat and
brought her into harbour. "The bravest man who ever lived,
who ought to have been turned out of the Service years ago"
was a contemporary judgment.

In *Mæander*, once more in the Far East, he took a grave
risk of another kind. He was senior officer of a small force
assembled off the Portuguese port of Macao for a regatta when
he learnt that a certain Mr Summers, a British subject, had
been imprisoned for a trifling act (failing to take his hat off to
the Governor). When it was clear that a formal application for
release would not succeed Keppel decided on other measures,
for "to dance attendance beyond this point on Portuguese
justice seemed to me unworthy of my position and hopeless as
to the object." The defences of the jail having been recon-
noitred by a visitor bringing fruit to the prisoner and the
Governor being embarked in one of the ships, lying three
miles offshore, to witness the regatta, *Mæander*'s barge, with
twelve bluejackets and six marines, closed the pier. As soon as
the first race had been started Keppel, excusing himself on
some pretext, jumped into a cutter and joined his men on the
beach. Disposing his cutter's crew to cover the line of retreat,
he sent the barge's men to the prison. A few shots were exchanged, during which a soldier was killed, and Mr Summers
successfully brought away. That the fatal bullet had probably
been fired by the Portuguese themselves was, as Keppel appreciated, beside the point. For his exploit Keppel was once
again reprimanded by the Admiralty, and thanked by Lord
Palmerston. Reporting at Whitehall two years later, on his
return to England, Keppel was shown into the presence of the
First Lord, Sir Francis Baring, with the words: "Here's this
fellow Keppel. I can do nothing with him."

Ships like *Mæander* were, by modern standards, very small.
The food was bad, quarters were cramped; you needed luck
and a strong constitution to survive. In his early days in the
Tweed Keppel was one of a party of nine stricken with fever.

after a picnic ashore. The treatment was bleeding, from both arms, and shaving the head, and only Keppel and one other came through. After three and a half years abroad only 150 of the 360 who had originally commissioned *Mæander* returned to England.

Yet men like Keppel never had any difficulty in finding a crew. He sometimes preferred an intelligent rogue to a fool, as when he exchanged one of his warrant officers for a smart man, "under a cloud: strongly suspected of having set fire to the dockyard, that he might get credit for his exertions in extinguishing it." Under Keppel the "smart man" turned out very well.

Having been pretty wild himself he had sympathy, without sentimentality, for those who got into mischief. He could turn a blind eye, and knew when to do so. Commanding the Naval Brigade after the fall of Sebastopol in the Crimea he "saw a sailor coming from the town. As he was steering wildly, I thought it best to retire into the shade." But he had no use for fuddlers or for anything which looked like lack of zeal in the presence of the enemy. In the Baltic during the earlier stages of the Crimean War, with a Commander-in-Chief "more at home in Cowes roads" than at sea who "so long and so persistently avoided the neighbourhood of the enemy's ships" he was far from happy. Of the bombardment of Bomarsund carried out, as he believed, when the enemy had already evacuated their positions he wrote with disgust: "we had nothing to do, and we did it."

He was at his best when on his own. The rules by which others must be bound were not, on occasions, for him; as a member of a team he sometimes failed, for discipline must work both ways. But he had courage, fortitude, dignity, humour and kindliness. Though autocratic he was never pompous. During his last appointment, as Commander-in-Chief, Plymouth, he climbed on to a Devonport tram to the evident amazement of a young midshipman already esconced in that humble conveyance.

"Don't tell my flag-captain you've seen me here," whispered

Keppel, "he wouldn't like it." But he had insisted, when his ship *Raleigh* was sinking under him, her bottom torn away on an uncharted rock, in firing a formal salute for a French man-of-war in the vicinity as though nothing in the world was amiss. "Which was done in as good time and as well as it would have been done had the ship been in the same trim order as she was three hours before." Matters of form are sometimes, but not always, important.

The loss of the *Raleigh* at a time when he was nearing the top of the Captains' list and hoping for promotion to flag rank was a bitter blow. "Do not recollect that I ever had so great a damper to my prospects, hopes, etc." He had commissioned her only six months before, the pennant being hoisted by the boatswain's wife, a "good-looking woman, ought to bring luck!" Now his frigate was a total loss, though the guns, spars, rigging and stores were saved, including two pipes of Madeira wine which he hoped to bring home to England. The boatswain's wife, in spite of her charms, had proved in-efficacious. Outwardly Keppel was quite unmoved ("It is necessary to be jolly under such circumstances"), and in the end he fell on his feet.

The British Fleet he had been about to join was blockading the Canton River. About a hundred well-armed Chinese war junks were lying in Fatshan Creek, out of reach of our heavy ships and protected by their own guns and a fort. Keppel, being on the spot without a job, was given command of one of two divisions of light craft assembled to deal with the situation.

The plan was a simple one. Warships' boats full of armed men would be towed as far as possible by shallow-draft steamers and gunboats. When these ran aground the boats, under oars, would charge to the assault.

Reveille was sounded before dawn. Daylight was just break-ing as Keppel, in the paddle-wheeler *Hong Kong*, set off up the creek with his gunboats, each ship towing a line of boats full of armed men. The junks were in two groups, those allotted to Keppel being farthest up the creek; twenty junks, strongly manned, each mounting fourteen guns.

Below the junks the creek was divided by an island "shaped like a leg of mutton," forming two narrow channels, one of which the Chinamen had blocked by stakes driven into the mud. The junks were moored in a compact line at the knuckle end of the island, with all their guns, moved to the engaged side, covering the remaining channel—a narrow strip of navigable water through which our boats must pass in single file. This critical spot was some six hundred yards from the junks, a very effective range in those days.

The British gunboats grounded one by one. The *Hong Kong*, being of very shallow draught, got furthest, but she too stuck below the narrows. Leaving the larger vessels fast in the mud Keppel, followed by his dog Mike, jumped into his gig to lead the pulling boats to the assault. Except for an occasional ranging shot the Chinese held their fire until the boats were in the narrows. Then guns crashed out. Round-shot and grape-shot fell among them, unprotected and, at this stage, unable to retaliate. Oars were smashed, boats holed; men killed and wounded: to add to the racket the Chinese were shouting and beating gongs. The British responded with cheers as they continued to press forward, and as they cleared the narrows the boats spread out, the men pulling their hardest, racing to be the first to board the enemy. It was like a cavalry charge.

But, for the moment, the opposition was too strong. Keppel's galley, hit three times and badly holed, was sinking. All the six men at the oars had been hit; one killed, one mortally wounded, one without an arm. As the galley sank Keppel and the wounded were helped into another boat, but Mike refused to leave the dead man who had always looked after him. In good order the boats paddled back to the *Hong Kong*, to dispose of their wounded and take on reinforcements.

The *Hong Kong* was now under fire and Keppel had another narrow escape when an 18-lb shot crashed through the paddle box and came to rest just beside him. "A few more grains of powder or a bulkhead less, and my head would have been unshipped to a moral."

The tide was rising and the junks now showed signs of getting under way, to move further up the creek. Midshipman Montagu described how Keppel leapt on to the paddle box, shook his fist at the enemy and shouted:

"The beggars are making off. Man the boats! Man the boats! You rascals! I'll pay you out for this!"

Keppel jumped into a cutter. In a moment all the undamaged boats were manned. Cheering as they bent to their oars the bluejackets closed the enemy. So determined was this second onslaught that the Chinese broke and fled, abandoning most of the junks which were stormed and set on fire. A few managed to get under way and made off up the creek, pursued by the boats which captured all but three, continuing the pursuit for seven miles until recalled by a signal from the Admiral. As they turned to drop back down the creek to the *Hong Kong* Keppel stood up and shouted:

"You rascals. I'll come back again for you soon."

Passing the scene of the morning's battle, they saw a big dog swimming towards them: Mike, who survived to witness other fights and eventually to return to England.[1]

Casualties on both sides had been heavy. The British had over eighty killed and wounded, many of them seriously, for the grape-shot and bags of musket-balls fired by the enemy did terrible damage to unprotected men. Keppel, though in the thick of it throughout, had escaped unharmed.

The night that followed was a bad time as *Hong Kong* and the gunboats dropped back towards the Fleet. Exhausted men begrimed with smoke, many of them covered with blood, lay about the decks. It was dead calm; the cries of the wounded, for whom little could be done in the cramped and crowded ships, were pitiful.

Keppel enjoyed danger and was never happier than in the thick of a fight, but the waste and cruelty of war always affected him deeply. Later he was to write feelingly of the appalling things he witnessed in the Crimea. The Guards, reduced,

---

[1] Though not to retirement ashore. Away from the neighbourhood of ships and sailors Mike was unhappy, so Keppel left him to continue a seafaring life.

chiefly by disease, from 4,100 to 500 men; twelve half-starved
horses struggling to pull an ammunition waggon which four
fit beasts could have handled with ease. An old shipmate, dead
of cholera five hours after he had been taken ill. Many of his
own men were smitten with smallpox. He went through the
wards where they were lying "their heads . . . swollen into the
shape and appearance of huge plum-puddings, eyes closed,
their own mothers would not have recognised them." Getting
their names from the surgeon he had a cheerful word for each.
The leader who must shoulder the troubles of others can never
reveal that he has any of his own, but Keppel, brave as a lion,
was at heart a gentle man.

The engagement in Fatshan Creek was in 1857. Next year
he was back in England. The court-martial convened after the
loss of the *Raleigh* had acquitted him, for the pinnacle rock on
which she had struck was uncharted, nine feet below the surface in a deep water channel and so steep-to that a boat's anchor
would not lie on its summit. Acquittal was pretty certain, even
without a letter sent from the Palace to the First Lord, Sir
Charles Wood, hoping that Keppel was not to blame. "He is
so gallant and zealous an officer that the Queen would deeply
regret anything which would distress or disappoint him."
Keppel was duly promoted to Rear-Admiral and awarded the
K.C.B., but he had to put up with the usual long period on
half-pay before hoisting his flag. In 1859 his wife, who had
been ailing for some time, died. "This the saddest day of my
life."

Though Keppel was very proud of both his wives (he
married again, two years later) he was not cut out for the hum-
drum pleasures of domesticity. Even when he was in England
he was often away from home, hunting, shooting, racing or
visiting his many friends. His private feelings were something
he always kept to himself, but it is pretty clear that he found
married life rather cloying. His second wife was often ailing
and, one suspects, somewhat over solicitous for his very independent nature.

"How are you and where shall I find you?" wired Lady

Keppel, when Keppel had gone away for a change after one of his many riding accidents.

"Am quite well. You cannot find me," was the reply.

He hated a fuss, and was the despair of his doctors. Once he announced his intention of rising from a sick-bed and going to Goodwood. The doctor shook his head, declaring he could not be responsible.

"And who the devil," growled Harry Keppel, "asked you to take responsibility?" Later to someone enquiring after his health he replied that he was quite well "and all the better for not having seen that beast of a doctor of mine for some time."

He had more accidents than most men, some of them serious, but bobbed up as fit as ever after them all. At the age of sixty-five, when Commander-in-Chief, Plymouth, he was visiting a ship in Devonport Dockyard when he tumbled twenty feet on to a quay formed of the pig-iron blocks used as ballast in sailing-ship days. Someone called for water, though with little hope that the crumpled figure would ever move again.

"Put some whisky in it," murmured Harry Keppel.

Just before he hauled down his flag for the last time Keppel, aged sixty-seven, was out with the Blackmore Vale. Hounds were running strongly when the field, a large one, came to a stiffish fence. There was a gap "which I left for the fair sex." Keppel charged for a place he thought his horse could jump and came "the heaviest cropper I have ever experienced." A friend found "horse and self as quiet as if we had been shot in action." After several months in hospital Keppel was as good as new, growing old in body, but not at heart. He was again a widower, living in chambers in the Albany. As always he enjoyed seeing his many friends. He loved young people and took great pleasure in the company of his daughter May. He had the gift of bridging the gap between generations. Young Prince George (later King George V) wrote to him from the Mediterranean Fleet, a long and chatty epistle beginning: "Sir. That is the proper way for a lieutenant to address an

c

Admiral of the Fleet, but I hope I may begin 'My dear little Admiral' which I always call you."

The career of his son, a sailor like himself, was a constant source of interest. Colin Keppel earned early promotion in the Naval Brigade during the River War against the Mahdi in the Sudan. "I hope you will not think it very disrespectful of me to express the general opinion," wrote Admiral Sir John Fisher in a letter of congratulation, "—that he has behaved like a chip of the old block."

Harry Keppel was a man of simple faith though in this, as in other matters which really touched his heart, he did not approve of outward show, considering certain practices "hard on those who like to worship and pray to the Almighty in a quiet way." Clearly he believed that it was behaviour out of church that mattered most.

He was ninety-four when he died. Bluejackets drew the gun-carriage which brought the little coffin to the village churchyard. Amongst the flowers was a message from Her Majesty the Queen.

"In loving memory of my beloved Little Admiral, the best and bravest of men. Rest in Peace." Alexandra.

He had his faults. Perhaps he would not have risen quite so far in his profession without the help of friends in high places, though he was very capable and a born leader. He was apt to treat his ships as though they were his private property, but they were happy, efficient ships. He spent a lot of time amusing himself which might have been devoted to more serious matters, but when in danger or adversity people turned to him, as they instinctively did, he never failed them. He became an Admiral of the Fleet without ever serving at the Admiralty, and his only administrative appointment was his last post, as C.-in-C., Plymouth. During his service the Navy passed, quite suddenly, from centuries of technical stagnation to the rapid changes which have persisted ever since, but it was not on the shape of ships to come or their tactical employment that he left his mark. Materially he did very little; spiritually he was in the direct line of succession with the greatest days of the Royal

Navy. He handed on, by living it, a lesson in leadership. It was Harry Keppel and his kind who preserved through the long years of comparative peace the ethos of Nelson's victorious fleet; its self-reliance, willingness to take risks, and its unflinching courage. For courage is still the first virtue in a fighting Service and men will always count for more than machines.

PART TWO

The Builders

WILSON
1842-1921
Old 'ard 'eart

WHEN Commodore Keppel commissioned the frigate *Raleigh* in 1856 he took with him as one of his young officers the son of his friend and relative Commander George Wilson, R.N. Arthur Knyvet Wilson, fourteen years of age and five feet one inch tall, had already seen action in the Crimea, where he had watched the bombardment of Sebastopol. He had passed into the Service the year before, going straight to sea as a cadet without any previous naval training because of the war.

The *Raleigh*, a sailing ship like all the vessels commanded by Keppel, made a good passage to China, but was wrecked off Macao as already described. Her officers were dispersed to other ships and Arthur Wilson, greatly to his disgust, was not with Keppel for the battle of Fatshan Creek. His chance came later when he was landed from the *Calcutta* in charge of a twelve-pounder gun for the assault on Canton. "Splendid fun, but unfortunately I got very little fighting" is an extract from a long and lively letter to his father about his experiences ashore. He returned to his Norfolk home at Swaffham just in time for his seventeenth birthday after having spent nearly four very active years abroad.

It was 1859, and all sorts of startling developments, of which the Navy in general was still blissfully unaware, were afoot. The Crimean War had produced a need for floating batteries protected against shell-fire by iron plates, the first armoured ships ever built. In 1856 the French followed up this idea with a much more ambitious project—a seagoing armour-plated ship, the world's first iron-clad. With *La*

Gloire on the stocks the long period of static naval design was over and the race of material was on.

In Britain *La Gloire*, appearing when France was showing signs of recovering from her defeat in the Napoleonic Wars, started a first-class naval scare. All the ships building in English dockyards were wooden ships. As the public now learnt with dismay, recent tests with another innovation, the rifled gun, had shown that solid shot could now be hurled clean through the thick oaken sides of the hitherto impregnable line-of-battleships at ranges up to no less than 600 yards. The iron-clad, her vitals protected by thick plates, would be capable of overwhelming any number of older ships at her leisure. England's wooden walls were crumbling.

So sudden a collapse of the foundations upon which their policy was based was not readily assimilated by Their Lordships of the Admiralty. For two years they hesitated, but in 1861 Britain completed her first iron-clad.

The *Warrior* was claimed to be greatly superior to *La Gloire* —the fastest and most powerful warship in the world, capable of overtaking and overwhelming any other man-of-war. Iron plates four and a half inches thick protected her vitals. Fourteen of her forty guns were breech-loaders—another new departure.

The public was reassured, but the Navy received this forerunner of things to come with modified enthusiasm. Though fitted with a powerful steam engine she was also full-rigged. Being for those days a heavy ship (9,210 tons) her sail area per ton of displacement was only about half what had been considered minimal for wooden warships.[1] Judged by accepted naval standards—performance under sail—she was slow and clumsy. Though the old form of propulsion was doomed it would be nearly forty years before it finally made a reluctant exit.

Arthur Wilson was now in his twentieth year and once more serving abroad, on the west coast of North America. He was working hard to master his profession and chafed at the long

[1] 3.25 square feet against 6 to 14 square feet per ton.

Admiral of the Fleet Sir Arthur Knyvet Wilson, Bart,
VC, GCB, OM, GCVO, when commanding the Channel Squadron

Late 19th-century transitional. The third-class cruiser *Comus* in 1897

periods spent in harbour "perfectly idle for six months."
Luckily, the active years in China had already made him a
good practical seaman. Returning home for his examinations
for lieutenant he did well, getting "firsts" in all three subjects
—seamanship, navigation and gunnery. He was a clever, conscientious, rather serious-minded young man.

In 1866 he was appointed as a junior staff officer to the
gunnery school at Portsmouth. He was following in the
wake of Lieutenant John Arbuthnot Fisher, a man of very
advanced ideas who was already making his mark. Technical
progress in the Fleet had been fairly rapid. The new ships
coming into service bore little resemblance to the old wooden
line-of-battleships, though masts and sails were still retained.
The Navy is a conservative service and most of the officers
resented the changes forced upon them. The few who saw
that the old Navy must give way to the new were mostly young
and junior men, so far without much power.

Wilson's next appointment was to the *Caledonia* in the
Mediterranean. He found that the guns were a secondary
consideration. Exercises aloft were the standard form of training the crew and the manner in which they were performed the
measure of the efficiency of the ship. Wilson, himself an excellent seaman, knew that boldness, initiative and personal skill
were developed aloft. But the days when guns were fired in
broadsides at point-blank range, the real "aiming" being done
by the seamen who worked the ship into position, were over.
No ship, however well handled, could expect to win in battle
under modern conditions unless her armament was properly
served. To relegate gunnery practice to third place by putting
cleanliness before fighting efficiency was absurd, but all too
common.

In 1876 Wilson again followed Fisher, when he joined the
new torpedo school H.M.S. *Vernon*, commissioned as a tender
to the Gunnery School *Excellent* three years before and now an
entirely separate establishment.

Wilson had already served on a committee appointed some
years earlier to investigate the properties of the "submarine

locomotive torpedo" invented by Mr Whitehead, and had been
greatly struck by the possibilities of the new weapon. He had
a natural aptitude for things mechanical and had invented a
number of devices adopted by the Fleet, including the masthead semaphore and a heliograph signalling lamp. He was
now to embark on a branch of the service on which he left a
considerable mark.

"Torpedo" in those days covered any form of explosive
underwater weapon, including mines. Electricity was coming
into use afloat, both for firing charges and other purposes;
training and developing this novel form of power was also
undertaken by *Vernon*.

These new sciences demanded a new type of man. H.M.S.
Excellent, the gunnery school, was the Mecca of a certain sort
of discipline. Naval guns had grown greatly in size. The
larger ones needed a large crew to supplement the small amount
of machinery then in use. Training aimed at producing men
who could serve their noisy weapons almost automatically.
Drill was taught in the most precise detail and initiative discouraged. Speed, smartness and instant obedience were all.
Men moved at the double around the shining guns. Orders
were barked out; shells rammed home, breech-blocks slammed.
Everything was an "evolution."

Torpedoes and mines required a different approach. They
must be meticulously prepared, each detail checked thought-
fully, without undue haste. Military precision was out of place.
In the *Vernon* the decks were often littered with coils of wire,
electric cables and other paraphernalia amongst which men
moved quietly about their work. Discipline was strict, but it
was discipline of another sort. Junior ratings were no longer
simply extensions of the machine or numbers of a well-
directed team. They must think for themselves.

The appointment suited Wilson admirably. At thirty-seven
he was developing the qualities which, becoming more marked
as he grew older, made him a legendary figure. He was a
bachelor who rarely left his ship and had no known interests
outside his work. He spoke very little, but expressed himself

clearly and very much to the point. He was extremely observant and a good listener. He was often thoughtful and preoccupied, but his ideas, if new, were thoroughly practical. Though already rather an intimidating figure and very much in command he was patient with the mistakes of others and avoided imposing petty restrictions. Though too austere to be personally popular, his ship was a happy one.

But Wilson, in spite of his scientific bent, was a man of action. In 1881 he was appointed in command of the *Hecla*, a ship which carried a number of boats equipped to launch torpedoes.

A crisis was brewing in Egypt, where a nationalist party led by Arabi Pasha was daily becoming more powerful. In June 1882 Arabi, openly defying the Khedive, seized the port of Alexandria. Support of the legitimate Government was a joint Anglo-French responsibility at that time, but France was unwilling to act. After some hesitation Britain decided to "go it alone." A large fleet bombarded the forts, driving out the rebellious troops. A Naval Brigade was landed under Captain John Fisher with Commander Arthur Wilson as one of his officers. Between them they improvised an armoured train, which did good work, but Wilson was disappointed to see very little fighting, for the subsequent stages of the campaign, which ended in the Battle of Tel el Kebir, were chiefly a military affair.

With the Khedive safely re-installed in Cairo, life on the Mediterranean Station returned to normal. Captain John Fisher, who had caught dysentery during the operations ashore, was invalided home, leaving his ship the *Inflexible*, the most advanced warship of her day, in less dynamic hands.

Fisher's departure was unfortunate, for the *Inflexible* was in many ways a revolutionary vessel and a real step forward. Displacing 11,880 tons she mounted guns of unheard-of size— four 80-ton, 16-inch muzzle-loaders in twin turrents firing a projectile weighing 1,684 lbs. Machinery of 8,407 h.p. gave a speed of over 14 knots. Her armour was up to 24 inches thick; she carried torpedoes, and the very complicated interior was lit by electric light.

But tradition must be served. Though intended to fight under bare poles, she was brig-rigged, so that her crew could take part in evolutions aloft with the rest of the fleet. Under Fisher they had been spending most of their time below decks, learning how to fight their mechanical monster. At sail drill they showed up badly; so the new captain gave up the unpopular task of preparing for war and concentrated on the usual evolutions, where his ship earned a high reputation for efficiency—shifting topsails and crossing top-gallant and royal yards with the best of them.

In February 1883 *Hecla* received orders which were to have a considerable effect on Wilson's future. There was trouble in another part of the Khedive's dominions, where a rebellion led by the fanatical Mahdi had overrun most of the Sudan and had even carried his authority to the Red Sea littoral. British troops were helping the Egyptians and amongst reinforcements sent to Trinkitat were some Royal Marines from the Mediterranean Fleet which were embarked in the *Hecla*.

Wilson's orders were to carry the Marines to Egypt and return to Malta, but at Port Said he learnt that our forces at Trinkitat were seriously short of both bread and water. Four tank lighters were ready loaded, but the only tug available was old and unreliable.

Wilson saw his chance. Though a stickler for discipline he could ignore instructions at times. This, he reasoned, was an emergency which required instant action. In case his Commander-in-Chief thought otherwise he delayed wiring for covering approval until he had passed through the canal and was about to sail from Suez. In those pre-wireless days, whatever the reply, he would be beyond recall.

Passing down the Red Sea the *Hecla* sighted the horse-transport *Neera*, fast aground on an uncharted reef. Wilson knew that horses were as badly needed as water and bread, but the sea was rough, the weather threatening and *Hecla*, approaching as close as possible to the wreck, was still three cables off when she anchored on bad holding ground. It was

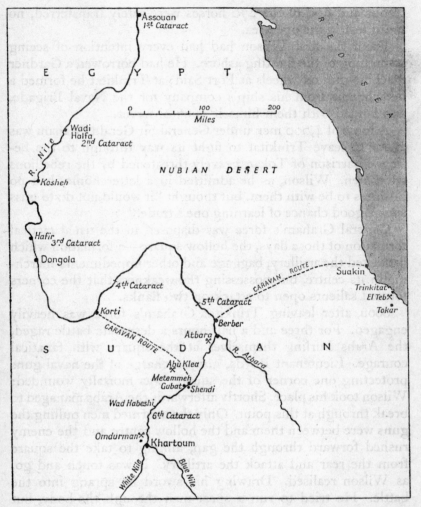

the sort of emergency in which Wilson delighted. Boatwork
was just practicable, so the thwarts were removed from *Hecla*'s
launch and pinnace and the transfer of men and beasts began without delay. Until nightfall, when the wind rose to a
gale, the work continued, the boats plunging up and down
alongside the wreck or fighting their way back to the *Hecla* full
of scared soldiers and frightened animals. In ten hours all the

troops and 200 of the 270 horses were safely transferred, no mean feat in the open sea.

From the first Wilson had had every intention of seeing something of the fighting ashore. He had borrowed a Gardner machine-gun on wheels at Port Said; at Trinkitat he formed a detachment from his ship's company for the Naval Brigade, and landed with them himself as an observer.

A force of 4,000 men under General Sir Gerald Graham was about to leave Trinkitat to fight its way through to the be-sieged garrison of Tokar, gravely threatened by the rebellious tribesmen. Wilson, as he admitted in a letter home, had no business to be with them, but thought "it would not do to miss such a good chance of learning one's trade."

General Graham's force was disposed in the usual tactical formation of those days, the hollow square—a formation which protected the artillery, baggage and other impedimenta march-ing in its centre, but possessing the weakness that the corners formed salients open to attack on two flanks.

Soon after leaving Trinkitat Graham's force was heavily engaged. For three and a half hours a desperate battle raged, the Arabs hurling themselves at the square with fanatical courage. Lieutenant Royds, R.N., in charge of the naval guns protecting one corner of the square, was mortally wounded; Wilson took his place. Shortly afterwards the Arabs managed to break through at this point. Only the unarmed men pulling the guns were between them and the hollow centre and the enemy rushed forward through the gap, aiming to take the square from the rear and attack the artillery. It was touch and go, as Wilson realised. Drawing his sword he sprang into the battle. He tried to run a spear-man through the body, but his sword snapped near the hilt. Wilson never hesitated, laying into the nearby Arabs with his fists. He was covered with blood from a head-wound (his old-fashioned pith helmet had saved his life) and looked so ferocious that the enemy hesitated.

It was all over in a moment, but Wilson's counter attack, carried out single-handed, had momentarily checked the advance, allowing some men of the Yorkshire and Lancashire Regiment to reach the threatened point.

Wilson, returning to his ship that night with his head done up with sticking-plaster, clearly thought no more of the matter, but Redvers Buller, one of the Brigadiers, was so impressed that he sent in an official report of the "distinguished act of bravery" which had saved the day. Wilson was the hero of the hour, though he took it all very modestly and coolly. As he wrote to a friend: "I only walked out in the morning as a loafer just to see the fight . . . as I happened to stumble into a hot corner I could not have possibly done anything but what I did, unless I took to my heels."

In some men this might have been false modesty, but Wilson was writing nothing less than the absolute truth. Physically and morally he was all his life quite without fear. He simply did what he conceived to be his duty. It never occurred to him to do otherwise.

El Teb, a battle in which, strictly speaking, he should never have taken part, made Wilson universally known, a national hero. Pictures of his exploit, some of them drawing on the imagination of the artist, appeared in the illustrated papers, greatly to Wilson's disgust, for he detested publicity. The *Hecla*, her commission abroad completed, had been ordered home to Portsmouth. The entry in his diary for 6 June is characteristic:

"Docked ship. Received the V.C."

That evening he was back in the workshop which he had rigged up on board. Next day he sailed, with relief, for Berehaven, escaping from the many invitations which were pouring in, including dinners by the press and the Savage Club. To all of them, including a telegram asking him to stay with the Queen at Balmoral, he answered politely but firmly that duty prevented him accepting. It is clear that Wilson owed none of his subsequent success to currying favour in high places.

Until 1887 the responsibility for naval armaments and ordnance stores had lain with the War Office. Now it was transferred to the Admiralty and a new Department, Naval

Ordnance and Torpedoes, was formed. The first Director was Captain J. A. Fisher with his old friend Wilson as deputy.

After two years at the Admiralty Wilson returned to the torpedo school (H.M.S. *Vernon*) as Commanding Officer. Material was developing at a tremendous rate and Wilson exerted considerable influence on the future of underwater weapons. The double-barrelled torpedo-tube for fast torpedo craft, the submerged torpedo-tube for larger ships, the develop-ment of the moored mine, boom and net defence for harbours and ships were amongst the matters to which he applied his inventive mind, backed by long practical experience at sea. Wilson, nearing fifty years of age, was still a bachelor, living alone in his cabin on board, landing only to take enough exer-cise to keep himself in his usual state of absolute physical fit-ness and entirely absorbed in his work.

After *Vernon* he did a further spell in command afloat, as Captain and Rear-Admiral. How and when he came by his nickname of "Tug" is not clear. There are various theories: that he was always pulling and tugging, forcing others to do his will; that he resembled a famous prize-fighter called Tug Wilson, renowned for his tenacity and pluck; that, as an Admiral, he had told a ship which reported that she could not sail until next day, when ordered to sea on urgent duty, that if she was not gone in four hours he would come and tow (tug) her out himself in front of the whole fleet. Whatever the truth the name stuck.

In 1898 he returned to the Admiralty as Controller of the Navy, charged with "all matters included in the designing, building and repairing of ships of war, the manufacture of armour, machinery, boilers and guns, torpedoes, and the pro-vision of stores and mechanical appliances." It was a key post, for a very large building programme had been authorised by Parliament—14 battleships, 27 cruisers, 52 destroyers, 2 sloops, 4 gunboats, 8 light draught steamers for special service and a Royal Yacht—and the public was keenly interested in the expansion of the Fleet.

During the next two years this interest was tinged with

alarm. It was widely believed that the Fleet, some of whose ships were still armed with muzzle-loading guns, had been allowed to become obsolete. Parliament noted with concern that, because of delays in building, large sums voted for naval expansion remained unspent.

Qualitatively, as well as quantitatively our ships were open to criticism. The new Royal Yacht, built to Admiralty designs in a Royal Dockyard, nearly capsized when put afloat, because the weights worked into her superstructure were far greater than they should have been. Public criticism became more vocal, much of it aimed at the Department of the Admiralty chiefly responsible, the Controller's. Then came the "battle of the boilers."

Hitherto our warships had been fitted with cylindrical boilers—reliable, but bulky, heavy, slow to raise steam. An entirely new type of boiler—lighter, smaller, quicker in operation and potentially of much greater steam-producing capacity —had made its appearance and the Admiralty had ordered a number for trial first in a gunboat, where they seemed quite successful, and then in the new cruiser *Powerful*.

Engineers ashore and afloat were by no means unanimous that the water-tube boiler was all it had been cracked up to be. Some went so far as to say that it was wrong in principle. The *Powerful*, sent on a voyage to China round the Cape, ran into trouble and the defects which her boilers developed were widely publicised. Leading the opposition was a Mr Allen, the Member of Parliament for Gateshead, a north-country engineer with a considerable reputation and the gift of the gab. He had a bluff, blunt, good-humoured manner which carried weight in the House of Commons. His arguments, clearly put, were easily followed by the public at large. They seemed most convincing. In the debate on the Navy Estimates for 1901 he remarked:

"I say briefly that the water-tube boiler for marine purposes cannot work . . . if you experiment more with these water-tubes you will come to grief again."

It sounds ridiculous enough in the light of later knowledge,

D

but with fears already growing that all was not well with Britain's first line of defence it brought matters to a head.

A General Election six months before had returned another Unionist Government to power, but Lord Selborne had replaced Mr Goschen as First Lord. On assuming office he had set up a Committee of Enquiry to investigate, amongst other things, whether the Controller's Department was unduly hampered by custom, and a further body, the Boiler Committee, to enquire into the Navy's policy on water-tube boilers. The Admiralty with 1,500 boilers on order, all of the same Belleville type which had been fitted in the *Powerful*, was heavily committed.

The interim report of the Boiler Committee appeared condemning the Belleville boiler, but recommending other types of water-tube boilers at present untried. Wilson felt very strongly that these conclusions had been arrived at without full consideration of all the relevant facts. The First Lord backed by all the other members of the Board supported the findings of the Committee. Clearly the position of the Controller had become impossible.

Wilson was a great commander rather than a great administrator. His habit of working alone, of issuing orders rather than laying down policy, his almost pathological reserve which prevented him from discussing matters with his subordinates and his consequent failure to decentralise, were grave handicaps. Fortunately his outstanding qualities were also fully recognised. He was offered, and accepted, the command of the Channel Squadron, an important post.

For out of partial failure was to come his greatest success. The Channel Squadron, already consisting of eight battleships and six cruisers, was to grow during the next few years into Britain's most important fleet as ships were recalled from abroad to meet the challenge of Germany's rapidly expanding navy. For the next six years Wilson was able to deploy to the full his great gifts for command afloat.

The squadron which he took over was efficient, but only in certain respects. The evolutions in which it excelled demanded a very high standard of discipline and skill, but often had little direct bearing on what should have been the underlying aim, defeat of an enemy fleet at sea. For too many years the Navy had been engaged in minor warlike operations, supporting the Army or the civil power on shore. Officers and men were of splendid quality, but lacking clarity of purpose. The ships were smart and clean, meticulously maintained, but the principal objective of a man-of-war, readiness for instant battle with a powerful foe, had become obscured. There was too much stress on the glories of the past; too little thought of the future. Tradition is a fine servant, but a poor master. Wilson set out to put all this right. He was exactly the man for the job, farseeing and technically very competent, a brilliant seaman, a fighter.

The very first time he took the Channel Squadron to sea he sailed them out of harbour in two parallel columns instead of a single line, halving the time to reach open water. He went on as he had begun, exercising his ships under conditions which at first surprised and alarmed his captains—at night without lights; in fog, without reducing speed; in every sort of adverse weather. He was daring, but he knew exactly what he was doing. Confidence grew. On manoeuvres he nearly always got the better of his opponents, often by some unorthodox move. Deep thought and a measure of intuitive genius gave him a knowledge of his adversaries' plans which seemed uncanny. Unruffled, composed, concise and clear in his orders, he was, as all were quick to appreciate, in complete command of any situation.

The influence which a single man can exert on thousands of his fellows, most of whom rarely see him, is an unceasing source of wonder. From the bridge of his flagship at sea, from the bare, unrevealing cabins which he used in harbour, Wilson imposed his will on every officer and man in his fleet. He was a hard taskmaster, for he worked them as he worked himself. Discipline and devotion to duty were the principles which guided him. "Duty," said Nelson, "is the great business of a Seaman." Wilson came very near to living this ideal.

The utmost effort of which a man was capable was the expected norm. Praise was superfluous, and rarely given. His signal to a cruiser, returning to port "sunk" by the umpires after performing particularly well on manoeuvres, "I am sorry to lose you," was so notably effusive as to be memorable. His inspection report on his crack battleship after admitting that she was "clean and well organised throughout . . . and had taken first place in General Exercises oftener than any other ship in the squadron," concluded with the frigid reminder that "more time should be devoted to the instruction of midshipmen in rifle and cutlass drill before breakfast."

His short, sturdy, upright body was as hard as nails, seemingly impervious to fatigue, heat or cold. Though always ready with a quick decision he would often seem to be away in a world of his own, deep in meditation. At such times nothing distracted him; guns firing within a few feet of the bridge at sea; men working heavy cables immediately above his cabin in harbour.

Though grudgingly admitting they were sometimes necessary he hated pomp and ceremony. One of the very few occasions when he lost his usual composure was when the German Emperor came in his yacht on an official visit to the fleet. It was foggy and a wireless signal announced that the *Hohenzollern*'s arrival was delayed. Wilson, who never minded what he wore so long as his clothes were comfortable, had postponed the evil hour of donning full dress with decorations as long as possible. He was walking the quarter deck, clad in an old "working" monkey-jacket when, without warning, the Emperor's yacht slid out of the mist. There was no time to go below to change. As bugles sent the men at the double to man the side Tug Wilson, helped by his coxswain and a trembling steward, struggled wrathfully into his gold-laced coat—an awesome sight.

Even off duty he lived to a rigid code. To clear his head and harden his body he would land for long tramps ashore with a gun and an old dog or with some perspiring companions. Dressed in a blue suit, wearing uniform boots and a black uniform tie he would cover the miles at high speed, usually in silence. The places he liked best were wild and desolate; lonely places where he could wear his old tweed cap, instead of the ancient bowler which acknowledged the greater formality demanded by a big seaport. He was never observed to enter a theatre or other place of amusement.

About once a year he would proceed on long leave to visit his sister in Norfolk. Mounting his bicycle, an ancient bone-shaker about ten years out of date, he would bump away over the Dockyard cobbles—the marine sentry presenting arms, officers and men standing strictly at attention, watching with some relief as he pedalled out of sight. But as often as not he would be back again several days earlier than expected, gladly taking up his task.

Indeed he seemed to have no taste for the relaxations of ordinary men. Let others enjoy music, cards or dancing (with the heavy proviso that they must never interfere with work), but such things were not for him. Though a kind and generous host he rarely smoked and bothered little what he ate or drank. He liked to entertain his officers at dinner, encouraging them to talk particularly on service matters. Alert and interested he would listen to their views, showing by his brief remarks that they had the whole of his attention. Though rarely seen with a book he was surprisingly well informed on the history and problems of any place where the Fleeet happened to be. In spite of his dictatorial ways he was without conceit, though he believed that age, experience and application had endowed him beyond his fellows. Personal merit did not come into it.

He was a man with a mission. Time was short; how short was apparent in 1905 when the Kaiser threatened France in a speech at Tangier and Wilson was told to be ready to attack the German coast. War, though avoided on this occasion, would come. Anything which hindered his preparations for battle must be avoided. Wilson liked to keep his ships in out-of-the-way places—Berehaven, Arosa Bay—where distractions were few. Twice he arranged for his fleet to go on "Christmas" leave early in December and to sail from its home ports for some desolate spot a week before the "festive season." Fighting men must learn to be not as other men; ships must be their homes, messmates their companions. Duty was the great business of a seaman.

Women, intrigued by the indifference behind a courteous manner, liked him. It is possible, but very doubtful, that had he been less of a confirmed bachelor he would have been more sympathetic with men who applied for compassionate leave to visit their homes, requests which were nearly always refused however good the grounds. Utterly indifferent to what others thought of him he never courted popularity to even the smallest degree. One afternoon the Admirals and Captains of the Fleet were racing against each other in their galleys. The weather was bad with a strong wind and a nasty lop. Several boats capsized. As the race progressed it was clear it would be a very close thing between those which were left. Spectators gradually assembled on the decks of the anchored ships, watching the plunging galleys fighting for the lead. Just short of the finishing line Wilson, who loved sailing a boat and did it very well, nosed ahead. It was a thrilling finish and when he returned to his flagship the crew broke out into a spontaneous cheer. To Wilson this was a failure in discipline. Hurrying up the gangway he ordered the "still" to be sounded and went below to his cabin without another word. Not for nothing did the sailors call him "old 'ard 'eart."

He was hardly the man to kindle enthusiasm or inspire love, yet men were proud to serve under this almost superhuman figure. He was utterly just. He had no favourites, and he was a splendid seaman.

With material already so costly as to breed a certain caution in its use he handled his ships with a daring disregard of the consequences of failure. Men recounted how he brought the Channel Squadron into a rock-strewn, tide-swept anchorage when all the leading marks were obscured by fog. Tug Wilson ordered a gangway to be lowered, walked down to just above water level, and led his ships into harbour by looking *under* the fog. When the mist lifted they were anchored in perfect station exactly where he had intended.

He was the finest commander of ships at sea whom any of them had ever known. His mastery of his profession, his un-ruffled composure, his consistency and his clarity of purpose won their allegiance; even, in spite of themselves, a sort of amazed affection. The Fleet he turned over to his successor, Lord Charles Beresford, if not exactly sorry to see him go, would have followed him anywhere. In war nine out of ten would have opted to serve under Tug Wilson in preference to any other admiral in the Navy.

Wilson gave strict orders that his departure should not be marked by the usual demonstration of manning the side and cheering. He went ashore alone, his barge passing through the silent ships without any fuss and ceremony. Inscrutable as ever he gave no sign of the poignancy of the moment. Though promoted to Admiral of the Fleet just before he turned over his command, his active connection with the Navy, his only interest for fifty-two years, was at an end, for he could not expect further employment.

He settled down in Swaffham with his sister, occupying himself with the small matters of country life. He bought a motor car which he maintained in the most meticulous con-dition. He even took up golf, studying the game with his usual diligence. Very soon he was as busy, and seemingly as content, as he had ever been in high places.

But all was not well with his beloved Navy. A year after Wilson retired the great controversy between the First Sea Lord, Admiral Sir John Fisher, and the principal commander afloat, Admiral Lord Charles Beresford, was coming to a head. Though many service officers remained loyally on the side-lines others were strongly partisan—in the "Fish-pond" or "Beresfordites." The rift was so deep that the discipline of the Navy was being undermined. Parliament, the press and the public joined in. Beresford, removed from his command afloat, wrote to the Prime Minister making serious allegations against the Admiralty. A committee at Cabinet level with Mr

Asquith in the chair found these charges unsubstantiated, but was profoundly disturbed by the schisms disrupting the Navy.

Harmony must be restored and harmony flows from the top. It was essential that the senior serving officer, the First Sea Lord, should be someone who had taken no active part in the dispute, a man without fear or favour, who commanded universal respect in the country and in the Navy.

Lord Fisher had recognised that his position had become untenable, but he still had a considerable say in who was to take his place. Fisher and Wilson had had their differences, but they had often worked together in the past. Wilson, in "Fisher's estimation," was "a very great man whose fighting views were absolutely impregnable." Wilson was no longer young, but he was physically very robust. He would be the right man in the right place. The Prime Minister agreed, and in January 1910, Sir Arthur Wilson returned to active duty as First Sea Lord.

The Fisher–Beresford dispute had aroused so much public interest that his appointment was front-page news. On the day he was to take up his post, pressmen and photographers were waiting outside the Admiralty, ready to report his arrival. Unlike Fisher and Beresford, Wilson had always shunned publicity. The assembled pressmen paid no attention when an elderly gentleman (he was sixty-eight) in a still more elderly frock-coat and top hat strolled up quite alone and unostentatiously entered the building. It is said that his first act was to order the removal of all chairs from his room but his own. Visitors would be encouraged to be brief.

Wilson moved into the official residence in Queen Anne's Gate where, except for the domestic staff, he lived quite alone. Bringing only the barest necessities he ignored the social side of his high office, immersing himself with his usual diligence in the business in hand. He had never shown the least favouritism. Confidence that their careers no longer depended on the success of either of the opposing factions gradually returned to the officers ashore and afloat. Firm leadership and Wilson's legendary personal integrity had cleared up a very nasty situation, but in other aspects of his work he was less successful.

The position of First Sea Lord is one of great personal power. The Government, through the First Lord, has the final say in directing policy, but the First Sea Lord, a nominee of the First Lord, has very wide terms of reference. They include sole responsibility for advising the Government on all major questions of naval policy and maritime warfare, including the preparations for war. He is directly responsible for the fighting and sea-going efficiency of the Fleet, its organisation and mobilisation, and the distribution and movements of all ships in commission or reserve. At that time control of the Intelligence, Hydrographic and Naval Ordnance Departments also came directly under his hand. The First Sea Lord was a *supremo,* with the other naval members of the Board subordinates rather than colleagues.

When the Admiralty was re-organised in 1832 material questions were already becoming more and more important. With no other country challenging Britain directly at sea the study of war faded into the background. The functions of executive action and supply were not separated and departmental duties, in particular the settling of endless questions involving material, tended to become the principal duties of all members of the Board. An immense amount of detail was brought directly to the First Sea Lord for final decision.

The steady pressure of their "daily round" left little time for thought on less immediate problems. There was no Naval War Staff in the modern sense—officers charged specifically with studying the past, thinking of the future and drawing up detailed plans, unencumbered by day-to-day departmental duties. The Navy's war plans were the individual province of the First Sea Lord, calling in what help or advice he thought fit.

The position was one which suited Wilson admirably. He had always preferred to work alone. As Commander-in-Chief afloat he had often acted as his own staff, writing out orders in his own hand. Even his second-in-command had rarely been shown his mind or asked for his views. Without a family or other personal ties, with an immense capacity for work, long experience and great ability he believed himself without pride and simply as a matter of fact to be perfectly capable of doing everything that was necessary.

In 1910 there was considerable public uneasiness about the fitness of our Fleet to combat the rapidly growing naval power of Germany. We had the ships, we had the men, but had we made the necessary arrangements to use them to the best advantage? What was the naval plan for war? If the Germans were to strike would we be ready? In the summer of 1911 the arrival of the German gunboat *Panther* in Agadir provoked a crisis. "Brinkmanship" on this scale must mean that the Germans felt themselves strong enough to risk aggression. In Winston Churchill's memorable words: "All the alarm bells throughout Europe began immediately to quiver."

In August the Prime Minister, Mr Asquith, secretly convened a meeting of the Committee of Imperial Defence, before which the heads of the armed services were told to explain what they thought might happen if the Kaiser was to march, and how we ought to react. The General Staff of the Army had detailed plans already prepared, but Sir Arthur Wilson, speaking for the Navy, revealed very little. Whatever naval war plans existed, says Churchill, remained "locked away in his own brain." The meeting made it clear that profound differences existed between the War Office and Admiralty, and that little or no discussion took place between the two Services. The Cabinet was far from satisfied. Next month Asquith invited Winston Churchill to become First Lord of the Admiralty.

Churchill had long been obsessed by a conviction that war with Germany was inevitable. Without plans, worked out in detail by the Army and Navy in full consultation, the threat could not be contained. The absence of a proper War Staff at the Admiralty was a crippling defect. In his own words we needed, "A brain more comprehensive than that of any single man however gifted—tireless and unceasing in its action— applied continuously to the scientific study of naval strategy and preparation." The Staff would be "an instrument capable of formulating any decision which has been taken, or may be taken, by the executive in terms of precise and exhaustive detail." Only then could we be sure that we had provided against every likely contingency.

It was a view to which Sir Arthur Wilson was wholly opposed. He believed that the First Sea Lord already had all the assistants he might need in the various Departmental heads. "The Service would have the most supreme contempt for any body of officers who professed to be specially trained to think . . . officers are judged by what they can do when afloat." The staff was himself, "and every soul inside the Admiralty, including the charwomen who empty the wastepaper baskets full of plans of the amateur strategists, *cabinet* or otherwise." A new First Sea Lord might require further assistance . . . "I see no necessity for any addition."

The differences between Wilson and the new First Lord on the broad lines of naval policy to be followed if war came were equally great. The Government believed that a British Expeditionary Force should immediately be sent to France. Wilson considered the effort involved would prevent the Navy carrying out its major function of destroying the enemy Fleet. The close blockade of German ports by the Fleet prescribed when Fisher was at the Admiralty was still supported by Wilson. The First Lord was convinced that the torpedo had rendered such a policy out of date.

"These," as Churchill remarked, "were large and vital differences."

The Board of the Admiralty is appointed by the First Lord. From the moment he arrived in Whitehall Churchill had been determined to have under him men willing to accept his views. Time was short, there was much to be done, the task could only be completed "by men who came together with consenting minds." Now, in a sweeping reorganisation, all but one of the Sea Lords were replaced.

Sir Arthur Wilson received the news with his usual equanimity. The Government, in the person of the First Lord, had

a perfect right to make what changes they chose. He had
done his duty. Orders were orders. It was now his duty to
make way for someone else. Calmly and without any literary
flourishes he wrote to his sister:

"When you return from your visit to Aunt Ellen you will
find me no longer a Lord of the Admiralty." He praised the
composition of the new Board, hoped that the change would be
made without any friction; he would be glad to get away. The
most he permitted himself was this gentle dig, "Whether they
will be more amenable than the present Board, I don't know."

Smiling his rather frosty smile Admiral of the Fleet Sir
Arthur Wilson withdrew once more into private life. He left
the Admiralty as he had arrived, without fuss or ceremony,
walking out alone through the north-west door and vanishing
into the crowds strolling in the Mall. It is an interesting commentary on the characters of two great men that Churchill retained the highest opinion of Wilson: "a man of highest quality
and stature."

Three years later Wilson was to return to the Admiralty to
work there with Churchill and Fisher during the war. When
Churchill was superseded after the failure to force the Dardanelles Wilson wrote to the Prime Minister saying that he
was not prepared to serve under any new First Lord "as the
strain under such circumstances would be beyond my strength."
At a time when Churchill seemed to have hardly a friend in the
world it was a tribute which he greatly valued. "I was as-
tounded to learn what he had done. It came as an absolute
surprise to me: and I do not mind saying that I felt as proud as
a young officer mentioned for the first time in despatches."

Praise from Tug Wilson, however indirect, was praise
indeed.

BERESFORD
1846-1919
The Sailor Politician

IF the building of the first iron-clad in 1856 was the fuse which set off the naval renaissance of the late nineteenth century it was the Naval Defence Act of 1889 which gave force to the explosion. Without the strong pressure of public opinion the Treasury's purse-strings would never have been sufficiently loosened to provide quantity as well as quality. The public had to foot the bill and it was Lord Charles Beresford, sailor and politician, who did so much to make the needs of the Navy known in Parliament, in the press and to the country at large.

For the thirty years around the turn of the century he was the most talked about figure in the Royal Navy. Afloat or ashore everyone knew of "Charlie B." To the man-in-the-street he was the ideal sailor; fearless, breezy, independent, but considerate of those under his command. He was rich, handsome and well-born, with a host of friends ranging from King Edward VII to simple A.B.'s. He had greatly distinguished himself in the fighting in Egypt and the Sudan. As a Member of Parliament he had hurled himself with equal zest into battle with parsimonious Governments for a stronger Navy. Such faults as impetuosity and love of the limelight were easily forgiven in this brave, high-spirited, sporting, generous and very charming man. To thousands up and down the country Lord Charles Beresford, a favourite bulldog squatting at his feet, was a symbol of Britain's might, majesty, dominion and power. In 1907 he assumed command of Britain's principal naval force, the Channel Fleet. Who could have predicted that twenty months later, a full year before the normal end of his appointment, he would be ordered by the Admiralty to haul down his flag?

The fairies who attended at the birth of Charles William de la Poer Beresford in 1846 had been generous in their gifts. Wealth, good looks, good health and an extraordinary capacity to survive the minor accidents of a reckless life were amongst them, good luck, which held for nearly sixty of his seventy-three years, and boundless energy. In his middle sixties he was still in better physical shape, except for an occasional twinge of gout, than many men twenty years younger, in spite of having broken chest-bone, pelvis, right leg, right hand, foot, five ribs, collar bones (four times) and nose (three times). He was hardly ever ailing, never poor and greatly loved. But he failed to achieve his lifelong ambition and died a disappointed man.

The de la Poers (or Pohers) were given a parcel of land in County Waterford in 1172. Early in the eighteenth century the family was joined by marriage to the Beresfords. The great Georgian house of Curraghmore was completed in 1771, seventeen years before a de la Poer Beresford became the first Marquess of Waterford. Charlie B. was the second of five brothers, three of whom served in the British Army. All were the sort who win the affection and respect of their fellow men— courageous, sporting, competent and kind; always ready to laugh or fight; slow to harbour a grudge.

They were a hardy, reckless lot. Charles' father inherited the title when his grandfather broke his neck in the hunting field in 1859. His mother, Christina, a very handsome woman with particularly beautiful eyes, was never on a horse until she was over forty years of age, but became a noted rider to hounds. Horses were an important part of life at Curraghmore and when the family and their friends were assembled for the hunting season there were up to a hundred beasts in the stables.

Young Charles was sent to school in England, first to Deal and then to the famous establishment at Stubbington which has prepared so many boys for the Royal Navy. The hulk *Britannia*, moored off Fort Blockhouse in Haslar Creek, had taken the place of the Royal Naval College in Portsmouth Dockyard. Cadets joined her before their thirteenth birthday and spent two years learning the rudiments of their trade— seamanship, navigation and gunnery with some ordinary school work. Charles was small for his age, but fearless, nimble and good with his hands. Sail drill aloft (the foremast had been retained for the purpose) and practical seamanship were the things in which he excelled. "Book work did not interest me" he confessed later. In 1861 he went to sea.

His first ship was the famous *Marlborough*, a wooden line-of-battleship pierced for 131 muzzle-loading, smooth-bore guns and closely resembling Nelson's *Victory*. The *Marlborough*, flagship of the Mediterranean Fleet, was renowned for her smartness and efficiency, meaning, in those days, the speed and precision with which her seamen could handle the sails. As young Beresford climbed her side to report on board two large men, the quartermaster and the boatswain's mate, peered down at him. "That white-faced little beggar ain't long for this world," said one in sepulchral tones. John (Chamfy) Glanville and Dicky Horne (it was like Charles Beresford to remember their names) were typical sailors of the day, free with their language, handy with their fists and afraid of nothing at all; ignorant, simple men knowing very little of life ashore, but magnificent in their own element.

A big sailing ship was a complicated thing: it was impossible for the work of the seamen to be supervised in detail and emergencies must be dealt with instantly, particularly in bad weather. Seamen were expected to act without orders, and did so. Life on board was always uncomfortable and often dangerous. Food was inadequate and very bad, quarters cramped, discipline severe, with floggings a frequent occurrence. Very little leave was given and the only use made of a run ashore, after months aboard, was to get roaring drunk. Yet this extraordinary life produced seamen whose professional skill, courage and hardihood has rarely, if ever, been equalled.

The older officers and men who taught young Beresford and his like their trade, were seamen of exactly the same type as

those who fought with Nelson at the Nile and Trafalgar.
Britannia ruled the waves and young British seamen had not the
slightest doubt that they belonged to the finest service in the
world.

The comradeship of the gunroom, the element of risk in-
separable from work aloft and the hard, practical work suited
young Charles Beresford admirably. In his autobiography he
refers to the *Marlborough* as "the ship of happiest memories."
It was indeed a good enough life for a healthy (as he soon became), high-spirited lad. The ambition of every young officer
was to become a proficient *seaman*, one of the men whose skill
would, in battle, place the ship in position alongside the enemy
at point-blank range. Gunnery was looked down upon, for
any fool could fire a gun after a little practice in loading those
primitive weapons. The *Marlborough* had a single screw and an
engine of 3,025 horse-power, but it was only used for entering
or leaving harbour. Work aloft was the work which mattered
and that was "a miracle of smartness and speed."

"No doubt the present fleet far excels the old wooden walls,"
wrote an old topmate to Admiral Beresford fifty years later,
"but the old wooden walls made sailors." The writer went on
to recall how he had stood bolt upright on the tiny platform
200 feet above the deck made by the truck or cap at the very
top of the royal mast. "No doubt a foolish practice. But in
those days fear never came our way."

But the wooden walls were on their way out. Beresford's
next ship was one of Britain's first iron-clads, the *Defence*. If
this was the Navy of the future he did not like it, . . . "a dreadful ship. After the immaculate decks, the glittering perfection, the spirit and fire and pride of the *Marlborough* . . . I was
condemned to a slovenly, unhandy, tin kettle which could not
sail without steam; which had not even royal-masts; and which
took minutes instead of seconds to cross (hoist) topgallant
yards. A disgusting spectacle. . . ." Charles wrote to his
father asking that he should be removed from the Navy, but
this unhappy interlude lasted less than a year and from 1865
to 1870 he served in vessels which successfully managed to

Admiral Lord Charles Beresford, Baron of Metemmeh and Curraghmore,
GCB, GCVO

ignore the greasy advent of machinery—the corvette *Clio* in
which he rounded the Horn and saw the Pacific Islands, the
frigates *Tribune*, *Sutlej* and *Galatea*. In the *Tribune* he served
under Captain Lord Gillford, afterwards Lord Clanwilliam, a
famous "taught hand" and a magnificent seaman whose exploits included sailing up the Fraser River in British Columbia,
cutting a new foremast out of the forest and rigging it without
outside help. Gillford had a saying "if a man is a lubber over a
job, you ought to be able to *show* him how to do it," a lesson
which Beresford, also a man of his hands, never forgot.
Amongst the many things this "sprig of the nobility" learnt in
the *Clio* was how to welt and sole a boot.

His captain in the *Galatea* was the Duke of Edinburgh,
another fine seaman. In a voyage lasting two and a half years
Charles saw South Africa, Australia, New Zealand, Tahiti,
the Sandwich Islands, Japan, China, India and the Falkland
Islands, learning much under that kind and wise Prince whom
he frequently accompanied during formal visits ashore. Here
also he was for the first time in regular contact with royalty.
On paying off the *Galatea* Beresford went as Flag-Lieutenant
to Admiral Sir Harry Keppel at Plymouth. They were a lively
combination, fond of sport and practical jokes. In spite of the
disparity in their ages they became and remained firm friends.

These were formative years which confirmed his love for
ships and the sea, taught him a lot about his fellow men and
gave him confidence in his own abilities as a seaman and a
leader.

His point of view remained essentially aristocratic. He
came from a great family which, while enjoying life to the full,
took its responsibilities very seriously. Leadership was not
something which you consciously acquired or even thought
about. You led, others followed. You knew, others didn't.
The Beresfords, popular as they might be, were a masterful
lot.

In 1874, at the request of his brother, now Lord Waterford, Charles Beresford stood for Parliament. In spite of his
opposition to Home Rule for Ireland, then a lively issue, he

E

was elected. He was to be in and out of Parliament for the next forty years. Never a party man, he confined himself almost entirely to naval affairs, on which he was a frequent speaker inside and outside the House. A great name, a lively wit and an easy, fluent style can be more potent assets than a profound intellect. His speeches, forceful but good-humoured, may have received more attention than they deserved, but there is no doubt that Beresford very soon became a well-known public figure. Though still only in his late twenties his influence was considerable.

In 1875, when the Prince of Wales visited India, Lieutenant Lord Charles Beresford was appointed A.D.C. Beresford, a very good organiser and a lively companion, was well suited to the post. His friendship with his royal master was to continue for very many years.

On his return Beresford, now a Commander, was appointed as second-in-command of the iron-clad *Thunderer* in the Channel Fleet. In those days a naval officer could continue to serve on full pay when a Member of Parliament. There was nothing to prevent this comparatively junior officer, M.P., standing up in the House of Commons and criticising the policy of the Board of Admiralty on such fundamental matters as the arrangements for training men joining the Navy, the more rapid promotion of officers and the number of cruisers needed to give proper protection to our seaborne trade. The Board, not unnaturally, became greatly incensed and the First Lord, George Ward Hunt, informed Beresford that he must choose between the careers of politician and sailor. Charles Beresford immediately appealed to the Prime Minister, claiming that the Admiralty's hint was a clear breach of Parliamentary privilege. Disraeli, a friend of the Beresford family, asked Charles what he intended to do. On being told that, if forced to make a choice, Beresford would resign his seat (which would probably be taken by a hot Home Ruler) Disraeli promised to have a word with the Secretariat. "And that," says Beresford, "was the last I heard of that affair."

But the Admiralty was right. The situation was an im-

possible one. A serving officer with access to some, but not all
of the facts, could attack the policy of the Board with all the
advantages of Parliament and publicity on his side. Even if
used with the utmost discretion, a powerful but possibly inaccurate weapon had been put into inexperienced hands. When
the young man concerned was an Irishman and used to getting
his own way a serious explosion was inevitable, though for the
time being nothing very startling occurred.

In 1878 Beresford married Miss Jeromina Gardner; all the
other members for County Waterford, strong Home Rulers to
a man, came to his wedding. That same year he was appointed
to command the Royal Yacht *Osborne* used by his friend the
Prince of Wales, a very pleasant post which he continued to
hold for the next three years until appointed to the sloop,
gun-vessel *Condor* in the Mediterranean.

Charles Beresford's appearance in a small ship (only 780
tons) on a foreign station when he might still have been enjoying a much more pleasant job in home waters was not entirely
fortuitous. For some time trouble had been brewing in Egypt
and there might be a chance of active service. Early in June
1882 *Condor* was lying off Alexandria with other units of the
Mediterranean Fleet under Admiral Sir Beauchamp Seymour.
Seymour's orders were equivocal. He was to support the
Khedive, who was being openly defied by a military dictatorship led by his own Minister of War, Arabi Pasha; but he had
little force at his disposal and the French, who shared the responsibility, were irresolute. Gladstone's Liberal government
was, indeed, unwilling to take up an increasingly open challenge.

It was at this point that Commander Beresford, never slow
to assume responsibility which did not properly belong to him,
decided to take a hand. He wrote to the Prince of Wales
stating his "conviction, formed at close quarters, that unless
Arabi's movements were forcibly arrested, England's position
in Egypt and her hold on the Suez canal were doomed." The
Prince discreetly informed the Foreign Secretary, Lord Glanville, of the contents of this personal letter, only to hear very

shortly afterwards that his impetuous friend had also forwarded his version of the political position to the ultra-conservative *Morning Post*, which was making full use of the information to belabour the Government. The Foreign Secretary was furious almost forgetting the dangers in Egypt in his indignation at the gross irregularity of a serving officer communicating with the press. The Prince was forced to intervene on his friend's behalf. "He is an Irishman," he wrote to Lord Glanville, "and in consequence hasty and impulsive, but I feel sure that the Queen does not possess a more zealous and loyal officer than he is, and as a rule a more punctilious observer of the regulations of the Service."

Beresford might have been taught a sharp lesson if a massacre of foreigners in Alexandria had not proved his point. The Government was forced into action, strengthened the Fleet and finally, on 11 July, ordered the bombardment of the forts manned by Arabi's rebellious troops. What King Edward VII's biographer Sir Sidney Lee so aptly terms Beresford's "Irish . . . native impulse to air in the press his political or professional views and grievances, to the embarrassment of his colleagues and superiors" was greatly encouraged by this confirmation of his prognosis.

Beresford's little *Condor* had been given only a minor role in the bombardment, which was carried out chiefly by eight large iron-clads including six of the most powerful battleships in the Navy. It was an imposing spectacle as the great ships poured their broadsides into the Egyptian batteries, which returned the fire bravely and with some precision. The bombardment continued all day, the forts gradually being reduced, though not until the battleships had fired off nearly all their ammunition.

Condor's part in the action was described in a letter written by her Captain at the time.

The Marabout Fort was the second largest fort, but a long way off from the place to be attacked by the ironclads. So the Admiral had decided not to attack it at all, as he could not spare one heavy ship, and of course he would not order the small ships down there as it was thought they would be sunk. The orders given to the small ships were to keep out of fire, and to watch for an opportunity to occur, after the forts were relieved, to assist. . . *Condor* [a] repeating ship for signals . . . took station just between the two attacking fleets.

Just as the action began the *Temeraire* parted her cables and got ashore. I ran down to her and towed her off, and while doing so, saw Fort Marabout giving pepper to *Monarch*, *Invincible* and *Penelope*. Not one of these ships could be spared, as they were getting it hot from the forts they were engaging. Seeing the difficulty . . . I steamed down at full speed and engaged Fort Marabout, on the principle that according to orders "an opportunity" had occurred . . . I thought we should have a real tough time of it, as I knew of the heavy guns, and I knew that one shot fairly placed must sink us. But I hoped to be able to dodge the shoals, of which there were many, and get close in, when I was quite sure they would fire over us.

Sir Beauchamp Seymour had just made a signal for the iron-clad *Monarch* to attack Fort Marabout as soon as she could be spared when he heard his own men cheering the little *Condor*. "Good God," cried the Admiral "she'll be sunk!" He was about to hoist her recall when he saw that the gunboat had virtually succeeded in silencing the big fort single-handed, so he hoisted instead "Well done *Condor*."

In a brilliant little action Beresford had shown his courage, initiative and fine leadership. Whatever his merits as a politician he was an excellent fighting man.

The remnants of Arabi's troops withdrew from the forts, leaving the great town of Alexandria at the mercy of the mob. Captain John Fisher of the *Inflexible* with a naval landing party occupied the outer defences. Beresford, at Fisher's request, was appointed Provost-Marshal and Chief of Police with a tiny force of sixty bluejackets and seventy marines to restore order in the great city itself. It was an unenviable assignment.

I never saw anything so awful as the town on that Friday, [wrote Beresford to a friend a fortnight later] streets, squares, blocks of buildings, all on fire . . . Arabs murdering each other for loot under my nose, wretches running about with fire-balls and torches to light up new places, all the main thoroughfares impassable from burning, falling houses, streets with many corpses in them . . . in fact a pandemonium of hell and its devils.

As more marines arrived from the Fleet the bluejackets were organised into fire-brigades, with artificers to keep the primitive appliances going. Natives, sometimes collected at the point of the bayonet, but well paid for their labours, were put to work clearing rubble and burying the dead. Europeans who had thought to seize the opportunity of paying off old scores were disarmed. Great firmness was necessary, but "I only had to shoot five men by drumhead court-martial, beside flogging a certain number." Very wisely Beresford had set up an Egyptian court to try the more serious cases where the penalty would be death or a long term of imprisonment for murder, looting and arson. Executions were only carried out by Egyptian soldiers. In five days order had been restored.

This impetuous man, sometimes so foolish in times of peace, was both wise and moderate when faced with a situation which would have dismayed and defeated most of those who got the better of him on the political stage.

He was, of course, always at his best and happiest when on active service. From Alexandria he tried to get to the front where the Army was preparing to advance on Cairo, around which the rebels were concentrated. He had been promoted to Captain for his services during the bombardment and relieved in the *Condor*, a Commander's command. The Khedive had offered him a post on his staff, but General Sir Garnet Wolseley, the Military Commander-in-Chief, declined to give his permission for Beresford to accept this appointment. On 13 September Arabi's army was defeated at Tel-el-Kebir. Before the end of the month the Egyptain campaign had ended with the victorious return of the Khedive to Cairo. Beresford went home to find himself something of a public hero.

There was still trouble elsewhere in the Khedive's dominions. In the Sudan Mahomet Ali, son of a boat-builder, had announced that he was the Mahdi and the chosen instrument for the reform of Islam. Expeditions sent against him were defeated by the fierce tribesmen who had flocked to his banner. In 1884 he was virtually in command of the whole of the country. After a great deal of procrastination and delay the British

Government decided to limit military action to rescuing loyal subjects left behind in the Eastern Sudan and Khartoum.

There is not much chance of the situation improving and every chance of it getting worse . . . [telegraphed General Gordon from Khartoum, where he had been sent to advise how this could be done]. You must, therefore, decide whether you will or will not make an attempt to save the two-thirds of the population who are well affected before these two-thirds retreat. Should you wish to intervene, send 200 British troops to Wady Halfa, . . . and then open up Souakin–Berber road . . . This will cause an immediate collapse of the revolt.

But the Government refused to accept Gordon's advice and continued to evacuate the Eastern Sudan. With the Souakin–Berber road abandoned there was only one route left open; the Nile. In April 1884 Gordon was closely besieged in Khartoum.

It is 1,650 miles from Cairo to Khartoum, almost as far as Newfoundland to Ireland, and a much more difficult journey. The Sudan, as big as India, was without roads or railways. Parts of the Nile are easily navigable at certain times of the year, but between Assouan and Khartoum are six great cataracts, hopelessly shallow when the river is low; fast-running, divided by many small islands and studded with hidden rocks when the Nile is high. Three of the cataracts can be by-passed by cutting across the desert along the caravan route between Korti and Metemmeh, but the route from Cairo to Khartoum is long and hazardous. (See map, p. 45.)

The Sudan campaign now followed the recognised British pattern; procrastination and delay having led to disaster, improvisation on an epic scale was used to overcome difficulties which were almost insuperable. It was decided to transport the Army to Korti in a fleet of 800 whale-boats thirty feet long, fitted with masts and sails as well as oars. Each would carry ten men. The navigation of the river, tricky at the best of times, being far beyond the capacity of the soldiers a force of Canadian *voyageurs* was engaged, two for each boat. The whale-boats were carried by road and rail to Assiout and towed to Assouan, hauled through the first cataract, which was not particularly fierce, and sailed 200 miles up the fairly easy stretch to Wadi Halfa. Here the real difficulties began.

Officers and men from the Mediterranean Fleet were already at work between Assouan and Korti and a Commander Hammill had surveyed the river as far upstream as Dongola. Working under great difficulties this officer had produced a report of extraordinary thoroughness from which it was clear that the passage of the second cataract, with its Beb-el-Kebir or great gate, was the crux of the water journey to Korti.

Lord Charles Beresford had been doing all he could to get sent to the front. Finally, in August 1884, when staying with the Duke of Fife at Mar Lodge, he was appointed to Lord Wolesley's staff. In September he was in Cairo.

Beresford's arrival in Egypt caused considerable misgiving in the breasts of the naval officers already on the spot, and Lord John Hay the C.-in-C. Mediterranean was at pains to point out that His Lordship was attached to the staff of the commanding general, not in command of the naval forces already on the river. In spite of these instructions Beresford very soon made his presence felt, taking an active part in passing the boats through the second cataract.

In October he was living in a small bell tent at Wadi Halfa "chiefly furnished with a penny whistle, a photograph of Lady Charles, my letters from home, and a stag beetle big enough to carry me to hounds, which I generally had to chase from my bed."

He was on active service again at last and very pleased with life, busying himself with arrangements for navigating the river and riding a racing camel for relaxation and on his journeys of inspection. The advance guard under Sir Herbert Stewart was at Dongola, but further movement south into increasingly hostile country depended on the assembling of troops and supplies.

At the end of November 687 boats including two comparatively large river steamers had passed the Second Cataract, negotiating eight miles of tortuous channels and three "gates" through which the current runs at twelve knots, much faster than the average mill-race. The upper of the gates, the notorious Beb-el-Kebir, was so narrow that the paddle wheels had to be removed from the steamers before they could squeeze through. Nine naval officers and seventy-one bluejackets assisted by hundreds of troops and native labourers had accomplished an "impossible" task, and though twenty-seven men had been drowned very few boats were lost, a little epic of ingenuity and skill. The river had been steadily falling since the end of August, greatly adding to the difficulties.

At the end of 1884 the expedition was concentrating at Korti, where the river makes its great loop north and east. On 31 December a message had come through written on a piece of paper the size of a postage stamp: "'Khartoum all right.' C. G. Gordon, 14th December 1884." The bearer had been told to explain that food was running very short, the enemy numerous. "We want you to come quickly."

On 8 January the Desert Column under Sir Herbert Stewart set off to march across the desert to Metemmeh, a distance of 176 miles. Here they hoped to meet four steamers sent down by Gordon which, manned by Beresford's Naval Brigade and a detachment of infantry, would proceed to Khartoum.

The column, about sixteen hundred strong, included five officers and fifty-three ratings under Beresford with a naval Gardner gun in four pieces carried on camels.

"All went well," wrote Colonel Sir Charles Wilson, "and the sailors, with Beresford on his white donkey, in high spirits, very amusing and nautical. 'Quartermaster, can't you make that man sit a little better on the camel?' 'Can't, Sir; camel's got his hump all a-starboard.'" Eight days after leaving Korti they had covered 150 miles and were approaching the wells of Abu Klea.

The only sign of the enemy had been tracks in the sand left by their scouts, but now the column was brought to a halt by a large force occupying the foothills surrounding the wells. Stewart formed a zariba and camped for the night. As darkness fell the enemy crept closer, firing into the lines. Beresford described how from around came the "noise of tom-toms, whose hollow and menacing beats endlessly and pitilessly repeated, haunts those who have heard it to the last day of their lives." The men, sleepless and very cold, waited impatiently for the dawn.

Stewart had expected the Arabs to attack, but when they did not do so he formed a square and continued his advance. Fire was exchanged as the square moved slowly forward. Then very suddenly, the Arabs charged.

The enemy rose from the ravine in which they were hidden, in the most perfect order. [wrote Colonel Wilson] It was a beautiful and shocking sight, such a one as Fitz-James must have seen when Rhoderick Dhu's men rose out of the heather. . . . How they managed to conceal their horses I know not, but they did so very effectively.

On came the Arabs, led by their Sheikhs, green and white banners floating in the breeze.

They were tearing down upon us with a roar like the roar of the sea [wrote Beresford] an immense surging wave of white-slashed black forms brandishing bright spears and long flashing swords; and all were chanting, as they leaped and ran . . . "La ilaha ili Allah Mohammeda rasul Allah."

Camels were still being driven through a gap in the angle of the square where the Naval Brigade had their Gardner gun when the Arabs charged and now, after firing a few rounds, the Gardner jammed. Beresford and the Chief Boatswain's mate were trying to clear it when the spearmen were on top of them, howling, thrusting. In a moment all the sailors around the gun had been killed. Beresford was knocked off his feet, but somehow swept along in the crush almost uninjured.

I can compare the press to nothing but the crush of a theatre crowd alarmed by a cry of fire. Immediately facing me was an Arab holding a spear over his head, the staff of the weapon jammed against his back by the pressure behind him. I could draw neither sword nor pistol. The front ranks of our men could not use rifle or bayonet for a few moments.

It was Inkerman on a small scale, a soldiers' battle. In furious hand to hand fighting the British gradually got the upper hand, but not until every Arab inside the square had been slain did the others waver and break away. In a few minutes over a thousand Arabs had been killed or mortally wounded, but the little British force had suffered heavily.

They still had twenty-five miles to cover before they reached the river and another battle to fight in which the square again repulsed the enemy. On 20 January, the exhausted men stumbled down to the Nile at Gubat. Twenty-seven officers and 263 men had been killed or wounded. The Desert Column had been badly mauled. Stewart himself was seriously wounded. Wilson, on whom the command now devolved, had not enough men on their feet to carry out the original plan. The Naval Brigade who were to have manned Gordon's four river steamers had been decimated. All its officers except Beresford and many of the best petty officers and seamen had been killed or wounded, and Beresford himself, with a bad attack of boils, was too ill to walk. Leaving enough men behind to defend the temporary hospital and the supplies, Wilson set off for Khartoum in two of the river steamers manned chiefly by native crews but carrying a dozen or so British troops.

Beresford offered to accompany me, [wrote Wilson] but there was every chance of his getting worse before he was better. Beside, I felt I could not deprive the force of its only naval officer, when it was quite possible that the steamers left behind might have to take part in a fight. Beresford gave me all the assistance and advice he could whilst lying in hospital, and let me have two of his artificers.

Left behind in spite of his pleas Beresford gradually recovered. One of the two remaining river steamers was in very poor condition, but the *Safieh* was put into fighting shape, the Gardner gun brought from Korti being mounted on board. There was no news of Wilson and waiting was anxious work. On 31 January the second division of the Naval Brigade arrived over the desert route, very welcome reinforcements which would enable Beresford, now out of hospital and living in the *Safieh*, to man her with a proper naval crew. In the small hours of 1 February he was roused by a shout from the river.

I ran to the rail, and there in the first light of the dawn was a boat, and Stuart Wortley's (one of the officers who had gone with Wilson) face was lifted to mine. He climbed aboard. "Gordon is killed and Khartoum has fallen," he said.

Five days after leaving Gubat, Wilson's two steamers, after many groundings and other adventures, were in sight of Khartoum. Under a hot fire from the shore they kept on until they reached the junction of the two Niles. Looking up the Blue Nile they could see the city of Khartoum with hundreds of dervishes ranged under their banners on the sandspit close to the town. But no flag flew over Government House, plainly viewed above the trees. They were too late.

Sadly, they started on the return journey, only to meet with further disaster. First one steamer ran aground, then the other. This time neither could be got off. Stuart Wortley, in an open boat manned by British and native soldiers, managed to pass through the enemy's lines to bring the news.

Beresford hurriedly set out to try and rescue Wilson forty miles upstream. The little *Safieh* built for peaceful uses on the Nile had been ingeniously converted into the semblance of a man-of-war. Round the guns and decks were bulwarks made of boiler plates and baulks of timber—bullet-proof, but not shot or shell-proof. The boiler being partly above deck was shielded by logs of wood. Abaft the funnel, on the roof of the saloon was a place for the riflemen. In the crowded space below decks was stacked gun and rifle ammunition, provisions, loot collected by the native crew and quantities of wood, the only fuel available, laboriously collected from on shore. "The filth was something indescribable," wrote Wilson, "the stench which rose from the holds overpowering; and the rats legion and ubiquitous—no place or person was too sacred for them."

It was a strange command for a Captain R.N., but the engines, though old, were clean and bright and well looked after. The crew had consisted of a very mixed bag of Sudanese and Egyptians with some regular Sudanese soldiers; most of these had been replaced by a detachment from the Naval

Brigades—including Sub-Lieutenant Colin R. Keppel (Harry Keppel's son) and Chief Engineer Henry Benbow. Twenty non-commissioned officers and men of the Mounted Infantry, all picked shots, manned the barricades on deck. Lieutenant Stuart Worley had come along to guide Beresford to Wilson.

The Nile in January is low and very difficult to navigate. Much would depend on the *reis* or native pilot. To guard against the sort of "accident" which might have been responsible for wrecking Wilson's steamers, Beresford informed his *reis* that he would be handsomely rewarded for a safe journey, but shot at once on any sign of treachery. The *reis* was then handcuffed to a stanchion, a bluejacket with a loaded revolver standing at his side.

Near where Wilson was stranded was the fort of Wad Habeshi. Because of the low river the *Safieh* must pass within eighty yards of a strong earthwork mounting four guns and manned by large numbers of riflemen. The guns, against which the *Safieh* was virtually defenceless, were the worst danger. Beresford gave orders that fire must be concentrated on the embrasures, hoping to demoralise the gun's crews. Rifle fire, against which the boiler plates and timber gave some protection, must be ignored. He had assembled and addressed his little ship's company the night before. "The men," he reported, "were as cheery and steady as possible."

The *Safieh*, though steaming at full speed, made slow progress against the current as she gradually approached the fort, her guns blazing away and the riflemen firing steadily at the embrasures. So accurate and effective was this onslaught that the *Safieh*, sustaining only minor casualties, drew level and left the fort astern. But suddenly a great cloud of steam poured out of the after hatchway and the engine began to slow down. Beresford immediately headed for the bank and dropped anchor.

Still under fire Beresford took stock of the situation. It was not very encouraging. The boiler had been hit and pierced. The fort was less than 300 yards away, the *Safieh* helpless, and no relief was possible. In this desperate strait the soldiers and sailors on board the little *Safieh*, taking their cue from their Commander, "were quite cool and jovial."

The boiler was pierced with a jagged hole some three inches across, which must somehow be sealed against a full head of steam. Both British engine-room artificers had been badly scalded. Chief Engineer Henry Benbow, now the only man on board who could handle tools, would have to make a patch a foot square, drill it, back it with an iron bar and bolt it in place. "I think I can do it," he said. It was about 10 a.m.

Meantime the fort continued to fire at the *Safieh* and the *Safieh* to return the fire. Bullets thudded into the timber baulks and clanged against the "armour," some of them penetrating the thin plates of the hull. Another shell or two would have put paid to the enterprise, so everything depended on preventing the enemy from manning or moving their guns. One of the Gardners was shifted into the stern immediately above the engine room. Down below in the stifling heat Benbow worked on.

Wilson, watching the battle from upstream, saw that the *Safieh* must have been damaged. Some of his men engaged the fort from the opposite bank whilst the remainder moved downstream. "I'll pick you up tomorrow," signalled Beresford. At 2 p.m. two engine-room artificers who had been with Wilson were brought on board the *Safieh*, a very welcome help to Mr Benbow toiling away single-handed in the stifling heat of the engine room.

At 5 p.m. the patch was ready, but the boiler was still so hot that it could not be entered. Cold water was pumped in and out. At 7 p.m. Benbow was able to report that the job was done; how well done was proved when the *Safieh* was visited thirteen years later. The patch was still in place!

But night had fallen; the *Safieh* was still above the fort and must run the gauntlet once more on her way downstream in daylight, for navigating the river in the dark was impossible. In the meantime Beresford tried to give the impression that his ship was still helpless and was being abandoned. Boats were ostentatiously hauled alongside as though to take off the crew;

the ship was darkened; even talking above a whisper was forbidden. At 5 a.m. the fires were lit. Except for the water lapping past the side everything was quiet. It was a tense moment as the steam pressure gradually rose. Then just before daylight an Arab opened an ash-pit door.

Immediately a great cloud of sparks shot from the funnel. In the stillness sounds carried clearly over the water—tom-toms beating in the fort, the shouts of men. Guns and rifles opened up as the *Safieh* weighed anchor and dashed past the fort, this time with the tide.

That night, after picking up Wilson's men, she was safely back at Gubat. In the dirty little cabin Beresford "slept so profoundly that I do not know when I should have awakened, had not first one rat, and then another, walked over my face."

Mr Benbow with a piece of plate and much skill and determination had saved the day.

The Arabs, so fanatically brave in battle, were disheartened. The garrison at Wad Habeshi which had suffered heavy casualties withdrew into the desert, allowing Wilson's column to extricate itself from its isolated position at Gubat without much further trouble.

Beresford, three times mentioned in despatches and awarded the C.B., returned to England. His exploits in the *Condor* and *Safieh* had made him extremely well-known. In the General Election of 1885 he was again elected to Parliament. Next year he went to the Admiralty, with a seat on the Board as Fourth Sea Lord, an appointment which he owed in some degree to the influence of his friend the Prince of Wales.

The not very interesting administrative problems which lay within his terms of reference were unlikely to satisfy the reforming zeal of Captain Lord Charles Beresford. Within six weeks of his arrival at Whitehall he had produced a paper criticising major matters of Admiralty policy which he laid before the Board. There was, he alleged, no proper organisation for rapidly mobilising reserves, or for using the Merchant Navy to supply the Fleet with coal and ammunition. The number of men available was insufficient to meet the war needs of the Navy. All of it sprang (and this was his major point) from the absence of a War Staff at the Admiralty. Without proper planning such deficiencies were inevitable.

The Board was nettled by this meddling in high matters by their latest recruit and considered his strictures grossly exaggerated. Beresford thereupon requested the First Lord's permission to show his memo to the Prime Minister, Lord Salisbury. The P.M. was kind, but firm. It was unreasonable to set the opinion of an officer who had never even commanded so much as a cruiser above that of Admirals past and present. Beresford concurred, and suggested that three well-known Admirals, not on the Board, should be asked for their views. The three Admirals agreed with Beresford. Lord Salisbury used his influence and Lord Charles got his way. A new Naval Intelligence Department was formed with Captain William H. Hall as its Director: "To organise war preparations, including naval mobilisation and the making out of plans for naval campaigns to meet all the contingencies probable in a war with different countries, corrected frequently and periodically."

It has been said that Beresford though an excellent commander of men was no administrator. Be that as it may he had put his finger on the greatest weakness of the Admiralty organisation. The new Intelligence Department might have been the beginnings of a proper Naval Staff, but there was still so much opposition to this "monstrous" idea that the infant failed to survive. In 1887 the salaries of the Naval Intelligence Department were cut. Beresford resigned from the Board, publicly declaring his reasons for doing so. Twenty-six years were to elapse before Winston Churchill, in 1911, forced the Admiralty to do what was so badly needed.

Fortunately, the augmented N.I.D. had had time to produce an estimate of the proper minimum strength of the Fleet. The figures made alarming reading. Beresford, though no longer at the Admiralty, was continuing inside and outside the House to urge the Government to strengthen the Navy. In 1888, whilst staying at Wilton with Lord Pembroke, he told the

Chancellor of the Exchequer, Mr Goschen, that an additional seventy-six ships were needed. Goschen was furious. "You won't get them . . . and for a very simple reason. They are not wanted." Beresford stuck to his guns. "Before very long you will order seventy ships at the cost of twenty million. And for a very simple reason. Because you must."

Speaking on the shipbuilding Vote (Vote 8) in the House of Commons in December he urged the adoption of a programme which included four first-class iron-clads, ten second class iron-clads, forty cruisers and torpedo craft.

Action was still delayed, but things were at last on the move. Public opinion was becoming more and more disturbed by the apparent weakness of the Fleet. The obviously well-informed articles in the *Pall Mall Gazette*, "The Truth about the Navy" by W. T. Stead (much of his material came from Captain J. A. Fisher), had been followed by a general agitation in the press. In July 1888 the Admiralty was told by the Prime Minister to make a confidential survey on the requirements for a war with France and Russia. Early next year the report of three distinguished Admirals on the state of the Fleet, a masterly document which went far beyond its term of reference, was laid before both Houses of Parliament. Very shortly afterwards the Naval Defence Act of 1889 which authorised very substantial additions to the building programme became law, authorising a programme of seventy new ships costing £21,500,000. It would be foolish to claim that Beresford was the cause of all this, but his influence had been considerable.

Beresford had been right, but his methods had made him very unpopular in some quarters. The Prince of Wales, always a good friend and a much wiser man, thought that it was high time he went to sea again. In July 1888 he had written to Lord Charles suggesting he should apply for a ship: "it will be a change also after the House of Commons and London Society." Whilst appreciating Lord Charles' many qualities he had a justly modest view of his political acumen. The Prince of Wales was annoyed when Beresford, whose judgment was never his strong point, delayed for another year, but was

F

eventually appointed to the command of the first-class armoured cruiser *Undaunted* in the Mediterranean Fleet.

For three and a half years he held this post with great success. As a leader of men he was without an equal in the Victorian Navy. *Undaunted* was smart and efficient; well-disciplined, but very happy. On board his ship the abounding energy which got him into hot water with the politicians was skilfully directed. This rich, Tory aristocrat was, in many ways, much more liberal-minded than most of his contemporaries. He refused to accept, as a sort of divine law, the enormous differences which then existed between the life of officer and rating. Ships of war, full of equipment and carrying large crews, must often be rather uncomfortable. In those days life on board many of them was, for the lower deck, quite unnecessarily disagreeable. Beresford carried out a number of improvements, trifling in themselves (such as more tin baths for the stokers) which added up to a real increase in general well-being.

Even more appreciated was his attitude to his crew. The basis of Beresford's success as a leader was his genuine liking for his fellow men. Stokers or seamen were juniors, but not inferiors. It had struck him from his earliest days afloat that, though the slightest fault was severely condemned, praise for good results was very rarely given. Condemnation rather than commendation. Good men needed recognition, though lubbers and idlers should be severely dealt with.

The defaulters' table where the Captain stands in judgment over wrongdoers is also a place where the Captain's own reputation can be made or marred. Beresford was strict, but he avoided inflicting penalties which had too lasting an effect on a man's career. He would also try to send a man away, even after a severe sentence, if not exactly smiling, without a feeling of resentment. Being a very good judge of men with a witty, but never a sarcastic tongue he was frequently successful. In December 1891, the third year of her commission, *Undaunted* won twenty-two of the twenty-nine prizes at the Fleet pulling regatta, a pretty good indication of the spirit of her crew.

Officers and men were sorry when the paying-off pennant was hoisted after three and a half happy and fruitful years.

For the next seven years, until he was promoted to Rear-Admiral in 1900, Beresford was away from the Fleet, though an appointment to the Dockyard at Chatham, which he held in 1894–96, entailed commanding ships at sea during their trials. In 1897 he re-entered Parliament and in 1898 and 1899 undertook a long tour of China and Japan on behalf of the Associated Chambers of Commerce of Great Britain, returning *via* the United States, where he made a number of political speeches. In command afloat or faced with some definite task, as in Egypt, he was capable of a single-minded concentration which made him very successful. Under less pressing circumstances he was apt to have too many interests, social, political and naval. Later he would be criticised for avoiding his share of the more tedious and unglamorous jobs afloat and ashore which are the solid background of essential experience.

On promotion to flag rank he resigned from Parliament and returned to the Mediterranean as second-in-command. The Commander-in-Chief was Sir John Fisher. Charlie B. and Jacky Fisher were the best known figures in the Service. Both in their different way had done much for the Navy and they had always been on friendly terms.

It has been suggested that the great Fisher–Beresford quarrel which later divided the Service into two warring camps dates from this period. Certainly Fisher, perhaps influenced by Beresford's reputation for flouting authority, seemed to go out of his way to assert himself on a number of occasions— incidents which soon became well-known to the Fleet.

The first occurred quite soon after Beresford's arrival in the Mediterranean. Without asking permission, as was required by stations orders, Beresford sent his signalmen to exercise ashore, making a signal to the Fleet suggesting that other ships should take part. It was a tactless thing to do, but not very venal. Fisher took the unusual step of administering a public rebuke to his second-in-command.

"*Ramillies* signalmen to return to their ship immediately," semaphored the flagship. "Report in writing why station orders have not been obeyed."

Signals are public property. Other ships took it in. Lower deck and wardroom wondered what would happen next.

A few months later came the second and far more serious incident.

Malta harbour is narrow and tortuous. All round are hills covered in houses and ancient fortifications. From one of them, the Barracca, the Grand Harbour lies below like a lovely moving panorama—blue sea, trim ships, fussy little boats—framed by the yellow sandstone rising steeply from the water's edge. It was Fisher's habit to lead the Fleet in, land from his flagship, and watch the other ships picking up their mooring from the Barracca.

Ships are handled by their captain, not the Admiral whose flag they may fly. Beresford was an expert seaman, but his flag-captain was not a good ship-handler. *Ramillies* came past the breakwater into Bighi Bay and started to swing round to pick up her buoys. In such confined waters the manoeuvre required a certain degree of skill and nerve, and *Ramillies* made a botch of it, blocking the narrow harbour as she tried to turn. The rest of the Fleet, still outside the breakwater, was delayed. Jacky Fisher lost his temper. Plain for all to read he signalled to his second-in-command. "Your flagship is to proceed to sea and come in again in a seamanlike manner."

It was a stupid thing to do. Admiral-of-the-Fleet Lord Chatfield, who was serving in the Fleet at the time as a commander, calls it "A lamentable example of bad leadership." In a matter of minutes the signal was being discussed in wardroom and mess-deck. In a matter of hours the Fleet had taken sides; pro-Jacky, pro-Charlie B.

Beresford, essentially a very loyal person, gave no outward sign, but a proud man of his age and background must have deeply resented Fisher's public rudeness. In private he was quite capable of giving as good as he got. A few months earlier Fisher had sent him a note asking how such a reputable paper as the *Morning Post* could have printed a news item that "the

Mediterranean Fleet under the command of Lord Charles Beresford" had returned from a cruise in the Adriatic.

Dear Sir John, [was the prompt reply] From the enclosure you have sent me it appears that the great British Public are accustomed to the name of Lord Charles Beresford, but as yet ignorant of the name of Sir John Fisher. I would suggest that the remedy lies entirely in your own hands.

Admirals living on board their flagships are much in the public eye. However carefully they observe the forms of ceremonial and courtesy their personal likes and dislikes are soon known. If any permanent damage had been done between the principal protagonists it was not apparent. When he had been six months on the station Beresford was offered the command of the Australian Station, but refused, preferring to remain in the Mediterranean where he could learn to handle a fleet. He recognised and admired what Fisher was doing to improve fighting efficiency; his exercises based not on tradition but the probabilities of war; the long range target practices; the insistence on high speed cruising which had converted a 12-knot fleet with breakdowns to a 15-knot fleet without breakdowns. He did not always agree with Fisher's methods; the hasty signals of a type which should never be made and the brusque overriding of contrary opinion, but he was in full agreement with Fisher's policy. What he felt about Fisher as a man (and a social inferior) he kept to himself, at any rate in public.

Fisher, who often said more than he really meant and expected to be taken with a grain of salt, quite clearly had no grudge against his second-in-command. Six years later, when the feud was at its height, he often wrote and spoke slightingly of Beresford, but in 1901 he evidently held a high opinion of his subordinate's capabilities, both as a leader and as a tactician.

"Beresford did uncommonly well," he wrote after the manoeuvres of 1900, "and is much pleased at my praising him, which he thoroughly deserved." Again, in 1901 "Wilson (the C.-in-C. of the Home Fleet, carrying out combined exercises with the Mediteranean Fleet) and Beresford handled their squadrons most admirably." Again, writing to Earl Spencer in 1902: "Charley Beresford is a first-rate officer afloat, no better exists in my opinion (which is a good deal to say!) and in the two years he has been under my command he has never failed to do everything he has been ordered, cheerfully and zealously and *has always done it well*."

This last letter was written three months after Beresford, after completing the usual two years in his appointment, had hauled down his flag and returned home.

The two men had continued to correspond. Fisher, though sometimes complaining of Beresford's passion for publicity, was not above using him to further his schemes. "The 'hoi polloi' believe in him and listen to him like no one else . . . he could do so much good for the Navy." Beresford had again been elected to the House of Commons, as M.P. for Woolwich, whilst still serving in the Mediterranean Fleet. Before the Naval Estimates of 1902 Fisher wrote him a very frank, friendly and highly confidential letter of advice, but was annoyed when Beresford, never notable for good judgment, mishandled the matter by going too far. Fisher's subsequent letter to Earl Spencer is an early indication of the coming rift in the lute.

There is a good deal in what Beresford urges, but he exaggerates so much that his good ideas become deformities . . . and his want of taste and his uncontrolled desire for notoriety alienates his brother officers. He promised me faithfully (for we have been great friends) that he would be circumspect and judicious . . . he has been neither.

Not long afterwards Fisher returned to the Admiralty as Second Sea Lord and immediately began to put into practice the first of the great reforms in the structure of the Navy which he had long been planning, the so-called Selborne Scheme which entirely altered the training of young officers. Beresford, who was later to become the leader of the opposition to the scheme, was strongly in favour. He had resigned his seat in Parliament and had assumed command of the Channel Fleet.

It was subsequently said, when Beresford's allegations of

gross mishandling of naval affairs by the Admiralty was being investigated by a committee at Cabinet level, that Lord Charles was lacking in experience in responsible positions at sea. It is true that he only did one commission afloat as a captain, but for over seven years, between January 1900 and March 1909, he was almost continuously in command of what were then the most important squadrons and fleets. As a seagoing Admiral he was markedly successful. Though not himself a technician he was fully alive to the importance of technical developments. He understood, and practised, the difficult art of delegating authority and allowed a well-chosen staff to be progressive. As a leader of men he was quite outstanding and his extraordinary popularity was well-deserved. Discipline, far from being relaxed under his command, was improved by introducing a much better relationship between officers and men and by removing unnecessary restrictions. It is true that his fleets were grossly over-centralised, but that was a fault of the age. As a captain he had chafed at the custom of "following the flagship's motions," often carried to ridiculous lengths; at the fecundity which produced orders from the flag on the most trivial matters ("dry up decks" after a shower of rain); the mountains of written instruction on every conceivable subject. As a captain he had realised the dangerous effects on initiative that such a system might produce; as an admiral he was as bad as the rest of his contemporaries and the Channel Fleet order book was a volume of 600 pages. It was to take the greatest battle in naval history to show up that particular weakness.

In 1904 Fisher became First Sea Lord. He was bent on altering the Navy to his ideas. Obsessed by a sense of urgency (Germany was fast building a great navy) he was prepared to ride roughshod over any opposition. One of his first actions was to order a major redistribution of the ships in the various fleets.

In 1905 Beresford became C.-in-C. Mediterranean. Lord Charles was ambitious. In the ordinary way he could have expected eventually to relieve Fisher at the top of the tree, as

First Sea Lord. But in December Lord Fisher was appointed as an additional Admiral of the Fleet. Instead of retiring next year on reaching the age of sixty-five he would continue at the Admiralty, perhaps for five more years; certainly until Beresford's chance of succeeding him had vanished. The blow fell at a time when Beresford was already exasperated by the removal, on Admiralty instructions, of some of his best ships to strengthen the Fleet in home waters—a redistribution which he believed to be thoroughly undesirable. Fisher's methods were dictatorial, "Never explain, never apologise" was a favourite dictum. Beresford was not the only senior officer in a highly responsible position afloat who felt that things were done, which very much affected their commands, without their being given a chance to state their views. "The Admiralty," as everybody knew, meant Fisher; "*l'état c'est* Jacky." Beresford, always a rebel at heart and with a strong propensity for being "agin the Government," had a good cause to which he could nail his colours. After Fisher he was unquestionably the most influential figure in the Navy, the natural leader of the opposition. Personal disappointment and the memory of humiliations inflicted on him in the past added fuel to the fire. Fisher was a menace to the Navy and a public danger.

It was a view which was pretty widely held, particularly amongst the older officers, and Beresford soon found himself heading a crusade which became more and more outspoken in its criticism of the Admiralty. The cold war rapidly became an obsession with both protagonists, each automatically opposing any suggestion made by the other.

From the Mediterranean Beresford, after a few months' leave, was appointed to the Command of what was then generally regarded as the most important naval force, the Channel Fleet. His arrival coincided with a major reorganisation of the Channel, Home and Atlantic Fleets which seemed to Lord Charles to weaken the former and to prejudice his position as Supreme Commander designate of the Fleets in home waters in time of war. It was the last straw. But the battle which ensued, bringing Beresford's naval career to a close and eventually unseating his antagonist, is best dealt with in another chapter.

As in the Mediterranean he was an excellent Commander-in-Chief. His quarrel with Fisher was public property, but many of the officers and by far the majority of the lower deck wisely refused to be involved. To them Charlie B. was a much respected and very popular commander who had passed into the ranks of the legendary figures whom men are always proud to serve. He took a very active interest in their welfare. He had a tremendous presence and made the most of it. (One of his midshipmen recalls seeing him carried by four Royal Marines to the bridge of his flagship when he had gout, looking very like a Roman Emperor.) He was competent and kind and his foibles, such as absolute silence in all boats underway, orders being given only by signs, were the sort which men curse about, but rather glory in. His smart friends, with their beautiful womenfolk, were a pleasant change after the austerities of "Tug" Wilson, his immediate predecessor, though Lady Charles, playfully referred to as "my little painted frigate," was not often seen on board. His fleet was smart and very clean and the practices and exercises introduced by Wilson were continued and developed. Unfortunately everything was overshadowed by his constant battles with the Admiralty; warfare of increasing bitterness which found its way into the press and finally began to sour the Fleet itself. It was a state of affairs that could not be allowed to continue.

After hauling down his flag for the last time in March 1908 Admiral Lord Charles Beresford returned once more to Parliament as Member for Portsmouth. He continued to fulminate against the alleged mishandling of naval affairs, but his influence was on the wane. In 1911 he was raised to the peerage as the first Baron of Metemmeh, a good title for an always gallant if often ill-advised figure. He died in 1919 and was buried in St Paul's, remembered and loved by very many of the thousands who served under his command.

One lasting monument remains to his memory: a proper Naval Staff.

FISHER

1841-1920

The Navy Builder

FOR nearly forty years Jacky Fisher was the most controversial figure in the British Navy. Even after he had left the Admiralty for the last time in 1915 his influence continued to be strongly felt. The Fleet which was victorious in the 1914–18 war and the ships which were the backbone of the Navy for many years afterwards were largely his creation. Whether Fisher himself was a great genius or a great menace is a point upon which opinions still differ sharply. That he was a great man is indisputable—a figure of almost Churchillian proportions with the same gift for expressing himself in vivid language, the same prophetic vision and the same dominating personality. Fisher was very often right, but was often equally successful in imposing his ideas when he was wrong. For better or for worse, the Navy of the opening decades of this century was Fisher's Navy.

Jacky Fisher was born in Ceylon in 1841. He came from sound middle-class stock—a long line of clergymen broken only when his father joined the Army. His mother, daughter of a London wine-merchant, was with her brother Frederick Lambe on his coffee plantation in Ceylon when she met and married the Governor's A.D.C. There were eleven children, seven of whom survived infancy. Sophia, a woman of tremendous vitality and great determination, retained her good looks into middle age.

Captain Fisher left the Army, but remained in Ceylon. Young Jack was sent to school in England where the ex-Governor and his wife continued to keep an eye on him. The

Wilmot-Hortons had a great house in Derbyshire to which he was invited. There were rabbits to be stalked and shot, perch to be caught in the River Trent. The butler, a pompous fellow, unbent sufficiently to give advice: "Don't hesitate. Shoot quickly." He underestimated the rapid reactions of his pupil. Jacky saw a movement in the bushes and immediately fired. It was the butler who had come to watch progress. The results were not serious but "I was disallowed a gun."

Living near Catton Hall was the last of Nelson's Captains, Admiral Sir W. Parker. As Commander-in-Chief, Plymouth, he had two nominations for naval cadetships and readily obliged his friend and neighbour Lady Wilmot-Horton. Jacky, aged thirteen, presented himself for the entrance examination.

"I wrote out the Lord's prayer, and the doctor made me jump over a chair naked, and I was given a glass of Sherry on being in the Navy."

There was no naval college or training ship at that time. He bought his uniform and reported on board the *Victory*, in which he was to fly his flag as Commander-in-Chief, Portsmouth, fifty years later.

"They were holystoning the decks, and the white-haired First Lieutenant, with his trousers turned up above his knees and no shoes or stockings, roared at me like the Bull of Bashan and afterwards gave me an orange when he met me outside his cabin in the cockpit."

Young Jack, "penniless, friendless and forlorn," went almost immediately to his first seagoing ship, the *Calcutta*. Life in a sailing ship never had the same appeal for him as for Charles Beresford. For one thing he was very seasick. On a voyage from Plymouth to Portsmouth, which took fourteen days because of strong contrary winds, he summed up his feeling in a little jingle:

> Now sailors all take my advice
> Let steamships be your motta
> And never go to sea again
> In the sailing ship *Calcutta*.

He saw the closing stages of the war against Russia in the Baltic, sailed to the Black Sea to bring back troops returning from the Crimea and went, now a fully-fledged midshipman, to China in the *Highflyer*, where he received his baptism of fire.

At seventeen he was acting as A.D.C. to his Captain during the attempt, in 1858, to force the mouth of the Pei Ho.[1] Gunboats fired at the Taku forts whilst seamen and marines struggled to advance along the banks of the river. The operation was a costly failure. The forts were much stronger than expected and the landing parties, subjected to a murderous fire, made slow progress through the mud in which they floundered. Casualties were heavy. Four of the seven gunboats were sunk. The British Admiral had his leg shot away but continued, with great gallantry, to urge on his men from a cot slung on a pole carried in a boat. "Nothing but blood and men rolling about with arms and legs off," wrote Jacky later. "We pitch them overboard as they are killed or dead. One soon gets used to it."

Jacky was at one point stuck in the mud from which he was hauled by one of the bluejackets—fortunately for him, for at nightfall the Chinese came out and beheaded those who remained in this predicament. Physically and morally quite without fear he took it all as it came. "I am certain I am not born to be shot," he wrote to his friend Mrs Edmund Warden.

This lady, whose husband was the head of the P. & O. Company in the Far East, played an important part in his life at that time. His own family was far away in Ceylon and Mrs Warden had more than taken their place. The Wardens' house in Shanghai provided the background of home and affection which he sadly missed, for in spite of his experiences he was only a lad. When the *Highflyer* was at sea he wrote long, affectionate letters to "My dear Mams" by every mail, in which he told in detail of his doings. Like many other very manly men Fisher had to have a woman to think about and confide in.

A photograph of Midshipman J. A. Fisher of H.M.S.

[1] See map on page 176.

Admiral of the Fleet Baron Fisher of Kilverstone, GCB, GCVO, OM, from the painting by H. van Herkomer (1911)

Highflyer shows a pleasant-looking lad with thoughtful, pene-trating eyes, firm mouth and a determined chin. The face is rather flat and broad, with a wide forehead over which, by accident or design, the lock of dark hair is already falling. A strong, kindly, slightly mischievous face; boyish yet mature.

The same mixture of wisdom beyond his years and irre-pressible youth comes out in his letters. They are full of high spirits and impish, humorous remarks, but his judgment of his fellow men has an asperity unusual in a lad of his age; a fellow midshipman "thinks everybody is honest till he finds out they are rogues, instead of treating them as rogues till he finds them to be honest." Fisher had the gift of writing as he spoke, fluent, pungent, making the people he met and the things he did come alive. "I like putting down things as I think of them, and if I was to read them over twice I should get disgusted with the stuff."

After the action at Taku he was transferred to the flagship, the *Chesapeake*, where he was "mate" (A.D.C.) to Admiral Sir James Hope. Here he had "nothing to do with anyone in the ship except the Admiral himself, and, no mistake, he keeps me going. He hardly takes his boots off without sending for me and informing me officially of it . . . It is very jolly in one way. I can give some of these Lieutenants a good snubbing sometimes."

But Fisher was no prig. He was popular with his seniors and contemporaries and with the lower deck, for he was full of drive and guts, good at his job, with a keen sense of humour. Christmas-time, when discipline was relaxed and most of the ship's company got very drunk on smuggled and hoarded liquor, was something of an ordeal for the junior officers. "Just been carried round the deck four times by about thirty bluejackets," wrote Fisher, "all of them making me taste their grog, etc., etc., with a fiddle and a big drum playing in front of me. I'd like to give them two dozen all round, the brutes."

He was working hard for his examination for Mate (later Sub-Lieutenant), and passed top of the whole station with a

first-class certificate. Being poor and very keen he spent a lot
of time on board even when the ship was at Hongkong.
Sometimes he would get gloomy fits, but usually he was an
irrepressibly cheerful lad, even in his next ship, the *Furious*,
where Captain Oliver Jones was "an awful scoundrel" who
kept the best table in the Fleet, but was a terror to his crew—a
great contrast to dear old Captain Shadwell of the *Highflyer*,
affectionately but irreverently known on the lower deck as
"Our Heavenly Father."

Captain Jones, tyrant though he might be, was a fine seaman and navigator; a man of parts who spoke several languages
and was a Master of Hounds when in England.

Fisher took it all as it came; controlling the simple but
unruly bluejackets, steering his way around the foibles of
eccentric seniors; learning, thinking and fast growing into a
man.

At home again after four years abroad he underwent the
courses and examinations in gunnery and navigation. Clever,
thorough, and with an excellent memory, as good with his
books as he had been on board, he got a "first" in both subjects and was awarded the Beaufort Testimonial for the best
examination of the year in navigation. Promoted to Lieutenant, he was appointed to the staff of the Portsmouth gunnery
school, H.M.S. *Excellent*.

An old seaman serving there at that time as a powder-
monkey tells a story of the young Lieutenant. Their Lordships
of the Admiralty arrived on a visit of inspection. Fisher, in
charge of the drill at one of the guns, overheard one Admiral
say to another:

"Is this Lieutenant Fisher as good a seaman as he is a
gunnery man?"

Fisher at once stepped forward.

"My Lords, I am Lieutenant Fisher, just as good a seaman
as a gunnery man."

His self-confidence was indeed remarkable, but there was
nothing stuck-up about him. Very strict on duty, with a
natural dignity which earned him ready respect, he was the life

and soul of the wardroom; full of fun, noisy, gay and very popular with his messmates. Gunnery Lieutenants in those days were people of small account—it was easy to fire the guns after the seamen had placed the ship in position, but Fisher, appointed to the *Warrior*, Britain's first iron-clad (but a full-rigged ship), managed by drive, cajolery and cunning to get a reasonable amount of time devoted to gun drill from the "essential" work of sail drill, scrubbing, polishing and painting.

In 1866 he married Frances Katherine Delves-Broughton. He was only twenty-five and neither of them had any money, but the marriage was a very happy one. The Navy continued to come first (it always would), but Fisher now had the home background which was essential to him. Three years later he was promoted to Commander at the early age of twenty-eight and appointed as executive officer of the *Donegal* on the China Station.

The Captain of a major warship is a remote god-like figure, but the Commander is constantly on view. He is responsible for all the things which touch the crew personally—organisation, routine, discipline, leave; their efficiency and happiness depend on him to a very great extent. Under Fisher there was no fumbling. Everything seemed to have been provided for in advance. Though a strict disciplinarian he was just, humorous and humane; self-confident, but prepared to listen to the opinions of others. His orders must be meticulously carried out, but none felt he was a mere cog in a machine. In a very short time he not only knew the big ship's company of the *Donegal* by name, but something about them.

His wife had remained at home. He had little spare cash when his mess bills were paid and not much private life. He was busy, but there was plenty of time for reflection. It was already clear to him that the Navy was overdue for great and fundamental changes. A revolution in material was under way —steam ousting sail, the breech-loading, quick-firing gun developing at an astonishing rate. Ships had suddenly become faster, more mobile and independent of the weather; their

weapons deadly at unheard-of ranges. His seniors and contemporaries found the upheaval highly unsettling, an evil to be
kept at bay as long as possible. But Fisher, a Junior Commander, already considered himself vitally implicated.

"The great failing of *Excellent*," he wrote to the Captain of
that establishment in 1871, "is an aversion to change . . ."
He went on to put his finger unerringly on a major weakness of
the Admiralty organisation. "The Admiralty is subordinate
to and dependent on the War Office for almost any species of
warlike store, from a 35 ton gun to a boarding pike and a
common shovel."

He would have to wait sixteen years before, as Director of
Naval Ordnance, he was able to put this right, but already his
eyes were on the summit. Major matters of policy were *his*
business.

Happy as he was in his work, it irked him to be so far
away from England, out of sight and out of mind if a good
billet fell vacant. He knew in his heart he was destined
for much greater things and he was anxious to be on his
way.

It was something above and beyond himself. His seniors
and contemporaries already recognised it. "The Captains and
Commanders of the China Fleet," as he wrote to his wife,
"make me out such a marvellous fellow. I do feel such a hum-
bug." For at heart he was a humble man, deeply conscious
that he was only what God made him. "I am astonished myself that I have done so well, and I thank God most heartily
for it, as I am sure it was not in me naturally." His Chris-
tianity, never spoken of to his messmates but so frequently
mentioned in his long, affectionate letters to his wife, was real
and tangible. His pay was only £360 a year, but from their
severely limited means they set aside £20 a year for charity,
for them a very considerable sum.

Of course, his great success caused some jealousy. His
relations with his own Captain were not always easy.

"I wish," wrote Fisher, "I could feel he knew more than I
did."

Nevertheless the commission reached a very successful conclusion with the *Donegal* returning from her three years abroad to pay off, and the Dockyard Admiral reporting a crew which "whilst in most perfect discipline . . . are most contented, active and cheerful."

Appointed to the gunnery school (H.M.S. *Excellent*) Fisher was told to start a new section for "Torpedo"—all forms of underwater weapons except the torpedo itself, which had not yet appeared. As an instructor he was most successful: an excellent lecturer, pithy, humorous and able to communicate his own clear vision of the reason why. His passionate belief in the importance of his work was infectious. Elderly post captains, sent on a course to fill in time, found themselves, in Jacky Fisher's classes, pulling an oar in a boat, laying out mines and hauling on slimy moorings with youthful enthusiasm.

If you are a gunnery man, [he told them] you must believe and teach that the world must be saved by gunnery, and will only be saved by gunnery. If you are a torpedoman you must lecture and teach the same thing about torpedoes. But be in earnest, terribly in earnest. The man who doubts, or who is half-hearted, never does anything for himself or his country.

On his promotion to Captain in 1874 at the early age of thirty-three, "Torpedo" became a separate branch of the Service with its own school where experimental work was carried out, H.M.S. *Vernon*.

As Captain of the *Vernon* he was a member of a committee sent to Fiume to witness trials of Mr Whitehead's locomotive torpedo—then a slow-moving, rather primitive contrivance carrying only a small explosive charge. But Fisher was impressed. In 1876 he wrote: ". . . the issue of the next naval war will chiefly depend upon the use that is made of the torpedo, not only in naval warfare, but for the purposes of blockade." Prophetic words indeed.

Fisher recognised that the new Navy would cost a great deal of public money, money which would only be forthcoming if the public and the politicians accepted the need. Displays

G

were arranged to which he invited Members of Parliament
and the press. The visitors were impressed, but there were
many raised eyebrows on the faces of officers of the older
school.

After these shore appointments, he went to sea again,
serving for the next six years in command of various ships
abroad. A short time under Captain Fisher was enough to
convert a slack ship into a model of disciplined efficiency.

"Now," he told the ship's company of the *Bellerophon*, "I
intend to give you hell for three months, and if you have not
come up to my standard in that time you will have hell for
another three months."

Sea and harbour, they would be at it every day, drilling and
exercising under his smouldering eye. But he was liked and
respected as well as feared. His most ferocious dressing-down
was salted with humour, and when after three months the ship
had reached his very exacting standard, he organised recreation
and amusements with equal fervour.

His ships surpassed themselves—150 runs with Whitehead
torpedoes by the *Northampton* in ten days when the whole
Navy had only done two hundred in a year. He was already
becoming something of a legend: the very short frock coat,
faded green with age, which he donned when a particularly
strenuous day might be expected; his habit of holding up his
left hand when addressing his men, fingers and thumb extended, closing them in turn with the other hand as he made his
points, "the four bananas and the baby's leg," as they were
irreverently called, disappearing one by one into a clenched
fist. His caustic remarks: "Do right and fear no man. Don't
write and fear no woman"—though he was never heard to say
small, uncharitable things. His high spirits and unquenchable
optimism. His passion for dancing—at a ball given by the
lieutenants of the flagship at Bermuda he was awarded the
prize for the best "cakewalk" by popular acclaim. The ebul-
lience which made it natural for him to enjoy what much
younger men enjoyed without ever losing his dignity.

He remained the least pompous of men. Travelling in plain

clothes from Malta to Constantinople to join a ship at short notice, he took passage in a scruffy old tramp. The skipper regarded his arrival with disfavour.

"There ain't room; there's only one bunk and when I ain't in it the Mate is."

"All right, I don't want a bunk."

"We ain't got no cook."

"That don't matter either."

Fisher and the skipper became fast friends and remained so over the years.

His reputation had been spreading far beyond his own ships and when a Captain was required for the latest and greatest of the Navy's new battleships, the *Inflexible*, Fisher was selected over the heads of many much more senior men.

The appointment was another turning point. *Inflexible* was detailed for guard duty at Mentone where Queen Victoria was in residence at her villa. The Queen had no particular liking for the Navy or for naval officers (their Lordships of the Admiralty had objected to making Prince Albert an Admiral of the Fleet), but Fisher's mixture of frankness and respect, fearlessness and utter loyalty appealed to her. When *Inflexible* left at short notice to take part in the bombardment of Alexandria, the Queen continued to follow his fortunes with interest.

The bombardment of the forts manned by Arabi Pasha's rebellious soldiers was the first occasion since the Crimean War that British battleships had been in action. It is interesting, in the light of later events, that Fisher, in charge of the party landed after the bombardment, should have specially asked for Beresford as his Naval Provost Martial. Between them these two men produced calm out of chaos in an astonishingly short time with the very meagre force at their disposal. When the soldiers arrived to take over, Fisher remained ashore with his Naval Brigade, living in the Ras-el-Tin palace, "very magnificent, but a mass of fleas and dirt." As a result he had a sharp attack of dysentery and was very ill.

Alexandria has been much in the news and Fisher had

become a public figure. Queen Victoria sent her congratulations, and her regret at the casualties sustained by *Inflexible*.

"The Queen had little thought," wrote her private secretary, "how soon the splendid guardship at Mentone would be actively engaged, and trusts that the capabilities of the vessel have proved equal to your expectations."

But Fisher was gravely ill. He could not afford to go home on leave at his own expense and was most unwilling to give up his ship. He was making his mother an allowance as well as supporting his own family, and a period on half-pay was an unwelcome prospect. In the end the First Lord, Lord Northbrook, stepped in and brought him back. "We can get many *Inflexibles*, but only one Jack Fisher."

A letter sent by the lower deck which followed him home shows the respect and affection of the men under his command. They wished him a speedy recovery, hoped to see him back again. "May you receive your share of rewards and laurels," it concluded, "and your Ship's Company will then feel as proud and prouder than if it was bestowed on themselves." Fisher was deeply moved by this unusual tribute.

After convalescence, he was invited to stay with the Queen at Osborne House, the first of a series of visits. The atmosphere was formal, though Fisher was not unduly repressed. At dinner only those speaking to the Queen used a normal tone; elsewhere around the table voices were hushed. A burst of merriment from those around Captain Fisher caused Her Majesty to ask the cause of their amusement.

"I was telling Lady Ely, Ma'am," said Jack, "that I had enough flannel round my tummy to go all round this room."

There was a horrified silence, but the Queen, for once, was amused.

So far he had been in appointments where his opportunities for applying his principles for reform of the Navy were limited. As a senior captain and on reaching flag rank this situation gradually altered. *Excellent* which he commanded from 1883 to 1886, was a museum of out-of-date notions—obsolete equipment and a staff of ancient pensioners who gabbled out the formulae they had learnt by heart. Fisher went through the place like a cyclone, sweeping out the old and useless and ruthlessly overcoming the opposition of comfortably established interests.

On promotion to Rear Admiral he became the Director of Naval Ordnance and Torpedoes, a new Admiralty Department. The supply of guns and ordnance, as already mentioned, was through the War Office; money for naval guns was included in the Army Estimates and reserves of ammunition were pooled. The situation was not unlike that which obtained between World Wars I and II when the R.A.F. was responsible for the Navy's aircraft. Army needs came first and the Navy's requirements for guns and ammunition of a different design received scant attention. Opposition to a change was powerful and sustained. It was Fisher's first serious engagement with the ponderous lethargy of a very conservative administrative machine, but he succeeded in getting naval war stores transferred to the Admiralty, which was also to become responsible for the design of its own ordnance.

The battle, which was bitter and prolonged, brought Fisher into intimate contact with many of the leading figures in the great armament firms, including Josiah Vavasseur of Armstrong, Whitworth and Co. Seventeen years later Vavasseur, who had no children of his own, was to adopt Cecil, Jack Fisher's only son, as his heir and leave him Kilverstone Hall, in Norfolk, from which his father took his title.

After four strenuous years at the Admiralty, Fisher went as Admiral Superintendent to H.M. Dockyard, Portsmouth. In the Dockyards, as at the Admiralty, apathy and procrastination ruled. Naval officers occupied many of the senior appointments, but they were birds of passage. The civilian element went on, if not for ever, at any rate until the sailors were safely back at sea. It was like fighting an enormous bolster. Your fist went in, but it got you nowhere. Robbed of the support of the rigid discipline by which they had hitherto been upheld many naval officers felt helpless, but Fisher succeeded in reducing

the time taken to build a battleship from three years to two.
His methods were personal and direct. He seemed to be
everywhere, and to know everything.

A battleship came alongside to have a damaged gun changed
in one of her main turrets. Fisher arrived to watch progress.
Under his eye the work went forward unusually quickly without any of the customary breaks. No doubt he would soon go
away. But at one o'clock a table and a chair appeared. Lunch
was served to the Admiral Superintendent whose interest in
the work was unabated. As a result the job was completed in
hours instead of days.

In 1892 he became a Member of the Board of Admiralty.
The Controller, or Third Sea Lord, is responsible for the
design, building and repair of the ships of the Fleet and of
their armament and machinery. It is an arduous and difficult
post in which the sea experience of a senior naval officer must
be combined with the qualities of the managing director of a
great armaments firm. He must anticipate future trends,
earn the respect and co-operation of the leaders of industry (not
unnaturally suspicious of the "amateur") and fire them with
his vision.

It was a difficult time in a difficult post. The changes made
practicable by the very rapid growth of technical knowledge
opened up all sorts of possibilities for the large number of ships
authorised by the Naval Defence Act of 1889. But inventors
are notoriously optimistic. Early trials with many of the new
"toys" had shown them to be unreliable. It would be several
years before decisions made now could be proved right or
wrong. If wrong, the effects on the Fleet would be disastrous.
"*Festina lente*" was the motto advised. Fisher had another of
his own invention. "He who strains at the gnat of perfection
will swallow the camel of unreadiness."

He took the very wise course of appointing an advisory committee of some of the cleverest shipbuilders and engineers in the
country. Amongst the innovations which they supported was a
new type of very fast torpedo-carrying vessel driven by turbines
supplied with steam from water-tube boilers, the destroyer.

One of his fiercest battles was about these same water-tube boilers. As he wrote later he "put the fire where the water used to be and the water where the fire used to be, so that a ship could get up steam in twenty minutes instead of taking five and a half hours." Most of the engineering world was dubious of these claims and heavily committed to boilers of the old type, but Fisher won his point.

In 1893 Fisher had his first serious brush with the politicians. The Liberal Government was trying to whittle down expenditure on the Navy. Matters came to a head over the estimates for 1893–94, the Naval members of the Board of Admiralty, headed by Admiral Sir Frederick Richards the First Sea Lord, threatening to resign if they were not passed. Richards was a very competent seaman and an excellent administrator, but no match in debate for the genial ruffianism of the Chancellor of the Exchequer, Sir William Harcourt, sent by Gladstone to bring the recalcitrant Board into line. As Richards was "as dumb as Moses" Fisher did most of the talking. The Board stood firm. Gladstone was forced to give way. Fisher's low opinion of politicians as a class, their lack of principle and short-sighted love of expediency, dates from this time.

After six years as Controller during which he left a decided mark on the technical development of the Fleet, Fisher hoisted his flag in the *Renown* on the North American Station. It was his first sea command since *Inflexible*, but his reputation had preceded him. A shipmate has described the awe in which he was held, "though he never did most of us any harm." Yet when he came up from below, as Captain the Hon. Barry Bingham, v.c., recalls, "the quarter deck shook, and all hands shook with it. The word was quickly passed 'Look out, here comes Jack.' Everyone stood terribly to attention as the great one passed on and away."

Always immaculately turned out, though taking considerable liberties with the dress regulations (blue spats were a Fisher touch), he would pace up and down like a tiger, immersed in thought. Like the great cats, he conveyed an impression of suppressed, but easily released power. Catlike were the expressionless eyes when he listened, without the least indication of how he would react, to something upon which he was asked to decide. In spite of the humour which laced his vivid speech and the kindliness he often showed to those in trouble he was an awe-inspiring figure.

In 1899 he was selected to represent Great Britain at the First Hague Naval Conference. Amongst the great naval powers assembled Britain was unquestionably the most important. "Fisher was like a little god," wrote W. T. Stead, the famous editor of the *Pall Mall Gazette*, "but as he was personally most gracious, put on no airs, and danced like a middy till all hours in the morning; no man at the Hague was more popular than he."

But he astonished and shocked many of the delegates by the strength and violence of his opinions and the way in which he tore away the veil which conventionally masked the brutalities of war.

"The essence of war is violence."

"Moderation in war is imbecility."

"Hit first, hit hard, and hit anywhere."

Fisher believed that talk like this was far less dangerous to peace than the suave evasions of diplomacy.

"My sole object is peace. What you call my truculence is all for peace. If you rub it in, at home and abroad, that you are ready for instant war with every unit of your strength in the front line, and intend to be the first in, and hit your enemy in the belly, and kick him when he is down, and boil your prisoners in oil ... and torture his women and children, then people will keep clear of you."

His sayings were repeated and quoted in the press. When the delegates dispersed the reputation of the genial, able, but seemingly ruthless Admiral was international. It was not without its effect.

From the Hague he went as C.-in-C. Mediterranean. During the next few years, using his ships and their crews as guinea-pigs, he was able to probe their weaknesses and consolidate his plans for the sweeping changes he intended to make when he reached the positions of ultimate responsibility, now almost within his grasp. But first he must revolutionise Britain's principal fleet, by shock tactics.

He started at once, cancelling all the official calls, the paying and returning of which normally took several days. Instead, Commanding Officers were invited to assemble in the flagship at 10 a.m. By noon it was all over. As he had begun, so it went on. Tradition, unless it served a useful purpose, was swept aside. Recognising that the older and more senior officers, soaked for years in out-of-date ideas, conservative, suspicious of change, would oppose him as much as they dared, he concentrated on discovering and bringing forward the best of the younger officers—the men upon whom the heaviest responsibility would fall in any future war. He set up a committee of Captains and Commanders to put forward proposals for the next manoeuvres, an innovation which caused much heart-burning in older breasts. To make known his own ideas he used to give frequent lectures to the flag and commanding officers, their second in command and engineer officers, "voluntary" lectures (but those who did not show up were ordered to be present at a repeat sitting).

His object, never lost sight of, was to prepare the Fleet for battle. Official inspections probed uncomfortably below the surface of an outwardly smart ship, looking for weaknesses in organisation. Lack of forward thinking in her officers could not be atoned for by polished brasswork, shining enamel, snowy decks and a well turned out crew.

Not that he was averse from that sort of thing. Fisher loved a show. He liked his barge to leave the gangway in a flurry of foam; to reverse alongside at "full astern." The Admiral's flag he flew was the biggest anyone had ever seen. He delighted in putting on a performance for important foreign visitors and royalty. His Fleet was the finest in the world and everyone should know it.

But his ships must be *war*ships. The shooting of the Fleet was greatly improved, though still leaving much to be desired because of material deficiencies. He insisted, in spite of all protests, in making ships steam at high speed for long periods, not just a few hours once a year. Breakdowns were frequent but the defects that caused them were gradually eliminated.

In 1902 Fisher hauled down his flag to take up another Admiralty appointment, as Second Sea Lord and chief of Personnel. It was exactly where he wished to be. He was convinced that a drastic change in the system of entering and training young officers was necessary. The motive power had been sails; now it was machinery. In the great days of sail officers had understood every detail of their ships; now the majority "had not stooped to oil their fingers, and the real masters of the Navy were the despised engineers, whose mammas were not asked to tea by other mammas."

The remark about the mammas is highly relevant. It is difficult, in 1961, to appreciate the reality of the barriers which separated the social classes sixty years ago. The engineer officers of the Fleet, entered direct from the Dockyards or Industry, were not "gentlemen" and mechanical matters were beneath the notice of executive officers mostly coming from the upper middle class. On the other hand, as Fisher realised, without a proper feeling for machinery officers afloat could not get the best out of the ships with which they would one day have to fight, and the "user" would be unqualified to exercise his very necessary influence over the design of ships and weapons.

As C.-in-C. Mediterranean Fisher had become friendly with Lord Selborne, now First Lord of the Admiralty. With this powerful support Fisher brought out the "Selborne Scheme." Boys would be entered as cadets at the tender age of twelve and henceforth educated in general as well as naval subjects by the Navy. The entry would be sufficient to provide all the officers needed to man the executive and engineering branches of the Navy and the Royal Marines. Trained together, knowing one another from boyhood, the officers of the Fleet would be a socially homogeneous body with enough basic engineering knowledge to meet the demands of the age. Later

their paths would diverge, some specialising in navigation, gunnery, torpedo or engineering, some in the duties of the sea-soldier. But in the junior ranks, all would be fitted to play a fully responsible part in the life of their ships; not divided, as had all too frequently been the case, into those who gave orders without really knowing how they could be carried out and those who did what they were told without a chance of deciding what the policy should be.

The Selborne Scheme struck at the very foundation of the "Establishment" and was viewed with horror by many. It was "making greasers of us all." The new officers, jacks of all trades would be master of none. Fisher overrode all these objections, though the inclusion of Marine officers in the common entry was dropped. A new "junior" naval college was erected on the site of the old stables at Osborne House in the Isle of Wight.

It might in retrospect be added that the Selborne Scheme though sound in principle was too wide in scope. Defects became apparent and the opposition, bulldozed underground during Fisher's years of power, remained alive. In 1919 it emerged and the pendulum, pushed too far in one direction, swung too far back again. Engineer officers were deprived of their executive status and barred from the higher administrative posts for which some of them were well suited. It was not until 1954 that the matter was rectified by the introduction of the modified scheme, doing justice to all branches of the Service, which exists today. Fisher, as is now admitted, had been working on the right lines though his ideas were too revolutionary. Like Lewis Carroll's Snark he was "ages ahead of the fashion"—too far ahead to achieve the very necessary result.

Fisher's next appointment was to Portsmouth as C.-in-C., hoisting his flag in the *Victory*, which he had joined fifty years before "penniless, friendless and forlorn." In addition to his naval duties he was selected, at the instance of King Edward VII, to be a member of a small committee set up to recommend how the War Office, whose organisation had failed miserably to meet the needs of the South African War, should be reformed. Fisher's comments were typical.

"The military system is rotten to the very core!" he wrote to Lord Esher, another member of the Committee. "You want to begin *ab ovo*! The best of the Generals are even worse than the subalterns, because they are more hardened sinners!"

With that clear vision which amounted almost to second sight, he went to the root of the matter. The British Army was "a projectile to be fired by the Navy. The Navy embarks it and lands it where it can do most mischief! . . . Instead of . . . ineffectually opposing the vast Continental armies, we should be employing ourselves in joint naval and military manoeuvres." It all seems obvious enough today, but Fisher, writing in 1903, had anticipated the requirements of two great wars and the great combined operations used with such success forty years later.

On Trafalgar Day 1904, Fisher reached the top of the naval tree by becoming First Lord of the Admiralty. Owing nothing to birth or wealth or social connections, he had got there by drive, merit and personality; by being so indisputably an exceptional man.

In those ten years before the outbreak of World War I in 1914 successive British Governments were neither wholly convinced of the inevitability of a war, nor entirely unconscious of the approaching danger. Periods of calm were punctuated by incidents which gave fresh cause for alarm. In Sir Winston Churchill's words:

Those whose duty it was to watch over the safety of the country lived simultaneously in two different worlds of thought. There was the actual visible world with its peaceful activities; and there was a hypothetical world, a world "beneath the threshold" as it were, a world at one moment utterly fantastic, at the next seeming about to leap into reality—a world of monstrous shadows moving in convulsive combination through vistas of fathomless catastrophe.

For Fisher at the Admiralty the problem was simplified. It was his business, with the men and ships and money at his disposal, to assume that at any moment the Navy might be called upon. In an emergency everything would depend on naval readiness. His task was to forge a weapon disposed for instant use.

All his life had been a preparation for the time which had now come. There was much to be done. With the introduction of the Selborne Scheme the foundations had been laid for providing the future Navy with the right sort of officers. But this was a long-term plan, the fruits of which could not be gathered for many years. In the meantime there were urgent matters to be attended to, things which could be done *now* or during the next few years.

In December 1904, less than two months after his arrival in Whitehall, a memorandum was issued ordering a major re-distribution of the Fleet. France was no longer our enemy; Japan was an ally; America a friend. The threat which for years had been centred in the Mediterranean was now in the North Sea. The old Channel Fleet, re-named the Atlantic Fleet, was moved to Gibraltar where it could reinforce either home or foreign waters. The Home Fleet, re-named the Channel Fleet, was increased to ten battleships in full commission, closely supported by other ships in reserve, but now with nucleus crews. Men for the extra ships and nucleus crews could only be found by reductions elsewhere. Fisher took the drastic step of paying off no less than 174 of the very large number of smaller ships on the various foreign stations abroad.

A howl of protest greeted these changes, but Fisher was un-doubtedly right. Many of the ships on the more distant foreign stations were obsolete and very little use as men-of-war. Naval distribution abroad had been little changed for nearly a hundred years in spite of vastly altered political requirements. As one journalist put it at the time:

Though the old system of distribution was popular, there was one fatal mistake in it. For lawn tennis, waltzing, relief of distress, or ambulance work after an earthquake it was admirable; for war purposes it was useless, because the force was divided and sub-divided and was largely composed of ships that could neither fight an enemy nor escape him. The change was made on the principle that Germany, and not earthquakes, were the objective; that Teutonic, and not seismic, disturbances were the duty of the Navy.

The redistribution of the Fleet was not a popular measure. Many overseas commands were reduced in importance and a number of pleasant posts where life was a long holiday, pleasantly divided between sport and social activities and little disturbed by drills or practices, ceased to exist. That we would now have insufficient strength abroad to defend the shipping on which the very existence of the Empire depended was a more valid criticism.[1] British representatives abroad complained that the withdrawal of so many ships would have an adverse affect on our prestige and influence.

But the Admiralty, still without the naval war staff which Beresford had fought for twenty years before, had not the machinery for calculating possible future requirements in detail. Fisher was never one for half measures and he was working on a limited budget, particularly as regards officers and men. If the Fleet in home waters was defeated in battle the war would be lost. Setbacks abroad would be inconvenient, but not a major disaster.

The storm caused by the scrapping and redistribution programme of 1904 had scarcely subsided when Fisher announced a further re-organisation in home waters. Ships in reserve were formed into a new Home Fleet under the command of an Admiral. One division of this Fleet, based on the Nore, would have six battleships in full commission and nucleus crews were to be increased from two-fifths to three-fifths of full complement. To provide these extra ships and men meant withdrawals from the Mediterranean, Channel and Atlantic Fleets.

In 1905 Beresford had taken command of the reduced Mediterranean Fleet, up till then the most important post afloat. It was still arguable, in spite of our recent *rapprochement* with France, that the only fleets actually in being which seriously challenged British seapower were the French and

[1] In fact, when war did come, a number of old ships had to be hastily commissioned and sent against enemy warships and armed raiders.

Russian, acting, as was always possible, together. Germany had shown her intention of building a modern navy which would in time be a most serious threat, but some years must elapse before the ships and men would be available. Beresford wanted a stronger Mediterranean Fleet and the friction with Fisher, which had been lurking just below the surface, began to be apparent.

Doubts as to the wisdom of Fisher's drastic reorganisation were sincerely held by a number of other very experienced officers. Murmurs that the Admiralty under Fisher was a "one-man band" and that dictatorship had been substituted for rule by consultation with the remainder of the Board and the C.-in-C.'s afloat, were echoed from the fleets by a section of the press. Was Fisher a public menace? Many were beginning to think so, but the only figure whose stature was comparable to Fisher's was Lord Charles Beresford. Well-born, rich and influential, idolised by the British public and very popular in his own Service he was the natural leader of the opposition.

Beresford, essentially a man of great loyalty, gives no hint in the public record he left behind as to when the admiration and respect he undoubtedly felt for Fisher for many years was clouded by doubt as to the rightness of some of Fisher's schemes and finally changed to active opposition. But when the change came it was complete, going far beyond reasoned objections to what Fisher wished to do and rapidly extending to almost anything the latter had proposed. When the Selborne Scheme was first introduced Beresford had expressed almost unqualified approval. "The strongest opponents of the scheme," he had said in an interview a few years before, "will acknowledge that it is a brilliant, statesmanlike effort to grapple with the problem." Indeed Beresford had always believed that the seaman must have a good working knowledge of his ship and its means of propulsion, sail in the old days, engines in the new. "The executive has remained ignorant of one of the most important parts of the profession," he said in the same interview, "the Engineer has never received that recognition to which the importance of his duties and responsibilities fully entitles him." After further favourable comments he concluded by saying that it was a "thoroughly matured and well thought out" plan which would "make more complete the well-being, contentment and efficiency of [the] Service." Now all this seemed to have been forgotten.

Fisher's methods, "Ruthless, Remorseless, Relentless," had made him many enemies. As he grew older and had more power he often acted without regard to the feelings of others and sometimes with more than a trace of vindictiveness. On the other hand, he inspired his followers, not only with his own vision of a new and much more effective Navy, but with an affection for which love is not too strong a word. He was indeed, for all his explosiveness and dictatorial ways, a very lovable man; gay, witty, warm-hearted, kindly and generous: a fearsome enemy, but a wonderful friend. He got his way sometimes by savagely overriding opposition, but often by his extraordinary charm. At sixty-five he had a boyish enthusiasm which was infectious. Not only the younger naval officers, but politicians and hard-bitten leaders of industry became his willing slaves. It enabled him to push through one of the greatest naval reforms with which his name is associated, the building of the *Dreadnought*; a ship which gave her name to a type of warship which was the backbone of the Fleet of every major naval power for forty years—the all-big-gun battleship.

Progress in design since the coming of the first iron-clads had been quite rapid, but evolutionary. In 1905 the battleships coming into service in our own and other navies were ships with a mixed armament of large (12-inch) and smaller guns in their main battery. Torpedo tubes were also fitted. There were a number of smaller quick-firing guns for use against the enemy's torpedo craft, but built-in protection was primarily designed against the enemy's guns. Each new class of ship tended to be larger and more powerful than its predecessors, but otherwise similar.

For some years Fisher had felt that this steady evolution was

not giving us the type of ship we required and that a revolution in design was necessary. His reasoning is worth following
in some detail. Battle range had increased from two or three
thousand yards to six thousand yards or more; ranges of ten
thousand yards were already feasible, with even greater ranges
likely in the near future. The increase of range had been made
possible by the accuracy of the modern gun, and made essential
by the threat of torpedoes fired by the enemy. Actions at
point-blank range were no longer contemplated or feasible.
But though the guns were accurate the instruments which
controlled their fire had not made a corresponding advance.
There was only one way to get the enemy's range; salvo firing
of guns in groups, observing the great splashes made as the
shells hit the water and adjusting the elevation accordingly.

Ships with the popular mixed armament suffered from
serious disadvantages. The "spread" of the falling shells
was apt to be very great and the time of flight of the large
and smaller shells caused them to arrive, not together, but
at intervals. If only the biggest guns were used to get the
range they were insufficient in number unless fired as a broadside. The solution, an all-big-gun battleship, seems obvious
enough in retrospect. (So does the modern aircraft carrier's
angled deck, but it was twenty years before anyone thought
of it.)

As C.-in-C. Portsmouth, Fisher had used the resources of
the Dockyard drawing office to make a series of sketch designs
for an all-big-gun battleship and armoured cruiser. Turbine
machinery, another innovation for a heavy ship, would give
them greater speed than existing battleships and armoured
cruisers. They were revolutionary in almost every particular.
So drastic a change would certainly be opposed by the majority
in political, naval and shipbuilding circles unless even Fisher's
drive was powerfully reinforced. He therefore took the wise
and unusual step of appointing a design committee consisting
of seven outstanding naval officers, headed by Rear-Admiral
Prince Louis of Battenberg and including the Engineer-
in-Chief, with seven civilian members of such outstanding

H

qualifications that their support was incontrovertible.[1] The Committee was directed to assist the Board of Admiralty with their advice on the best types of naval vessel to meet future requirements. Fisher himself, though not a member of the Committee, acted as its Chairman.

The battleship was to carry as many 12-inch guns as possible, all mounted above the main deck. Her armour was to be adequate and her speed, 21 knots, was 2 knots higher than any existing British battleship. The battle-cruiser, with a speed of 25 knots, would also be armed with 12-inch guns, but her protection would be similar to that of the latest types of armoured cruiser. Both ships would have light anti-torpedo-craft guns. (It should be noticed at this point that the battle-cruiser was never intended to fight battleships, but to have the speed and gun-power to out-manoeuvre and overwhelm cruisers, and armed liners.)

After a number of meetings the Committee selected designs for the battleship and cruiser which eventually appeared as the *Dreadnought* and *Invincible*. The *Dreadnought* mounted ten 12-inch guns; the *Invincible* eight. Turbines replaced reciprocating engines in a major ship of war for the first time.

Another innovation was the subdivision of the interior into an unusually large number of watertight compartments to limit the effects of underwater damage by torpedo or mine. But protection was never a major consideration, coming low on the list of priorities which the designer had to meet. Fisher always believed that speed and gun-power were a substitute for armour. The fast ship with very big guns could keep her distance, and destroy the enemy without coming seriously under the fire of his smaller weapons. He encouraged the building of ships which could not stand up to the same sort of punishment as they were able to inflict. It was a very serious error.

---

[1] Lord Kelvin, Professor J. H. Biles of Glasgow University, Sir John Thornycroft and Alexander Gracie from the shipbuilding industry, the Director of Naval Construction, Philip Watts, R. E. Froude the Superintendent of Admiralty Experimental Works, and the Chief Constructor of Portsmouth Dockyard, W. H. Gard.

If, as Fisher was convinced, the *Dreadnought* marked a revolution in naval building other countries would be quick to follow our example, and speed of construction was essential. To save time the gun-turrets, the design and erection of which usually takes far longer than the building of the hull, were to be practically the same as those of earlier classes. Even so an immense amount of detailed work is necessary to design, build and equip a great ship. Spurred on by Fisher, all records were broken. On 3 January 1905 the Design Committee met for the first time. On 2 October, the keel of the *Dreadnought* was laid. She was launched only eighteen weeks later, in February 1906 and went to sea on her trials early in October, just a year and a day from laying down—an extraordinary feat, for which great credit must be given to Portsmouth Dockyard and the numerous sub-contractors involved.

The extraordinary success of the *Dreadnought* was proved by the fact that the principle she had established was only departed from in one major respect in subsequent design—the substitution of rather larger guns in the secondary armament for the small weapons inadequate to deal with destroyers armed with the longer-range modern torpedo.

In its day the building of the *Dreadnought* was a step forward comparable to the coming of the atomic submarine in our own times, but many people believed that her introduction, by making the older types of battleships obsolescent, had had the effect of reducing Britain's preponderance in the capital ships which were the backbone of the Fleet.

The all-big-gun armoured cruisers or battle-cruisers as they came to be called, could make short work of the older, slower and less heavily armed armoured cruisers. For commerce protection they were ideal, but they were also intended to work with the Fleet where they would eventually be opposed by other battle-cruisers of about the same speed and gun-power. Fisher's priorities in which protection took third place made the British version very vulnerable, as was to be tragically proved at the Battle of Jutland seven years later.

But Fisher was almost more delighted with his *Invincible*

than he had been with the *Dreadnought*. Laid down in 1906 she began her trials in 1908. Her speed was, for those days, phenomenal for a heavy ship—26·6 knots.

Fisher had planned to give Britain a useful lead in these all-big-gun ships. In this he was successful. In November 1909 the only Dreadnoughts in commission besides the seven in the Royal Navy were two German and one Japanese. Germany had a further eleven on the stocks and fitting out against Britain's thirteen. The United States, France, Japan, Russia and Italy were also building Dreadnoughts, and the mixed armament battleship, as Fisher had foreseen, was a thing of the past. The German Dreadnought cruisers were a little slower than the British, but they were much better protected—battle-cruisers in fact as well as name.

At the other end of the scale to the great battleships was the submarine, just becoming a practical proposition when Fisher went to the Admiralty. The early submarines were small, un-reliable and of very limited endurance; of not much use even for coast defence. Fisher was sure that they could be de-veloped, giving the new branch every encouragement and taking a personal interest in its doings. Backed by his drive the British Submarine Service forged ahead.

Amongst the officers Fisher had assembled to help him was one of whom much was to be heard—Captain John Jellicoe, now occupying Fisher's old post as Director of Naval Ord-nance. Working closely with him in a newly created appoint-ment was another brilliant gunnery officer, Rear-Admiral Percy Scott. As Director of Target Practices he was empowered to visit all the principal Fleets.

Fisher's detractors accuse him of being pre-occupied with *materiel* to the exclusion of other equally important matters. The record proves them wrong. Very liberal-minded in many ways he was determined to democratise the Navy. Amongst the reforms which he pushed through was an improved system of entry and training for the lower deck with special reference to the engine-room branch, increased opportunities for pro-motion to warrant rank and better victualling arrangements.

Concurrently he re-organised the Naval Dockyards and introduced simpler and more efficient schemes for the supply of
naval stores. No detail seemed to escape the probing eye of
this man who had "the energy of a steam engine, the pertinacity
of a debt collector, and no reverence . . . for anything but
facts."

Though now in the middle sixties, Fisher's capacity for hard
work seemed unimpaired. He was often up and at his desk
in the small hours of the morning, getting through a vast
amount of detailed administrative work before breakfast. His
astonishing memory was as good as ever and he still found
time to write voluminous letters and memoranda in his own
hand. By lengthening his working day he kept ahead of the
many jobs in hand, a volcano of seemingly inexhaustible
energy. He was, in many ways, a superhuman figure, but he
was not immune from the influences which lie in wait for those
of his attainments. "All power corrupts." As time went on
his characteristics became more marked. Driven by a sense of
urgency, of having so little time to accomplish what he felt to
be necessary, he became increasingly dictatorial. The number
of his enemies in and outside the Navy grew. Some of them
were in high places.

Fisher's enemies called him a dictator, but he had always
believed in seeking the opinion of others. When he was C.-in-C.
Mediterranean, he constantly picked the brains of his subordinates. As First Sea Lord he continued with this practice.
With a contempt for convention which was typical he encouraged a number of comparatively junior officers whose
acumen he respected to write to him privately on service
matters. It was a practice that was open to the most serious
objections. Discretion was never Fisher's strong point and it
was soon suspected that the First Sea Lord had a private intelligence system of his own. Senior officers strongly objected
to being reported upon by their subordinates. "Espionage"
was the term they used. Officers who in all honesty had been
opposed to some of his reforms and were not therefore "in the
Fish-pond" felt that their careers might well be prejudiced.

The sort of thing which was going on is contained in a letter which later received wide publicity. In it an officer in the Mediterranean Fleet—Captain R. H. Bacon—gives a long account of an interview with the Prince of Wales and his discussion with H.R.H. about the effects of some of Fisher's reforms on officers afloat.

Bacon, dealing with a remark by the Prince of Wales about "unrest" in the Service, lists what he believed to be the principal grievances under these headings.

(1) Want of information.
(2) Not being consulted more by the Admiralty.
(3) Captains being treated with little consideration.
(4) Notion spread by [Fisher's] detractors that he overrides everyone else.
(5) A total misconception of the [Selborne] Scheme, especially as regards interchangeability.

"About this," says Bacon, "the wildest statements are flying about."

Bacon's letters are very frank and it is clear that he was not afraid to bring to light unpalatable truths. Neither, and less admirably, does he avoid mentioning by name some of the Admirals whom he felt had "got at" the Prince of Wales— the C.-in-C. China, Sir Arthur Moore, the C.-in-C. East Indies, Sir Edmund Poë, "and probably the two Admirals here [Lord Charles Beresford and Admiral Lambton]." Criticism of these officers, which includes Bacon's own C.-in-C., was certainly implied. Describing a talk with the King, Bacon wrote how he "told His Majesty straight out that the Navy was suffering from a want of loyalty to the Admiralty among the Admirals afloat. . . . The King and the Prince of Wales were always most loyal (if such a term may be used) to you personally," he concludes, "and to the whole of the schemes of reform, but very much disturbed at the Service agitation headed by Lord Charles Beresford and Admiral Lambton."

This letter was dated 15 April 1906. It cannot have been

entirely fortuitous that on 24 April Fisher wrote to the First
Lord.

It is with extreme reluctance that I feel compelled in the interests
of the Navy and the maintenance of its hitherto unquestioned discipline
and loyalty to bring before the Board the unprecedented conduct of the
Commander in Chief of the Mediterranean Fleet in publicly reflecting
on the conduct of the Admiralty and in discrediting the policy of the
Board and inciting those under his command to ridicule the decision
of the Board.

But Fisher, alas, was now hardly the man to speak of conduct prejudicial to discipline. Even the King was unable to
make him behave with greater circumspection. Fisher's
friendship with the King was of long standing and very
greatly valued. The Crown, to which he was intensely loyal,
appealed to his sense of pageantry and mysticism and he
appreciated to the full the qualities of restraint, excellent
judgment and political acumen not notably prominent in his
own character. The very great interest which the King had
always taken in the Navy led Fisher often to discuss matters
with him. The King, on his part, enjoyed the frankness of
Fisher's views.

(On one occasion in the past Fisher had been a little too
frank. The Prince of Wales, as he then was, saw across the
dinner table Fisher talking animatedly to a lady who evidently
was much entertained.

"Be careful," he warned her. "They say these sailors have a
wife in every port."

"Ah, Sir," said Fisher, "aren't you sorry not to be a sailor."

There was a pregnant pause before the Prince broke into a
hearty laugh.)

The King was indeed greatly disturbed by what was going
on in the Navy. Lord Charles Beresford was another close
friend. Knowing both men very well he used his influence to
prevent a calamity, but in vain.

In April 1907 Admiral Lord Charles Beresford assumed
command of what had hitherto been by far the most powerful
British naval force, the Channel Fleet—fourteen battleships,

seven cruisers and a number of smaller craft, a total of sixty-
eight ships. His arrival coincided with yet another re-organisation, reducing its strength to eight battleships. True, the intention was that in time of war the C.-in-C. Channel Fleet
would be the supremo, with the Atlantic and Home Fleets
under his orders, but once again Lord Charles had taken over
a great Fleet only to have it reduced in size. He had no control
of the training of a large part of his wartime command.
Further, he was not supplied with any overall strategical plan
of how the Fleets for which he would be responsible were to be
used.

This last complaint was a very valid one. The efforts
Beresford had made to have a proper Naval Staff at the
Admiralty specifically charged with the task of studying war
and producing detailed plans for its prosecution had been
nullified and never put into practice. If plans existed they were
locked up in Fisher's brain. True the C.-in-C. Channel Fleet
had been sent an "Order of Battle," but the instructions it
contained were brief and insufficiently comprehensive.

After some increasingly acrimonious correspondence a
meeting was held at the Admiralty on 5 July 1907 between
Lord Tweedmouth, the First Lord, Fisher and Beresford at
which some very plain speaking took place. Tweedmouth had
been greatly disturbed by the growing tension between the
Admiralty and its principal executive afloat, the C.-in-C.
Channel Fleet. The matter was already the subject of gossip
and hints of trouble were appearing in the press. The questions which the First Lord now put to Lord Charles brought
the principal differences into the open—the number and type
of ships he considered he should have under his command; the
further information he needed. Why did he not try to culti-
vate good and cordial relations with the Admiralty, who were
most anxious to achieve this end?

Beresford, never very strong in argument, was inclined to
hedge when directly confronted in this way.

The First Lord returned to what was in fact his major
point, relations with the Admiralty. Beresford tried to pass it

off lightly: "You will allow me to smile for at least ten minutes over Question No. 3. There is no question of cordial relations. I do not care about having rows with anybody." But Lord Tweedmouth gently stuck to his guns. On 30 June Beresford had written: "The Home Fleet, as at present constituted, is a fraud and a danger to the State." He had said this again and again and his views were generally known. If, as Beresford now argued, it was a private letter it was a strong statement which must be substantiated.

"What you want to say to us now is, 'You must not take my letter in that way,'" said Fisher. "'I was only doing it as giving you a friendly criticism, and not meaning you to take it as anything insubordinate?'"

"Certainly," said Lord Charles. "That I had any notion of insubordination I absolutely deny."

The discussion continued on equally frank lines, Fisher pointing out in detail that Beresford's requests had always been met. The composition and disposition of the Fleet were matters of high policy decided not even by the Admiralty, but by the Government. When it came to training the ships and their crews the Admiralty had and would accede to the reasonable requests of the C.-in-C. The important matter of war plans was not gone into very thoroughly for Beresford climbed down. "I have no right to put myself up against the constituted authority of the Admiralty."

Unfortunately this interview failed to clear the air. Some weeks earlier Beresford had written to Fisher:

There is not the slightest chance of any friction between me and you, or between me and anyone else. When the friction begins I am off. If a senior and a junior have a row the junior is wrong under any conceivable condition, or discipline could not go on. So long as I am here I will do my best to make the Admiralty policy a success.

But the quarrel went on. Beresford continued to bombard the Admiralty with criticisms of their plans and policy, often going far beyond the limits (which he had so frankly acknowledged) of what was proper for an officer in his position. Fisher on his part had clearly come to the opinion that Beresford was "impossible." He had been, he felt, very patient and had leant over backwards to avoid undesirable friction. Now he was through. Being the man he was he joined battle with every weapon at his disposal. On both sides the gloves were off. Each had their fervent supporters and though a considerable body of moderate opinion refused to attach itself to either camp, there was a very real danger of the discipline of the whole Navy being undermined. A letter from Lord Charles to the Admiralty written in November 1907 is typical of the open way in which the feud was now conducted.

It has come to my notice that a feeling has arisen in the Service that it is prejudicial to an officer's career to be personally connected with me on Service matters. This may not be a fact, but the impression I know exists.

This letter concludes with this paragraph.

The ordinary etiquette, civilities and courteous dealings which officers in high and distinguished command have heretofore so markedly received from the Admiralty have been entirely absent in my case. I have not been honoured by one word from the Lord Commissioners of the Admiralty as to two of these momentous changes affecting me so vitally in the management and administration of the great office assigned to me. I make no requests, but I desire to state officially that such incidents as I have recorded cannot induce to the efficiency of the Fleet or assist me in my numerous labours.

The Admiralty replied asking for specific evidence (which was not forthcoming) about the very serious allegations that association with Beresford was prejudicial to an officer's career. In conclusion Their Lordships "must remind you once more that the responsibility for the naval defence of the Empire, whether in Home waters or elsewhere, rests with the Board of Admiralty."

. . . my Lords cannot understand on what grounds your allegation of discourtesy on their part is based. They would, however, observe that it becomes increasingly difficult for them in their correspondence with you to avoid overstepping the usual limits of official reserve while you continue to employ language which has no parallel within their experience as coming from a subordinate and addressed to the Board of Admiralty.

It seems in retrospect that the limits of official reserve had long been overstepped on both sides and the end of this sorry episode was not yet. With the Navy, Parliament, the press and the public taking sides an explosion was daily becoming imminent. Early in 1908, Rear-Admiral Percy Scott relinquished his post as Director of Target Services to take command of a cruiser squadron in the Channel Fleet. A few months later he was involved in an incident with Beresford which lit the fuse.

Scott, an ardent Fisherite, was at sea for target practice in the *Good Hope* with the *Roxburgh* when he received a signal from his Commander-in-Chief to return to harbour and prepare for a visit by foreign royalty to the Fleet. Scott thereupon signalled to *Roxburgh*: "As paintwork is more important than efficiency we must go back to Portland to make ourselves pretty."

Beresford ordered Scott to repair on board the flagship and publicly rebuked him in a stormy scene. Not content with this he made a general signal to the Channel Fleet.

In regard to my order made to the Fleet to paint ships the signal made by the Rear Admiral, First Cruiser Squadron is contemptuous in tone and insubordinate in character. The Rear Admiral is to issue orders to *Good Hope* and *Roxburgh* to expunge the signal from their signal logs and to report to me by signal when my orders have been obeyed.

Scott subsequently alleged that he was simply following the well-known naval practice of sometimes making rather facetious signals. Beresford thought otherwise and asked the Admiralty that his insubordinate subordinate should be relieved of his command. The Admiralty did nothing and Beresford, knowing Scott's relations with Fisher, drew his own conclusions.

There was a lull, but not for long. In July 1908 came another incident which, reported in the press, brought the great Fisher–Beresford quarrel to a head.

The cruisers of the Channel Fleet were steaming in parallel columns, one line led by Scott's flagship *Good Hope*, when they were ordered by the C.-in-C. to alter course, both lines turning inwards. Scott alleged that the columns were only 1,200 yards apart. As the diameter of the turning circles of the leading ships were more than half this distance a collision would have resulted (the sinking of the *Victoria* and *Camperdown* in the Mediterranean had been the result of a similar manoeuvre). Scott therefore disregarded Beresford's order, turning outwards instead of inwards. Told to give his reasons for failing to obey a signal he had a perfectly adequate reply, and there the matter might have ended, but for a very strange series of events.

On 6 July *The Times*, a pro-Fisher newspaper, published a letter from an ex-Civil Lord of the Admiralty, which mentioned the incident. Next day there was an article headed:

A STRANGE OCCURRENCE IN THE CHANNEL FLEET

"We have received the following account from a correspondent," it began. Who was this mysterious "correspondent" who could get his message into print when the Fleet was still at sea on its way to Norway? Evidently a man of influence. The timing of his message was certainly most convenient. On 8 July *The Times* first leader was headed:

DISUNION IN THE NAVY

The situation . . . manifestly demands, [roared the 'Thunderer'] if it has not already received, the prompt consideration of the Cabinet . . . It was . . . the duty of all those who serve the country in the Navy not to allow their personal opinions of this or that act of policy to abate in any way that noble habit of ready and cheerful obedience to all who are set in authority over them . . . if, as alleged, Lord Charles Beresford is at loggerheads with the Board of Admiralty, or with any individual member of it, he is, in our judgment, ipso facto in the wrong . . . If, as alleged, he is not on speaking terms with one of his flag officers he is equally in the wrong . . . The 'strange occurrence' which we recorded yesterday . . . which appears to have led to a misunderstanding between himself and Sir Percy Scott is a significant case in point. On the merits of the case, in the present state of our information, *we can offer no opinion*,[1] but would it have occurred at all if relations between Commander in Chief and subordinate had been as normal and cordial as they ought to have been?

[1] My italic.

The Commander in Chief of the Channel Fleet must be confronted with the historic alternative *se soumettre ou se demettre*. Lord Charles Beresford, so long as he holds his present position, is not free to let it be known, whether by his actions or demeanour, either to his Fleet or to the world at large, that his attitude to the Board of Admiralty is one of scant respect for its authority and avowed dissent from its policy . . .

Strong words indeed and not, perhaps, as unbiased as we would normally expect from such a source, and next day *The Times* offered a very decided opinion on the case by publishing a diagram purporting to show exactly what had happened in the "strange occurrence" and what the result might have been. The caption to this diagram, with the *Good Hope* and *Argyle* in collision, read, "Fig. II shows what would inevitably have happened if both ships had obeyed the signal." That everything depended on the correctness of the assumption that the two ships had been only 1,200 yards apart was not mentioned.

One side of the case had been made public. What about the other? The Press Association had sent a telegram to Lord Charles Beresford asking if they could publish a statement from him. The reply dated 9 July from Skagen was brief and very correct. "Thanks. Cannot communicate with anybody but Admiralty. Beresford."

His enemies were less restrained. In the House of Commons on 10 July H. C. Lea brought up the "strange occurrence," asking whether a Court of Enquiry had been ordered to assemble and whether, if there was a prima facie case for such an enquiry, Lord Charles Beresford would be relieved of his command.

Defence of the absent Admiral came from an unexpected quarter when Redmond, the Irish Nationalist, asked whether Lea "in considering this matter would be careful to receive with the utmost caution any charges made against Lord Charles Beresford, or any other Irishman by *The Times* newspaper" and "whether there was any possible way of preventing *The Times* newspaper from constantly circulating scandals of every kind."

Cheers and laughter greeted this sally, but indeed the matter was serious enough with the dispute which had long raged within the Navy spreading to Parliament and the country at large, and with leading newspapers ranged behind the antagonists.

It was clear that the position had become intolerable. Fisher, Beresford and Scott had served the Navy and the country very well, but antagonisms had been aroused which struck at the foundations of the Service by undermining its discipline. Scott, still flying his flag in the *Good Hope*, was transferred to the South African Station. The First Lord, Reginald McKenna, was in favour of using the excuse of a further reorganisation of the Channel and Home Fleets to terminate Beresford's appointment, but the Cabinet, apprehensive of the influence of the popular Lord Charles and his many friends in high places, and not convinced that all the errors had been on his side, would not for a time agree. In the lull which followed McKenna became more and more convinced that Lord Charles must go. Finally he got his way. In December he informed Lord Charles officially that "after much deliberation" he had "decided that the present commands of the Channel and Home Fleets should be held for a period of two years" and that Beresford would be relieved in March 1909. This was a year before the end of the usual term. "Under the circumstances," wrote Lord Charles in his reply, "you cannot wonder that I feel deeply that my career afloat, which has extended over nearly fifty years, should be so abruptly terminated."

Fisher had long realised that his dictatorial ways might lead to a situation which would eventually bring him down, but methods and man were indivisible. "A negative attitude is *never* successful. An attack should always be met by a counter-attack." "Never explain." "It is only damn fools who argue." "I am going to kick other people's shins if they kick mine." Even the influence of the King was unable to make him alter his ways. Indeed constant opposition had tended to make him even readier to strike out and inflict unnecessary wounds. It was his way of salving his own injuries, for he had been deeply hurt by the attack made upon him. "When I retire," he said to a friend, "I shall write my reminiscences. I shall call them 'Hell. By One Who Has Been There.'"

Early in the New Year came the great Navy Scare of 1909. Its basis was a widely held opinion that the greatly accelerated pace at which the German Navy was being strengthened was not being matched by British warship building. Critics pointed out that in the three years 1906–09 our original estimates had actually been *reduced* by a total of four battleships. Now McKenna, presenting the Navy Estimate for 1909–10, confessed that the Government did "not know, as we thought we did, the rate at which German construction is taking place." He went on to ask for six instead of two battleships in the current programme, a minimum requirement if by 1912 the German Navy was not to have too great a relative strength in capital ships.

The cat was properly out of the bag. How had such a situation been allowed to develop? Had the Government overriden the advice of its naval advisers, and if so why had not the naval members of the Board, and particularly the supremo who arrogated so much power to himself, resigned? "The sole responsibility," stormed the *Daily Express*, "for the fact that in a few months Great Britain will be in a more vulnerable position than she has been since Trafalgar belongs to the First Sea Lord."

It need hardly be said that Fisher was the very last man who was likely to have understated the requirements of his beloved Navy, but he was always a realist. The public and the Treasury held the purse strings. It was useless to demand more than they were prepared to pay for. A few days later he wrote to Sir Arthur Davidson: "I welcome this scare—the Radicals swear I engineered it to 'dish' them! The Public wants pepper always to make them wake up!" In the end eight, not six, Dreadnoughts were authorised, but a residue of discontent remained which was to be stirred up later on.

It was the moment when Lord Charles Beresford hauled down his flag for the last time. Leaving his flagship he drove in a carriage through Portsmouth Dockyard to the harbour

station to take the train to London. For hours every tram
bound for the Hard had been crammed with people; old ship-
mates and members of the public who wished to express their
feelings—that he was the victim of a very raw deal—by giving
him a rousing send-off. No naval officer since Nelson's time
had ever received such an ovation. The cheering and the
singing of "For he's a jolly good fellow" continued until the
train had moved out of sight. At Waterloo huge crowds had
assembled to give him an enthusiastic welcome.

Lord Charles, his naval career at an end and suffering from
a strong sense of having been unfairly treated, was no doubt
encouraged by this very tangible evidence of public support.
In 1910 he re-entered Parliament as the Member for Portsmouth, a seat he was to hold until he was raised to the peerage
in 1916.

Immediately after hauling down his flag he had written
to the Prime Minister Asquith drawing his attention to matters
which he considered to be of grave public importance—matters
of such moment that the Government now decided they should
be investigated without delay by a sub-committee of the Committee of Imperial Defence.

The sub-committee, under the chairmanship of Asquith
himself, was composed of Haldane, Sir Edward Grey, Lord
Crewe and Lord Morley with Sir C. L. Ottley as Secretary—a
clear indication of the importance given to Beresford's allegations.

The gravamen of his charges was that the Channel Fleet
had never been equal to the force it might have to encounter
in home waters, was not organised in readiness for war, was
gravely deficient in small craft and destroyers and was not
backed by a proper strategical plan which could immediately be
put into execution.

Fifteen meetings of the sub-committee heard evidence and
studied documents which would fill a long book and can only
be touched on here. Beresford was cross-examined at length.
Fisher, though present, had promised not to open his mouth
unless directly called upon, the principal exponent of the

Admiralty's case being the First Lord, Reginald McKenna. Personal altercations between Sir John and Lord Charles were thereby avoided, but a lot of dirty linen was exposed to view by both sides. Attempts were made to discredit Beresford as an expert witness by tabulating the comparatively short time he had spent actually in command at sea. A witness called by Lord Charles—an officer serving at the Admiralty under the Director of Naval Intelligence—stated that he had been threatened with damage to his career if he took an active part in the enquiry on Beresford's behalf.

There was a very long and complex wrangle about the question of war plans, the Admiralty restating its responsibility for the strategic distribution of the Fleet and for the general plan of operations to be carried out on the outbreak of hostilities; Beresford maintaining that Commanders-in-Chief must have sufficient background information (a need which he said had never been met) to meet their responsibilities for training in peace and for drawing up their tactical plans for war.

In August the sub-committee published its report as a Parliamentary paper. The investigation had shown that "no danger to the country resulted from the Admiralty arrangements for war, whether considered from the standpoint of the organisation and distribution of the Fleets, the number of ships, or the preparation of War Plans."

Beresford's main charges had not been upheld, but the absence of cordial relations between the Board of Admiralty and the Commander-in-Chief of the Channel Fleet was given the prominence which the Committee very evidently considered was their due.

The Board of Admiralty do not appear to have taken Lord Charles Beresford sufficiently into their confidence as to the reasons for dispositions to which he took exception; and Lord Charles Beresford, on the other hand, appears to have failed to appreciate and carry out the spirit of the instructions of the Board, and to recognize their paramount authority.

Fisher was bitterly disappointed by the Committee's Report. "*It's a most cowardly production*," he wrote to Commander

I

Crease, his Naval Secretary. The fact that a junior officer had arraigned the Board of Admiralty before a court at Cabinet level and had failed to substantiate his charges had barely been touched upon, thus cutting away one of the foundations of naval discipline.

He was very hurt by what he called a red herring about the Naval War Staff. The Committee had been "impressed with the difference of opinion amongst officers of high rank and professional attainments regarding important principles of naval strategy and tactics," and had looked forward to the "further development of a Naval War Staff, from which the Naval members of the Board and Flag officers and their staffs at sea may be expected to derive common benefit."

The truth is always particularly odious. Although a Naval War College had been established at Portsmouth with Fisher's blessing there *was* no proper Naval Staff for the very good reason that Fisher didn't want one. Though not averse to seeking advice he was far too much a dictator to allow comparatively junior officers to meddle in matters of high policy. Neither Fisher, nor his successor at the Admiralty, Wilson, believed in delegating responsibility for the preparation of war plans. It was indeed a grave weakness in the Admiralty organisation, and not put right until the advent of Churchill two years later. Even after the war Fisher was unrepentant. In 1919 he wrote:

A Naval War Staff at the Admiralty is a very excellent organization for cutting out and arranging foreign newspaper clippings in such an intelligent disposition as will enable the First Sea Lord to take in at a glance who is likely amongst the foreigners to be the greatest fool or the greatest poltroon . . . So far as the Navy is concerned, the tendency of these 'Thinking Establishments' on shore is to convert splendid sea officers into very indifferent clerks.

Whilst the Beresford Enquiry Committee was sitting, Fisher's critics had been given further ammunition of which full use was made. His habit of corresponding with certain trusted junior officers has already been mentioned. He had gone even further, causing extracts from their letters, which he thought contained valuable comments, to be printed for restricted circulation. Now the inevitable occurred. Parts of these circulars found their way into the press, including a section of Captain Bacon's letter to Sir John describing his discussion with the Prince of Wales about "unrest" in the Service due to Fisher's schemes of reform. Newspapers hostile to Fisher seized on this evidence of espionage in the Navy with joyful cries. Questions were asked in the Commons and although the First Lord appealed to the House "not to be misled by any such trumpery matters as these into censuring a man who has given the very best service to the public that any man could give" an unfortunate impression remained.

The summer ended with rumours flying about that Fisher was about to leave the Admiralty and receive a peerage. As his friend Lord Esher has told us, for more than two years Fisher had felt that he was "standing on the edge of a precipice to which all great reformers are led, and over which they ultimately fall."

Of course he had undermined his own foothold. As level-headed a naval officer as Admiral Prince Louis of Battenberg had written to Sir George Clarke as far back as 1905 of the "senseless way in which Fisher insults and alienates our senior men" and as the years went by with their conflicts over the Selborne Scheme, the re-distribution of the Fleet, the *Dreadnought* and many other matters, this characteristic of over-riding opposition with little or no attempt to placate it, of driving rather than leading, had become much more marked. "It is small wonder," wrote Winston Churchill, "that he left so many foes foaming in his wake." Though physically still very robust, memory unimpaired, mind as keen as ever, his judgment was neither as sound nor as detached as it had been in the past. The attacks coming from within the Service to which he had given his life were like a physical injury from which the pain never ceased. He had loved the Navy with all the strength of his strong and affectionate personality. Nothing he had done had been for himself. But now the thing which he loved had turned against him. Fighter that he was he struck back, without much regard to his choice of weapons. His friend and biographer Admiral Sir R. H. Bacon was to write later that Fisher's "old saying that 'he would break anyone for the good of the Navy,' became that 'he would break anyone who opposed him.'"

He had always been prone to express himself both in speech and on paper in picturesque and rather exaggerated terms and this tendency, growing with the years, left him open to accusations of being an unbalanced megalomaniac. His unguarded dictions were quoted by his enemies and even alienated some of his friends. "*I am not going till I am kicked out!* I am going to stick to it, and stick to it in silence," he wrote in May to Sir Archibald Hurd, but silence was not his way.

In August he went off on leave to the Tirol still smarting over the implications of the Beresford Committee's report and the failure to bring an insubordinate officer to book.

"Let discipline go and politics triumph!" he wrote to Rear Admiral Sir Charles Ottley. The rest and change revived him. Back at Whitehall in October he wrote to a friend:

I am going to have fierce fighting at the Admiralty, I expect, but I am quite ready for it, as I feel a giant refreshed. Of course, I am always living from hand to mouth, and though no one knows it, I have very often been on the verge of leaving the Admiralty during the whole of the last five years. I've had about enough of it now.

Fisher was indeed making up his mind to go. Fortunately the man by whom he wished to be succeeded was entirely acceptable to the government. Indeed Sir Arthur Wilson was probably the only senior naval officer whose prestige and influence were equal to the task ahead. He was universally respected and had no "label" either of the Fish-pond or the Beresfordites.

"Elisha is right underneath; all expectant for the mantle dropping on him!" wrote Fisher to Stead at the end of October. The Prime Minister had proposed a peerage on the King's Birthday in November. Fisher was disappointed it was not a Viscountcy. "I don't think I can look a gift horse in the mouth, but I've been urged to demur being a common or garden Peer, like the man who makes linoleum or lends money for elections." But he was ready to forget this on receiving "the very best letter I ever received in my life" from King Edward.

Nobody deserves the thanks of your Sovereign and your Country more warmly than you do. Time will show what admirable reform you have created in the Royal Navy, and you can afford to treat with the contempt that it deserves those back biters who have endeavoured to calumniate you. . . .

Baron Fisher of Kilverstone was to live to see the Navy which he had created become one of the chief instruments in winning the First Great War, but for a time his work was done. He had made his mistakes, but they were as nothing compared to what he had accomplished. Let the greatest Englishman of our own time confirm the reality of Jacky Fisher's stature in the words he wrote in 1920.

There is no doubt whatever that Fisher was right in nine-tenths of what he fought for. His greatest reforms sustained the power of the Royal Navy at the most critical period of its history. He gave the Navy the kind of shock which the British Army received at the time of the South African war. After a long period of serene and unchallenged complacency, the mutter of distant thunder could be heard. It was Fisher who hoisted the storm-signal and beat all hands to quarters. He forced every department of the Naval Service to review its position and question its own existence. He shook them and beat them and cajoled them out of slumber into intense activity. But the Navy was not a pleasant place while this was going on. The "Band of Brothers" tradition which Nelson handed down was for the time, but only for the time, discarded . . .

For some months Fisher lived at his son's house, Kilverstone Hall, Norfolk. Several publishers approached him with very lucrative offers for an autobiography, which he refused—a great loss, for his graphic, pungent style and ready wit would have given us a highly individual book. Though not a rich man money never tempted him. In the past he had more than once been offered positions of great power and affluence in industry. But the Navy was his only real interest. He continued to keep in close touch with naval affairs and exchanged frequent letters with the First Lord, Reginald McKenna.

As a relaxation he busied himself in the garden. "So Jacky is growing roses, is he?" muttered an old shipmate. "Well, all I've got to say is that those roses will damned well have to grow . . ."

For years Fisher had been an advocate of Anglo-American friendship and had always opposed the obstacle of the Anglo-Japanese alliance. In the winter of 1910 he visited the U.S.A. to attend his son's wedding and returned "*immensely* impressed by the *magnitude* of the *men* and the *things* and the *ideas.*"

He was living on the Continent having a holiday when Winston Churchill became First Lord of the Admiralty in 1911.

In spite of the difference in their ages Fisher and Churchill had much in common. Both were men of vision, convinced of the inevitability of war with Germany and of the vital necessity of keeping a jump ahead of the enemy. Wilson had been most successful in healing the Fisher–Beresford rift in the Navy, but he was unprogressive, stubborn and rather unimaginative. It was natural that Churchill should turn to Fisher "a veritable volcano of knowledge and inspiration." Admiral Sir Francis Bridgeman succeeded Wilson as First Sea Lord, but the association continued. Long letters were followed by a "secret" meeting of several days in the Admiralty Yacht *Enchantress*. To avoid embarrassing brother officers on the Board Fisher returned to the Continent, but the letters continued and there were other meetings.

In almost every way Fisher's influence on Winston Churchill was considerable. It can be seen in the latter's courageous decision to increase the size of future big ships' guns to fifteen inches without waiting for the trials of the prototype to be completed, and the laying down of a division of fast battleships armed with this weapon—the famous *Queen Elizabeth* class, one of the most successful type of warship ever produced which proved their worth in both world wars. It was

Fisher who pressed for more rapid democratisation of the Navy, which he felt was lagging behind the times in improving conditions and opportunities on the lower deck. Measures introduced by Churchill's administration stimulated recruiting and stilled unrest at a very critical time, for a series of outspoken articles by Fred T. Jane,[1] which appeared in the *London Magazine* of 1912 entitled "The Dogs of War," give a picture of poor pay, out-of-date disciplinary methods and a lack of opportunity for promotion to commissioned rank. It was Fisher who pressed ceaselessly for the development of submarines and of naval aviation, both aircraft and airships, and for greater attention to be given to internal combustion engines which he felt would eventually supplant steam turbines, as they had supplanted reciprocating engines. In all these matters he found in Churchill a willing ally; quick to take a point and forceful in promoting action.

The greatly increased power demanded from the machinery of future ships was forcing a change from coal to oil. The *Queen Elizabeth* class were the first heavy warships with exclusively oil-fired boilers—a major step for a nation whose only native fuel was coal. Oil fuel was the fuel of the future, burnt in the boilers of turbine-driven ships or used directly in the internal combustion engine. It was essential that Britain should be sure of getting all the oil she would need. In 1912 a Royal Commission was appointed to study the problem and Fisher, after a great deal of persuasion, which included a special trip abroad by the Prime Minister and First Lord in the *Enchantress*, consented to act as chairman, on his own terms.

He tackled the job with his usual vigour and thoroughness and produced a report in just over six months. The change to oil was shown to be practicable, but the ramifications were very extensive, including the vital necessity of obtaining a controlling interest in Middle East oilfields and the provision of huge storage facilities in Britain and abroad. To protect our supplies in war would now become a major article in British foreign policy and military strategy. With Churchill brilliantly

[1] The well-known compiler of *Jane's Fighting Ships*.

pressing the case on the political side, against strong opposition, the change, based on the recommendations of the Fisher Committee, was carried through in 1913.

War was coming very close. In August 1914 the Royal Navy consisted of 60 battleships, 9 battle cruisers, 46 armoured cruisers, 62 light cruisers, 215 torpedo boats and torpedo boat destroyers and 76 submarines.

In November 1914, Fisher was recalled to active duty as First Sea Lord. Things had not gone well in the first few months of the war. The German High Seas Fleet was bottled up in harbour, but there had been heavy British losses in home and foreign waters. The old Admiral had only been at Whitehall for twenty-four hours when the shattering news came through of the defeat of Admiral Cradock's Squadron by von Spee at the Battle of Coronel.

Fisher was seventy-four, but his extraordinary energy seemed undiminished. Now he knew exactly what he wanted to do and how to get it done.

With the active backing of the First Lord he insisted that battle-cruisers should immediately be despatched from the Grand Fleet to South American waters. *Inflexible* and *Invincible* had certain defects which must be rectified before the long voyage. "Not less than a week," was the minimum estimated by Devonport Dockyard. "Three days," snorted Fisher. If necessary, dockyardmen must sail in the ships. The battle-cruisers left on time, reached Port Stanley in the Falkland Islands on 7 December and were coaling when von Spee, sure that reinforcements could not possibly have yet arrived, hove in sight next morning. Von Spee made off at full speed, but *Inflexible* and *Invincible* had the heels of him. The Germans fought bravely, but the twelve-inch guns of the battle-cruisers overwhelmed them. *Scharnhorst*, *Gneisenau*, *Leipzig* and *Nürnberg* were sunk almost without casualties on the British side. Within six weeks Coronel had been more than avenged in a victory which gave the nation and the Navy the fillip they needed at just the right moment. It was a splendid justification not only of Fisher's return to the Admiralty, but of the ships which he had sponsored.

Fisher's return to the old buildings in Whitehall acted as a universally administered pep-pill. Inertia vanished overnight. "His drive and life-force made the Admiralty quiver like one of his great ships at its highest speed," said Churchill.

Fisher did not subscribe to the widely held opinion that the war would be a short one. On 4 November he called a conference and put in hand a vast building programme, using his wonderful persuasive powers to fire the leaders of the ship-building and engineering industries with his own enthusiasm. No one could be more charming than Fisher when he wished to be, and long experience prevented him from asking the altogether impossible. "Knowledge is power. When you have been a kitchen maid no one can tell you how to boil potatoes." The ships laid down in 1914 were of inestimable value two years later. Churchill called this move "one of the greatest services which the nation has owed to the genius and energy of Lord Fisher."

In strategy his policy had three objectives—to drive the enemy off the seas, to pin his ships into their harbours and finally to strike a great blow where he least expected it, forcing the High Seas Fleet to come out to fight and be annihilated. The blow, in Fisher's opinion, should fall in the Baltic—sea-borne Russian armies landing within ninety miles of Berlin. The armada of 612 ships which he had put in hand included many vessels specially designed for the shallow Baltic waters from 33-knot battle-cruisers (5) to monitors (37) and motor barges (200).[1]

Churchill shared Fisher's views that a naval offensive was essential, but did not agree as to its location. The alternatives were an advance by the Army up the Belgian coast with strong naval support, or the forcing of the Dardanelles.

[1] The larger ships were very fast, heavily armed and lightly protected. In reply to critics Fisher remarked that they were "not built for salvoes, but for Berlin." Three of them (the largest tin-clads afloat) were converted to aircraft-carriers after the war.

It had always been doubtful whether two such explosive and strong-willed characters could work in double harness. Fisher out of office as the power behind the throne was one thing. The close and complex relationship of First Lord and First Sea Lord was another. The methods of both men were autocratic and Churchill had long been accustomed to go far outside the normal province of his office, not only deciding policy, but taking a very active part in the details of implementation. The position was aggravated by their different hours of work. Fisher rose at four in the morning and was at his desk soon afterwards. By 8 a.m. when, as was often his custom, he attended Holy Communion in Westminster Abbey, he had got through a vast amount of work. Later in the day he would deal with less exacting matters, but little of importance escaped his prying eye which in his own phraseology was "like an elephant's trunk—one moment picking up a pin, the next rooting up an oak." By evening even his giant strength was visibly tiring and he went very early to his bed. Relaxations were few, but he would sometimes disappear to his beloved Abbey where he would sit in silent contemplation. Churchill, always a late starter, preferred to tackle the most important problems after dinner. But at first the two great men worked well together, honouring their agreement to keep each other mutually informed of their decisions. Fisher's statement to the Dardanelles commission in 1916 that "Mr Churchill and I worked in absolute accord at the Admiralty until it came to the question of the Dardanelles" is an exaggeration, but there were no serious differences in the closing months of 1914 and much valuable work was done.

In January 1915 the mounting of a naval offensive against the Dardanelles was definitely put forward. Fisher, always lukewarm, came to the conclusion that to embark on so large a project so far from home would make demands which would seriously reduce the necessary margin of superiority of the Grand Fleet. He indicated his objections in a meeting which he and Churchill had with the Prime Minister. If the Baltic project was not at the moment practicable he preferred an advance up the Belgian coast. Asquith, moved by the urgent necessity of doing something which would relieve Turkish pressure on the Russian armies in the Caucasus, decided in favour of the Dardanelles.

At a meeting of the War Council immediately afterwards Fisher was only prevented from resigning by Lord Kitchener, who pointed out that he was the only dissentient. After this Fisher loyally did his best, going into the campaign "*totus porcus*," though increasingly at odds with Churchill.

Early in May 1915 it was evident that failure in the Dardanelles was likely. A proposal to send out more ships revived all Fisher's fears, reinforced by Jellicoe's protests that the strength of the Grand Fleet was being prejudiced. But on 14 May, Churchill, working far into the night, gave orders for additional ships to be despatched.

The matter had been discussed with Fisher earlier in the day, but the operational instructions now sent out included a number of extra vessels. Fisher, sitting down to work in the small hours next morning, found these orders on his desk with a covering note: "I hope you will agree." He saw at once that the First Lord had gone far beyond their decision a few hours earlier. It was the last straw. Before breakfast he had sent in his resignation and left his office, never to return. Even a note from the Prime Minister, "In the King's name I order you to remain at your post," failed to bring him back into the Admiralty building, though he continued to see important papers in his official house next door.

The failure of the Dardanelles campaign and Lord Fisher's resignation coincided with reports of a serious shortage of shells for the Army in France and precipitated a first-class crisis in which Asquith's Liberal Administration was reconstructed as a Coalition. Bonar Law replaced Churchill at the Admiralty. At first it seemed that Lord Fisher would be asked to remain, but the old Admiral made this impossible by presenting the conditions under which he was prepared to do so in the form of what was virtually an ultimatum. No Prime Minister could have swallowed such dictatorial demands and

Fisher finally severed his connection with the Admiralty. For the rest of the war he was doomed to remain on the sidelines, though appointed a few months later as head of the Board of Invention and Research. He continued to press the claims of attacking Germany in the Baltic, believing that the war could be brought to a speedy conclusion by a project; "Napoleonic in Audacity—Cromwellian in Thoroughness—Nelsonic in Execution! Big Conceptions and Quick Decisions! Think in Oceans—Shoot at Sight!"

At seventy-six he was still full of fire and physically very vigorous. "I *now* can dance twelve waltzes without stopping!" he wrote in July 1917, "(and hum my own waltz music!) I did it only the other day."

In July 1918 his happy married life was suddenly brought to an end by the unexpected death of Lady Fisher. She had been a constant support to him for fifty-two stormy and eventful years and he missed her very much. But the old volcano was by no means extinct. In 1919 he erupted in a series of articles in *The Times*. Amongst other things he stated his conviction that "air fighting dominates future war, both by land and sea; by sea the only way of avoiding the air is to get under water." He was a prophet to the end and his powers of vivid self-expression never deserted him.

The savage instinct is still strong, and every human hates change—especially a change for the better. If you invent new cures for disease, they will burn you; if you are a patriot, they will shoot you; if you build up a business that employs a thousand men, you are a blighted capitalist, grinding the faces of the poor; if you compose divine music, you will die in a garret.

In 1920, lying in hospital during his last fatal illness he had written characteristically, "No mourning, no flowers, and the nearest cemetery," but when he died only the death of a beloved King could have witnessed a more genuine display of public grief. Even his enemies recognised his genius and to the common people he had long been one of those rare beings who really touch their hearts. The gun-carriage which bore his body to rest in Westminster Abbey where he had spent so many reverent, reflective hours passed through great bare-headed crowds. "This man's Fame is safe with history," wrote *The Times*. "The people knew him and loved him. His body is buried in peace, but his name liveth for evermore."

> A seer of signs, few had he read amiss
> In those blind days ere yet the strong Foe braved us.
> Ah, be his epitaph, dear Mourner, this—
> He built the Fleet that saved us.[1]

[1] From "In Memory of Lord Fisher" by Sir William Watson, *Nineteenth Century*, September 1920.

SCOTT

1853-1924

"Aim Straight"[1]

PERCY SCOTT was born in London in 1853. His father was a solicitor, his grandfather a surgeon with a taste for research and his great-grandfather a captain in the Royal Navy. Percy, good seaman, inventor and sea-lawyer was a mixture of the three—a turbulent, litigious man with a very original mind who has his place in history as the father of the gunnery renaissance which enormously increased the deadliness of naval gunfire between 1904 and 1914.

Percy Scott's early years followed the usual pattern of the age. In 1866 he joined the old three-decker *Britannia*, moored in Portsmouth harbour as a naval training ship, a small and unremarkable cadet of thirteen who had passed in forty-sixth out of sixty-four entrants. Two years later he was appointed to his first sea-going ship, the 50-gun frigate *Forte* in which he sailed for Bombay round the Cape of Good Hope. The *Forte* had engines, which were hardly ever used. Neither were the guns. The wooden carriages were french polished; the shot, painted blue with white tops and a gold band, decorated the gun-deck. The fact that these shot were now too large to enter the muzzle-loading guns was of small account.

Young Scott learnt no gunnery in the *Forte*, but was taught a lot of other useful things. Midshipmen in those days were in constant close contact with their men, aloft in all sorts of weather and away for long hours in the boats under oars and sail. In spite of rigid social barriers young officers learnt the

[1] Motto of Scott of Witley.

lower-deck point of view in a way which is often difficult to achieve in these more democratic days.

A year in an armoured ship in home waters followed this long commission abroad, and in 1873 Percy now a Sub-Lieutenant volunteered for service on the West Coast of Africa where he scented chances of a more adventurous life. He saw the closing stages of the Ashanti War and took part in operations against pirates up the Congo River, where he achieved his first independent command, a steamboat protected with steel plating, manned with seamen and marines. Life in the boat was exciting, but uncomfortable—seventy officers and men crowded together in a very small space which was usually insufferably hot. The long tropical nights were particularly trying and young Scott complained of the noisy belching of the hippopotami which came to the surface close alongside, breathing through their wide-open mouths. He must have done well, for he was promoted to Lieutenant and mentioned in despatches by the renowned fighting sailor Commodore Sir William Hewett, who had won the Victoria Cross in the Crimea and was a great hero at that time, fearless, bold and extremely self-reliant.

Returning home Lieutenant Scott, aged twenty-five, joined the Gunnery School at Portsmouth, H.M.S. *Excellent*. The time was to come when ambitious young officers saw, in specialising in gunnery, a road to early advancement, but this was far from being the case in 1878. Gunnery was still a neglected art. Ships were judged, not by the results of target practice, but by their appearance and the seamanlike smartness of their crews. Steam was slowly ousting sail, but many ships still had masts, fully rigged in the old-fashioned way. Work aloft was the hall-mark of efficiency. Where the sails had vanished other "stick and string" evolutions had taken their place—laying out anchors, hoisting in and out boats, spreading and furling awnings—drills which required good organisation and discipline and made men quick and self-reliant, but had little direct influence on fighting efficiency. A certain amount of ammunition had to be fired off once a quarter, but this was

often a perfunctory business. As ships expected to do battle
with the enemy at point-blank range the neglect of gunnery was
not so idiotic as it might appear, but with guns coming into
service capable of accurate fire over much greater distances a
change was long overdue. The Admiralty had so far done
nothing to lead the way. The important report rendered once
a year by an Admiral inspecting his Squadron which sum-
marised the state of efficiency of his ships under various
printed headings, forbore from even mentioning the results
she had obtained at target practice. (It was 1903 before this
question was included.) As late as 1901 the inspection report
of one of the best shooting ships in the Navy, the *Astrea*,
commended the physique, dress and bearing of her company,
the cleanliness of the ship and the smartness of her crew at
exercise, but makes no reference whatever to her value as a
fighting unit of the Fleet.

These reports, passing through the Commander-in-Chief to
the Admiralty, were regarded as having an influence on the
careers of the captains and senior officers. In the circumstances
it was accepted, not unnaturally, that a smart crew, a clean ship
and proficiency in evolutions were the things that mattered;
gunnery was a thing of small account.

The more ambitious of Percy Scott's contemporaries must
have thought he had made a strange choice. After qualifying
in the *Excellent* and serving for a while on the junior instructional staff he went back to sea as the gunnery lieutenant of the
Inconstant. The *Inconstant* was the flagship of the sail training
squadron, pretty barren ground for a keen young gunnery
officer. Two of the young Princes, Albert Victor and George
(later King George V), were serving in the Squadron which
spent the next two years on what Scott later described as "a sort
of yachting cruise with endless entertainments", to South
America, South Africa, Australia, New Zealand, Fiji, Japan,
China and Singapore. Even a dedicated young gunnery officer
could appreciate the very real benefits of sail training for both
nerve and body. Aloft men were often alone, learning to
act on their own initiative. "In gunnery we were no worse

Admiral Sir Percy Scott, Bart, KCB, KCVO, as a captain.
From the cartoon by 'Spy' in *Vanity Fair* (1903)

than any other ship," but Scott for the time had to be content with doing what he could at his own inconspicuous level. Nevertheless it was in *Inconstant* that he emerged for the first time as that rather unusual human animal, the man who sees something wrong and immediately sets about righting it with the means at his disposal.

On the rare occasions when the guns were fired he found himself badly handicapped by the absence of any means of quickly and certainly passing the range of the target from the masthead to the gun deck. In these days when boys are mechanically minded from childhood and pretty well cut their teeth on all sorts of machines, the profound ignorance about such matters eighty years ago is difficult to appreciate, but it was quite a feat for Scott to make drawings and to produce, his only assistant an armourer and with rudimentary workshop facilities, a simple but reliable electrical indicator-transmitter at the masthead and receiver on the gun-deck—which worked very well.

His next invention was equally practical. Fire broke out on board deep down in one of the holds. The after part of the ship was soon filled with smoke and no one could get to the seat of the blaze, for the smoke-respirator of German design supplied by the Admiralty proved ineffective. The situation was serious until Lieutenant Scott, using the diving dress supplied for work underwater, though encumbered by the weight of the helmet and its corselet—about as handy on ships' ladders as a set of medieval armour—managed to get down to the fire with a hose and put it out. Scott promptly set about designing a breathing apparatus of his own—a light helmet made out of a large butter tin fitted to a short jerkin banded at the waist and sleeves, the helmet connected to the ordinary diver's air pump by a length of hose. He had a very smoky fire lit in a safe place and tried it out. It worked admirably. The Captain and the Admiral were impressed and sent a full report to the Admiralty.

As both the inventions met a very real need, were cheaply and easily made and had shown their value in service Scott

K

may well have imagined that they would soon be adopted. It
was his first brush with bureaucracy, a skirmish which in later
life developed into a full-scale cold war. Official letters wan-
dered off on their leisurely orbit and, after a long delay, came
crawling back. Lieutenant P. Scott was to be thanked for his
diligence and zeal. The matters were under consideration.
Whitehall then relapsed into silence. Electrical range trans-
mitters were finally fitted in H.M. ships in 1904. The smoke
helmet fared even worse. It was 1910 before a light and
practical issue was finally made, though Scott alleges that his
smoke helmet was adopted almost instantly by the New York
Fire Brigade.

Such were the ways of officialdom in 1881. The effects, on a
keen but intolerant young officer, were lasting.

In 1882 the *Inconstant*, on her way home from the Cape, was
directed to the Mediterranean to join the British fleet anchored
off Alexandria to quell Arabi Pasha's revolt. *Inconstant* arrived
too late to take part in the bombardment of the forts, but
landed a detachment under Percy Scott as a part of Captain
John Fisher's naval brigade, sent to restore order and defend
the town. Arabi's troops, still investing the city, had a gun
which outranged any mobile artillery on the British side.
Captured forts were in the wrong place and faced the wrong
way. Could the guns be moved? Experts from the Royal
Artillery and Royal Engineers reported that it was impossible
without a lot of special gear. Major-General Sir Archibald
Alison referred the matter to the Navy and Scott was sent to
see what he could do.

The nearest suitable gun was mounted on a high bank over-
looking the sea. It weighed seven tons and was very far from
being of a mobile pattern. Scott describes how he sat for an
hour looking at it, determined not to be beaten, but wondering
how on earth he could manage with the very rudimentary
equipment available. The solution in the end had the sort of
inspired simplicity which distinguished all his work. His bluejackets dismounted the gun and allowed it to roll down the
embankment. The gun, immensely strong, was undamaged

and it was comparatively easy to lash it under a sling-wagon, move it right across Alexandria to the railway station and hoist it on to a truck. Comparatively easy, for the road gave way on a number of occasions en route. Unfortunately, the nearest point on the railway line was a hundred yards from and considerably below the point at which the gun had to be mounted, a steep slope of sandy soil intervening.

Scott constructed an "anchor" out of buried railway sleepers on the top of the hill to which he attached a very large block. A heavy hawser went from the gun through this block and down to two locomotives on the railway line. Backing them up was every available man; bluejackets, soldiers and native labourers. With the locomotives going full steam ahead and over a thousand men sweating away on the hawser the gun "went up in double time." After this it was a mere matter of lifting the 7-ton gun three feet on to its carriage. Brute strength, in the shape of hydraulic jacks and an inclined plane made of railway sleepers, got over this difficulty. "It took some time and some shoving, but we got it in place." Later two more 7-ton guns were brought up by similar means.

The Generals were very pleased. Alison wrote to Sir Evelyn Wood of "the excellent work which Lieutenant Scott of the *Inconstant* has rendered to me in bringing up heavy guns under almost insuperable difficulties. . . . He is one of those men with whom it is a perfect pleasure to act, he never makes difficulties and never finds anything impossible." The conditions were indeed those at which Percy Scott was always at his best—a task which others had said was impossible and no interference from above as to how he set about it.

Such opportunities, common enough in war, don't often come to young officers in peacetime and Scott's next appointment, to the staff of the Gunnery School, would have been regarded by most thirty-year-old bachelors who enjoyed social life as a good opportunity for catching up with some of the things they had missed in three years abroad. Percy Scott was as gay as the rest of them, out of working hours, but the itch to alter and reform, to shape things to his own pattern could not be denied. *Excellent* was still housed in two old wooden line-of-battleships moored in the harbour—cramped, badly equipped with instructional apparatus and unsuitable for the purpose. Not far off was Whale Island, a low expanse a few acres in extent, formed chiefly of the spoil excavated when making new dry docks at Portsmouth Dockyard. "Mud Island" as it was often called was used by *Excellent* for training men in shore fighting and as a rifle range, purposes for which this dreary, barren place was quite suitable. Scott was looked upon as a madman when he suggested that "Mud Island" could be converted into a splendid Gunnery School, with proper living accommodation, classrooms and gun batteries standing on drained and levelled ground sown with grass and planted with shrubs and trees. Quite undaunted Scott made a survey of the island and drew up detailed plans of what he proposed, explaining the great gain of efficiency which would result. The scheme would probably have finished up in some forgotten pigeon-hole if the captain of the Gunnery School had been any other than the redoubtable Jacky Fisher, who was immediately impressed with its possibilities. With Fisher's drive behind it the plan went to the Admiralty. In 1885 it was approved in principle to move *Excellent* ashore and though with Fisher and Scott leaving for other appointments progress was slow, some sort of a start was made.

Scott, now a Commander, went back to sea as executive officer of the *Duke of Edinburgh*, the most modern turret ship of her day. He arrived full of ideas for improving her gunnery efficiency only to find himself blocked by indifference. Why bother? It would add nothing to the reputation of the ship, which depended, not on shooting straight, but in looking like a yacht and performing creditably in "evolutions" most of which had little practical value. Here even Scott seems to have met his Waterloo. Training officers and men to hit the target with the guns which the ship had been designed and built to carry was an unpopular innovation.

So we gave up instruction in gunnery, spent money on enamel paint, burnished up every bit of brightwork on board, and soon got the reputation of being a very smart ship . . . The nuts of all the bolts on the aft deck were gilded, the magazine kegs were electro-plated, and statues of Mercury surmounted the revolver racks. In short, nothing was left undone to insure a good inspection.

The guns, as he bitterly commented, were not fired if it could be avoided, for the blast spoilt the paintwork. It was a frustrating period. His inventive urge could not be smothered, but a masthead signalling lamp—a long-felt need—which he produced in the *Edinburgh* was turned down by the Admiralty for no better reason, in Scott's opinion, than it was *his* idea; that it emanated from Percy Scott. Whitehall and Percy Scott were invariably at loggerheads.

After this commission in the Mediterranean Scott returned to the Gunnery School as executive officer and second-in-command. Five years had elapsed since official approval had been given to build a modern establishment on Whale Island. The work was far from complete with some buildings erected, some still going up and nothing attempted in the way of draining, levelling and road-making. For a sailor accustomed to the neatness and order of a ship it was a dismal scene of dirt and chaos. Some of the men were already living ashore; others were still accommodated in hulks in the harbour. Instruction was being carried out under great difficulties and his original vision of a smart, efficient, modern school was very far from being realised.

Scott, always at his best when confronted by great difficulties, persuaded his Captain to get all the men ashore, relying on the bluejacket's genius for making himself as comfortable as possible and his surroundings ship-shape. The sailors could not possibly do all the work needed alone and his method of spurring on the Admiralty to supply official help was ingenious. Money was collected by private subscription in the Fleet and a cricket pitch properly laid on a drained foundation and sown with grass—a green oasis of trim orderliness in the surrounding sea of mud and clay. The pitch was ready when the Lords Commissioners of the Admiralty came to the island on a periodical visit of inspection. After a morning spent ploughing through the mud he brought them to the cricket pitch, smooth, firm and comparatively dry. Their Lordships took the hint and official approval was given to level and drain the island at public expense. Four hundred convicts, working in gangs of twenty-five under self-elected leaders, were employed. The material seemed unlikely, but Scott managed to imbue these men with something of his own enthusiasm. There was plenty of talent amongst the prisoners and he gave them an interest in life, setting the gangs to compete with one another. He found their work "wonderfully good"—a remarkable tribute to Scott's gift for leadership. Whale Island was eventually to emerge as a naval establishment which for years was a model of its kind. Not for nothing does a portrait of Percy Scott hang in a place of honour in the wardroom.

After three years as a very efficient builder and contractor Scott was promoted to Captain and appointed to the Ordnance Committee. In 1894, at the age of forty-one he married the daughter of Sir Frederick Dixon-Hartland. In 1896 he was appointed to his first command, the little cruiser *Scylla*, 3,400 tons, in the Mediterranean Fleet.

It might be thought that as Captain of his own ship he would at last be free to put into practice his ideas for improving gunnery efficiency, but a small cruiser in a large fleet was very much bound by the orders of the Commander-in-Chief or senior officer present. Following the flagship's motions was as important as holystoning decks or shining the brightwork. A year was to pass before, with the arrival of a progressive Commander-in-Chief in the person of Admiral Sir John Hopkins, Scott was able to make a start on the series of improvements to the accuracy and speed of naval gunfire which gives him his place in history as the father of modern naval gunnery. He was forty-three.

Scott was essentially a practical man, inspired certainly, but not a visionary. His genius lay in finding practical solutions to the problems immediately in front of his nose. Added to this was his passion for gunnery; to hit the target, to hit it often and to go on hitting it at longer ranges were the objects to which he devoted the most fruitful years of his life, now about to begin.

In 1898 the *Scylla* was ordered to go on an independent cruise to the Eastern Mediterranean. Scott would be off on his own for some months, with the C.-in-C.'s permission to carry out any improvements which her captain believed would improve the *Scylla*'s shooting.

Although there was nothing wrong with the guns themselves the percentage of hits obtained at target practices even at the modest ranges then in use (1,600–2,000 yards) was very low. The guns were accurate, but the sights were primitive— open sights on the lines of those fitted to a rifle and depending, as with a rifle, too much on individual judgment. Clamping an ordinary watchkeeper's telescope fitted with cross-wires (a midshipman's hair) to the sight bar gave the layer a single, definite point of aim instead of having to judge when two points were in line and brought the accuracy of the average gunlayer up to that of the hitherto most skilful.

So far, so good, but ships must fight at sea in all sorts of weather. The gun platform is never steady and the layer must learn to fire "on the roll," pressing the trigger as the sights come on. Some men became extraordinarily proficient, but *average* results were poor. Fuel was rationed and ships spent weeks at a time in harbour. Some means must be found of simulating the roll of the ship; further it should then be possible to teach the layer to follow the target continuously, not just snap at it as it sailed past the crosswires. For quite a long time Scott was at a loss, but at length he hit on a solution.

Scott's genius was for improvisation. With strictly limited resources he would produce a device which was simple, practical and easily made—in this case a small target sliding up and down in a frame opposite the muzzle of the gun and imitating more or less exactly the apparent motion of a floating target viewed from a rolling ship. The layer kept the target in his sights, working the gun elevator wheel up and down to follow it. When he pressed the trigger an electrically operated pencil fixed to the gun-muzzle made a dot on the target. If he was "on" the dot was in the bull's eye. Errors, as in rifle shooting, were as easily apparent. The men christened this contrivance the "Dotter" and the name stuck.

By now the men of the *Scylla*, at first somewhat doubtful as to the necessity or even the sanity of all these changes, were becoming very keen. Scott had never lost the "common touch" learnt as a lad aloft and in ships' boats. He knew "what made men tick"; that competition with a clear object, simple rules and easily understood results were major incentives. But his men were getting too little firing practice. Full-bore ammunition was strictly rationed and the sub-calibre[1] guns supplied, which fired a cheaper, smaller shell, were inaccurate. By substituting a rifle barrel in a special rig made on board and devising a target which could be towed by his ship's boats at high speed he was able to give the men plenty of practice at negligible cost. The rifle was just as accurate as the big gun. Scores made in this way had a very close relation to what would happen when using service ammunition.

Scott's three years in the *Scylla* were drawing to a close. Before he was relieved she would take part, with the rest of the fleet, in what was known as the prize firing—a formal affair in which the number of hits scored in one minute was recorded. Forty per cent of hits was considered a very good result and twenty per cent was not unusual. Characteristically, Scott informed the Commander-in-Chief that he anticipated scoring over seventy per cent.

Three years almost to the day after he had assumed command the little *Scylla*, one of the smallest ships in the fleet, went out to do her prize firing. The result was almost unbelievable: fifty-six hits out of seventy rounds fired, an average of exactly *eighty* per cent.

Admiral of the Fleet Lord Chatfield, then serving as a Gunnery Officer in the Mediterranean Fleet, tells of the astonishment with which this amazing result was received.

Unfortunately, like other prophets, Scott was not always much honoured in his own country. For this he was himself

[1] A little gun fitted inside a big gun.

more than a little to blame. He was intolerant, very sure he was always right and openly contemptuous of those who differed from him. Maybe he was right in nine-tenths of what he strove for, but the past was neither as bad nor his more conservative contemporaries as foolish as he believed. Even the Admiralty, favourite Aunt Sally with all progressive young naval officers, had a fund of accumulated wisdom on which to draw which was often very valuable, irritating as the delays of bureaucracy might seem. Scott's methods of pushing his ideas would be less remarkable nowadays than they were sixty years ago. He believed that it paid to advertise, and acted accordingly. The ship's company of the *Scylla* were proud of themselves and of their captain, but Scott's contemporaries and seniors in other ships were not amused and an unnecessary resistance to Scott's very necessary reforms was built up by their dislike of Scott himself. At the back of this dislike was the suspicion, not entirely unjustified, that Scott was as much interested in helping himself as in helping the Navy—an accusation which even the bitterest of his opponents never levelled at Fisher.

Scott's next appointment, as Captain of the cruiser *Terrible*, brought him very much into the public eye. *Terrible*, on her way to China when the South African war broke out, was diverted to the Cape. Naval 4·7-inch guns on improvised mountings, designed by Scott in a few hours, assisted in the defence of Ladysmith. (Those of us who were children in the first decade of this century will remember the lead models— the long gun on its broad-tyred wheels which could be made to fire a little cylinder of wood—the sailors in their wide straw hats pulling the traces.) Scott's masterly improvisation made a very real contribution to the campaign. Unfortunately he also gave vent to some savage criticisms of his Admiral, Sir Robert Hastings Harris, criticisms which found their way into the press and caused a lot of unnecessary pain. At the worst Harris had been pompous and rather slow in reaching certain decisions; it was rumoured that he had refused to allow badly needed ammunition to be supplied in time. Even twenty years later Scott was to write that Ladysmith need never have endured such sufferings "had the amount of ammunition for which I pressed for gone with the guns." Harris, whose book appeared six years earlier than Scott's, has a different tale to tell. The Admiral is discreet and restrained, but he quite clearly believes that Scott had been responsible for spreading erroneous and misleading statements about him—all old history now, but an indication of what was thought of Captain Percy Scott by one of his seniors.

Terrible's section of the Brigade under her executive officer, Commander Limpus, saw much action. Scott was retained on the coast, where he was made military Commandant of Durban, the city being under martial law.

After the relief of Ladysmith *Terrible*'s gun-crews were no longer needed at the front and a soldier was appointed commandant of Durban. *Terrible* continued her interrupted voyage to China where she became famous for her shooting. Before this Scott had again crossed swords with his Admiral, this time Sir James Bruce. It was once again a matter of guns. Scott, anchored off Taku during the Boxer Rising, wanted to send some 12-pounders which he had prepared to assist in the defence of Tientsin. The Admiral refused to approve. As *The Times* commented later: "It was a grievous blunder not to send these guns to Tientsin with the relief column." But Bruce's opposition was almost certainly due to Scott's methods. In his memoirs Scott relates how he confided to an American officer at Taku that jealousy would prevent *Terrible*'s help being asked for if it could possibly be dispensed with—a sad commentary on Scott's relations with his superior.

Scott was working hard on the second stage of his campaign (Hit often), making successful efforts to increase the rate of fire without losing accuracy. In those days guns were loaded largely by hand. A medium-sized gun such as a six-inch needed a crew of ten which must learn to work very quickly and accurately together. The operations of inserting and ramming home the shell, which weighed 100 pounds, putting in the cordite charge, closing the breech, firing, opening the breech again, required an intricate series of closely co-ordinated movements. To do all this ten times a minute without mistake or accident needed constant practice, impossible with live ammunition. Scott devised a tray with a breech block in which conditions were accurately simulated; with it the crew would practise every day instead of once every few months. The Scott "loader" was later to be used throughout our own and other navies, though there is a record of one specimen which was polished and painted a variety of colours and kept as an almost untouchable ornament.

The Commander-in-Chief Sir Edward Seymour ordered that Scott's methods should be followed. Efficiency improved all round and the China Fleet's good shooting became legendary. Widespread and lasting good was done on this rare occasion when Percy Scott convinced and did not antagonise his colleagues and superiors. Loyalty to the Service is a very strong bond which Scott, an individualist to the point of egotism, often contemptuously ignored. As Admiral of the Fleet Lord Chatfield wrote much later in his memoirs, "Scott's ideas were often delayed in coming to fruition, great and good as they were."

But it was Scott's method to bulldoze rather than to convince. He was, by nature, a dictator. Given undisputed control he did very well—as Commandant of Durban under martial law, in his own ship on detached service. He was an exceptionally gifted man, but he had to be cock-of-the-walk. To persuade others to do what he wished, to work subtly so that his colleagues would believe his ideas their own, accepting with a shrug that it didn't matter provided that the job was done the right way, was not in his nature.

Returning to England after three years abroad the *Terrible* was given a tremendous reception. Portsmouth entertained Scott, his officers and men at an official banquet. The Navy League wrote him a letter referring in glowing terms to "the signal service performed by you in mounting heavy guns for use before Ladysmith and in the field," and "the improvement in gunnery practice of the Navy, which has largely been the

result of the record firing by His Majesty's Ship *Terrible*."
That he had done a splendid job was undeniable and the
award of the C.V.O. by King Edward VII (he had already
received the C.B.), was richly merited. The feeling remained
that there was too much emphasis on Percy Scott and too little
recognition of the part played by the Navy as a whole. Scott,
who had designed the improvised mounting for the Naval
guns, was better known to the public than Captain Lambton[1]
who had commanded the Naval Brigade in action.

Percy Scott returned to the Gunnery School in April 1903,
in command. The impact of his arrival was characteristic.
"The officers of the *Excellent*," he wrote, "were at first a little
loath to believe that all they had been doing was wrong." As
always he was soon successful in imbuing his subordinates
with his own enthusiasm and convincing them of the essential
rightness of his ideas. He worked on them directly. At 8.45
each morning he would sit in his office with the door wide open.
As he ate his breakfast the staff officers were required to
present themselves in turn, bid him good morning and say
their names. At lunch, which he took in the wardroom, he
would single out officers undergoing the long gunnery course,
officers who would shortly be distributed throughout the Fleet,
and question them about their daily doings. The methods
which he had used with such success in *Scylla* and *Terrible* were
applied to the instruction given at the school. Scott, demon-
strably right in most of what he stood for, did not take long to
win over the staff of the Gunnery School, who soon became his
enthusiastic supporters. With Whitehall he was less successful.
Even when Sir John Fisher became First Sea Lord in 1904 he
was often highly critical. Any decision with which he, Scott,
did not agree was wrong. He, and he alone, knew all the
answers. In particular he opposed Fisher's efforts to substitute battle practice—firing all guns in broadsides or salvoes
at realistic ranges (five to seven thousand yards)—for the short
range (1,600–2,000 yards) single-gun practices which had so
far been the test of gunnery efficiency. Scott realised that

[1] Later Admiral of the Fleet Sir Hedworth Meux.

longer ranges must be used in battle, but believed that until better sights and more instruments for fire control were available they were not practical. You must walk before you can run. It would be time enough to talk of firing broadsides at 6,000 yards when the individual guns could make eighty per cent hits at 2,000 yards. Fisher, of course, got his way. Much of Scott's opposition was due to the fact that some of his proposals for new gunsights and for certain experiments with broadside firing were not at first approved. "My two years as Captain of the *Excellent*," wrote Scott, "were one continuing battle with the Admiralty. They were as determined that the gunnery of the Fleet should not be improved as I was determined to improve it. Every suggestion that they could possibly delay, or turn down, they did."

Fortunately for Scott, and for the Navy, Jacky Fisher was neither ruffled nor deceived. He had a very high opinion of Scott's abilities. In 1905 a new post was created by Order in Council with Scott as its first incumbent with the title of "Inspector of Target Practices." Captain John Jellicoe, another Fisher nominee, was Director of Naval Ordnance at the Admiralty and Captain Hamilton, a friend of Scott, at the Gunnery School. It was a good team.

"I have a very strong additional and vital reason connected with the shooting of the Fleet which in my opinion renders it obligatory to have Jellicoe as D.N.O. and Percy Scott as Director of Shooting" wrote Fisher to the First Lord, the Earl of Selborne. "Hit, hit hard and keep on hitting," was one of Fisher's favourite dictums, and Scott, awkward personality though he might be, was the man to carry it out. After all, as Fisher wrote when speaking of Percy Scott in his memoirs, "Nelson was nothing if he was not insubordinate."

Scott attended the principal target practices of the Channel, Home, Atlantic and Mediterranean Fleets, analysed the results and made recommendations. Methods which had survived from the days of point-blank firing over open sights were rooted-out and the percentage of hits, which had been lamentably low, greatly increased.

Promoted to Rear-Admiral, he was at the apex of his career. In 1904 there had been 2,000 more misses than hits. In 1906 the position was reversed; 2,000 more hits than misses. With Fisher at his back Scott was a powerful figure. Captains began to realise that their future prospects no longer depended on spit and polish, but fighting efficiency. A cartoon in *Punch* by Bernard Partridge (reproduced opposite) reveals the very great public interest in the Navy in those days—an interest fed with frequent authoritive articles containing much detailed information about our ships and their performance on service which make strange reading after two great wars with their security regulations.

In 1905 Scott had been awarded £8,000 for his various inventions to improve efficiency. He makes no mention of this in his memoirs, an ungenerous omission, for the sum was a considerable one in those days. Scott felt that officers should be free to patent their inventions, but there is a good deal to be said for the Admiralty point of views: that they have a proprietary right in the ideas of those whom they have trained from boyhood.

When the *Dreadnought* was launched in 1906 Scott was included in a special honours list and it was as Sir Percy that he hoisted his flag as the Rear-Admiral of the Second Cruiser Squadron of the Channel Fleet the next year. The rows which developed with his Commander-in-Chief, Lord Charles Beresford; the notorious "paintwork is more important than efficiency" signal in 1907 and the *Good Hope*, *Argyll* affair in 1908 have already been described. From the first there was friction between Beresford and Scott, friction which Scott, rather astonishingly in view of his own record, somewhat smugly describes as being due to his unwillingness to side with Beresford in a cold war with Fisher about the organisation and composition of the Channel Fleet. "Very politely, I refused to join in a campaign against the Board of Admiralty." He realised that this would annoy his Commander-in-Chief, but "remained firm in my determination to do my duty to the country and the Admiralty as I saw it." Perhaps the key to this

PUNCH, OR THE LONDON CHARIVARI.—December 26, 1906.

WITHOUT PREJUDICE.

Britannia. "ACCEPT MY CONGRATULATIONS, SIRE, ON THE SPLENDID GROWTH OF YOUR NAVY. AND, SINCE I HAVE YOUR ASSURANCE THAT YOUR PROGRAMME IS NOT AN AGGRESSIVE ONE, I FEEL SURE YOU WILL BE INTERESTED TO SEE WHAT I HAVE BEEN DOING IN THE LAST THREE YEARS!"

rather strange picture of outraged virtue lies in the last four words.

When the great explosion occurred in 1908 which led to Beresford's suspension and, eventually, to Lord Fisher's leaving the Admiralty, Scott's Squadron was sent abroad, to the Cape and South America.

In 1909 he hauled down his flag. Early in 1910 he was made a K.C.B. and given an award of £2,000 for his improvement in gunnery apparatus, a "golden handshake," for he had been informed that he was unlikely to be employed at sea again. It was suggested that he should devote his talents to developing the system of gun control always connected with his name which proved its value so conclusively in the 1914–18 war—director firing.

Percy Scott was unquestionably the man who made director firing a practical proposition, but it was not his own invention. In 1885 Lieutenant R. H. Perse, R.N., designed an instrument known as a "director"—a sort of master gunsight located in the conning tower or aloft from which an officer could direct all the guns on to the target and fire them simultaneously. For various reasons the idea was never pursued. There were no proper instruments in those days for passing orders between director and gun. Firing at less than 2,000 yards at a stationary target from a slowly moving ship (as was then the practice), the man laying the gun could see where his shots were falling and make the necessary sighting correction. With longer ranges coming into use the position was now entirely different. The individual gunlayer could no longer see if he was hitting or not. Guns must be fired in salvoes, all set to similar ranges and deflections and corrected together until they were on the target. The master gunlayer, or director, must be placed high up; above the smoke of his own guns with a "spotting" officer close at hand to observe the fall of shot. The burden of constantly adjusting range and deflection to allow for the fact that both firing ship and target were moving on different courses must be removed from the gun, whose crew were no longer capable of these complicated calculations, to a "transmitting station"——a quiet and well-protected place in the bowels of the ship.

As far back as 1905 Scott had revived the question of director firing. Modern instruments could solve all the old difficulties. The matter had been "under consideration" for some years without a definite decision, though Scott had used a home-made version in the *Good Hope*. Scott himself is frank about why nothing had been done. "I was the pioneer of director firing, and to that fact was due the long delay in its introduction."

On half-pay after hauling down his flag in the *Good Hope*, he went to the great armament firm of Vickers with his ideas. With their assistance the details were hammered out. In June 1910 he was able to show the Director of Naval Ordnance a complete set of working drawings. With the strong support of Sir John Jellicoe, now a member of the Board, the scheme went through. Scott was appointed to the Admiralty in an advisory capacity and orders given to fit out the battleship *Neptune* for trials. Early in 1911 successful firings were carried out. Jellicoe, now Commander-in-Chief Atlantic Fleet, and the most outstanding of the younger Admirals, recommended that all ships should be fitted with directors, but there was considerable opposition in influential quarters. Admiral Sir Francis Bridgeman, the Commander-in-Chief Home Fleet whose flagship was the *Neptune*, was a prominent member of the opposition. It was the old story of clashing temperaments. But for the intervention of the First Lord of the Admiralty, Winston Churchill, director firing might once again have been shelved. Churchill ordered further trials using two of the latest battleships of the same class, one with and one without the director. *Orion* and *Thunderer* carried out firings under exactly similar conditions of range, light and sea. The results reported by Vice-Admiral Sir John Jellicoe proved "most conclusively the superiority of the Director System."

If Scott had not been behind it, that would most likely have ended the matter. The German Navy was adopting its own version of director firing. Efficient long-range fire was

L

virtually impossible without a director system, particularly in bad weather. Jellicoe, returning to the Admiralty in 1912 as Second Sea Lord, pressed that all our heavy ships should be fitted forthwith, but the name of Scott was a red rag to many in the Fleet and at the Admiralty and there was much procrastination and delay. When war came in 1914 only eight of our battleships had directors. The work of conversion was speeded up, urged on by Jellicoe, now Commander-in-Chief of the Grand Fleet. All the capital ships which fought at Jutland in 1916 had directors, but it was not until after the battle that its necessity for other classes of warships was finally accepted. A sad story, and further proof, if proof is needed, that human passions—jealousy and personal dislike—can blind honest, conscientious men, even when such vital matters as the fighting efficiency of the Fleet is at stake.

Sir Percy Scott, who had made very satisfactory financial arrangements with some of the armament firms for the production of his various inventions, was now a rich man. "This," says the *Dictionary of National Biography*, "enabled him to accept the offer of a baronetcy conferred upon him in 1913." He had divorced his first wife in 1911. In 1914 he married again.

For a man who had devoted practically the whole of his life to a single idea—gunnery efficiency—Scott was astonishingly free from bigotry. In June 1914 he suddenly appeared in a totally new guise.

The gun in 1914 was unchallenged as the principal weapon of war. The best-known gunnery officer in the country was Percy Scott. Coupled with his name was the battleship: gun and mounting in their most highly developed and elaborate form. There was consternation when this high-priest of the gunners' cult wrote to *The Times* suggesting in the strongest terms that no more battleships should be built and hinting that the submarine torpedo and the aircraft were the weapons of the future. A fifteen-inch shell in the middle of Fleet Street could not have caused a greater sensation.

Amongst the more restrained expression of disapproval was

the view expressed by the *Globe* that his letter was "premature, ill-advised and calculated to do serious harm to the cause of maintenance of British supremacy at sea." The *Manchester Guardian* summed up as follows:

Written by a literary man doing a scientific novel or scare tale, it would pass well enough. But is it what we have the right to expect from the most accomplished naval gunner, and a naval officer of approved capacity?

Anti-Scott Admirals on the retired list rushed joyfully into print and the battle of words was still raging when war was declared in August 1914.

In November when Fisher once more became First Sea Lord of the Admiralty, Scott was recalled as an adviser on naval gunnery matters to the Board. "I had but one answer to all his detractors and to the opposition to his return," said Fisher. "He hits the target." Jellicoe mentions the invaluable assistance of Scott in the work now at last being expedited, with Fisher's drive behind it, of fitting the rest of the battleships and battle-cruisers with director firing.

With Fisher's departure after the Dardanelles failure Scott found himself without much support. For curious reasons which need not be gone into here the Lord Commissioners of the Admiralty were responsible for the air defence of London, a responsibility they had largely neglected as was quickly apparent when a Zeppelin appeared over the city in September 1915. The First Lord, now A. J. Balfour, sent for Scott and gave him a free hand to do something as quickly as possible. He was sixty-two, but his genius for improvisation was unblunted by the many knocks he had received. Guns were obtained from all sorts of unexpected places, including the French Army, mounted on improvised carriages and manned by a scratch body which included university men, barristers, artists and city men dressed up in naval uniform. It was a job after his own heart.

In February 1916 a regular Anti-aircraft corps had been formed and the War Office took over. Sir Percy Scott continued to serve at the Admiralty, but his work was really done.

On 31 May 1916 the Battle of Jutland was fought, proving, amongst other things, the absolute necessity of director firing for all ships fitted with several guns. It was a pyrrhic victory for Scott whose son John, a midshipman of sixteen, was lost in the armoured cruiser *Defence*, sunk by the gunfire of the German High Seas Fleet with heavy loss of life. Approval had been given over a year before to fit *Defence* with director firing, but the work had never been done. Its absence cannot have been vital, but the feeling that his son's ship lacked the equipment necessary properly to fight her guns remained.

The reference to the death in action of his eldest son is almost the only mention of his family in his autobiography. Though twice married and the father of three children he was not a family man. The ruling passion of his life was his work, and in this they had no part. Neither, for that matter, did any intimate friend of either sex. Percy Scott walked by himself, suspicious, decks cleared for action. He cannot have been an easy man to live with, and it is not surprising that his first marriage ended in the divorce court after seventeen years marked by long separations and little real companionship. Family and friends were secondary considerations, and, although he enjoyed the company of women, it was purely as a relaxation.

In the last chapter of his memoirs he makes a few remarks about the future navy. Written in 1919 they were strangely prophetic:

I regarded the surface battleship as dead before the War, and I think her more dead now if that is possible. The battleship of today costs roughly £8,000,000; she carries . . . shells containing about 100,000 lbs. of high explosives; her effective range is, say, 15 miles, she is vulnerable to aircraft with bombs and aerial torpedoes, and to submarines . . . For £8,000,000 we could build many aeroplane-carrying ships, equipped with aeroplanes carrying over 100,000 lbs. of high explosives . . . their range would be about 150 miles. . . . The future is with the aeroplane.

He died in 1923, eighteen years before his "aeroplane-carrying ships" fought their naval battles in the Pacific between fleets just over 150 miles apart.

PART THREE

The Users

JELLICOE
1859-1935
The Head of the School

ON 18 July 1914 all the ships in the Royal Navy in home
waters of any military significance were assembling at Spithead for a review. As they came to their anchors in eleven
accurate lines they almost filled the wide stretch of mud-
coloured water which had witnessed so many gatherings of
naval might, though none like this.

The Admiralty had decided to substitute a Test Mobilisation for the usual annual manoeuvres. Churchill as First Lord
was behind the change, but tells us it had no connection with
the international situation. Whatever the motive it was an
inspired decision.

Three great Fleets were assembled. The First was in full
commission; the Second, ships with nucleus crews brought up
to full complement, and the Third manned mostly by reservists,
called to the colours for annual training.

Ten years had passed since Lord Fisher had started the
process of concentrating Britain's naval strength in home
waters and made plans for rapidly bringing ships in reserve to
full effectiveness. The review was the tangible fruit of his
prescience. Indeed the hand of Fisher was to be seen everywhere in that great assembly.

"All that is best and most modern here is the creation of
Lord Fisher," said Rear-Admiral Sir Robert Arbuthnot, a
man little given to eulogy and never "in the Fish-pond." The
dreadnoughts, the 13·5-inch guns carried by the latest "super-
dreadnoughts," the water-tube boilers and steam turbines
which drove them along at high speed; the many destroyers

fired by oil fuel, the submarines, the seaplanes roaring overhead—all bore evidence of his genius.

Beyond the English Channel the background was sombre.
War was in the air. The review, wrote the *Illustrated London
News*, was "a businesslike rather than ceremonial occasion."
King George V, due at Portsmouth at noon, was kept in London by a hurriedly called meeting of the Privy Council and
did not arrive until 5 p.m. The Fleet put on a great searchlight
display that night for the crowds assembled ashore, but the
true climax of the occasion was when the dark-grey ships, led
by the Royal Yacht, moved out to sea, so exactly spaced that
they might have been wired together, for exercises in the
Channel.

Flying his flag in one of the very latest battleships was the
Commander-in-Chief, Sir George Callaghan. It was a proud
moment for the old admiral, due to hand over Britain's most
responsible position afloat in a few months' time. Pride was
indeed the dominating emotion of the men who manned those
two hundred ships. No other country could match what they
saw around them, in numbers, in strength or (as they believed)
in quality. A month earlier many of the latest ships had visited
Kiel for the celebrations marking the re-opening of the canal,
enlarged to take the greatest vessels afloat. Hospitality had
been exchanged with the young German Fleet; smart men and
well-kept ships, though with no tradition to guide them (or
hold them back). The big guns of their heavy ships were of
smaller bore than ours, though calibre for calibre they fired a
larger shell. Their armour was thicker, but class for class they
were slower, because of their greater beam. Rumour spoke of
unusual powers of resistance to underwater damage.

How would they fare in battle? There were a few officers in
the British Fleet, mostly young and uninfluential, who wondered if too little thought had been given to the probable
course of modern war. It was more than a hundred years since
the Royal Navy had fought great battles at sea. Past experience was no guide and the exercises and manoeuvres in
vogue, rigidly directed from a highly centralised command,

Admiral of the Fleet Earl Jellicoe of Scapa, GCB, OM, GCVO,
on board H.M.S. *Iron Duke* when C.-in-C. Grand Fleet

The Grand Fleet at Sea, 1916

often seemed unrealistic. ("You be damned," signalled the angry admiral to the submarine which could clearly have sunk him half a dozen times.) But such doubting voices were few. Britannia had ruled the waves for generations. Evidently it was a law of nature.

The exercises over, the First Fleet anchored in Weymouth Bay, but the Second and Third Fleets dispersed to their home ports. The reservists, after some valuable experience in the ships they might be called upon to man at short notice, returned to their homes. In a day or two the extra men drafted to the Second Fleet would be back in the barracks and schools. The First Fleet was due to give manoeuvre leave. Soon all the great ships would be immobilised.

In Europe the situation was no easier, but as yet there was nothing to justify special action. Nevertheless on Sunday 26 July the First Sea Lord, Prince Louis of Battenberg, acting on his own initiative, ordered the First and Second Fleets to remain fully manned and to complete with fuel and ammunition.

All that week tension grew. On Tuesday the Admiralty (Churchill informing but not consulting the Prime Minister) ordered the First Fleet to Scapa Flow. That night the battle fleet, steaming without lights, passed Dover. Wrote Churchill: "Eighteen miles of warships running at high speed in absolute blackness through the narrow Straits, bearing with them into the broad waters of the North the safeguard of considerable affairs."

Callaghan was not with them. He had been told to report to the Admiralty and rejoin his Fleet at Scapa Flow. Sir George was a greatly respected commander, but he was sixty-one and not in the best of health. Would he be equal to the severe physical strain of the supreme command for even a few months of war?

On Saturday Germany declared war on Russia. There was no longer any doubt that hostilities were imminent. That night after dinner Churchill ordered general naval mobilisation without waiting for the Royal Proclamation, issued next day.

An officer who had been serving on the Board as Second Sea Lord, Vice-Admiral Sir John Jellicoe, was on his way to Scapa Flow, ostensibly to become Second-in-Command of the Grand Fleet. On Sunday night, as the signals warning of approaching war were going out, Jellicoe and Callaghan were told to open the secret envelopes they had been given—orders transferring the supreme command forthwith.

Fisher's fleet was ready, with the man Fisher had selected in command. As far back as 1905 he had picked Jellicoe as the outstanding officer of the decade, and arranged to shape his future accordingly. It was "the first fruits of ceaseless importunity" when Jellicoe took over the Atlantic Fleet in 1910. In 1911 one of Fisher's conditions for supporting Churchill had been that the new First Lord should continue the work "to get Jellicoe Commander-in-Chief of the Home Fleet prior to October 1914, which is the date of the Battle of Armaggedon." Fisher's prophecy of when the war would begin had been wonderfully accurate. Had he been equally inspired in his selection for "Admiralissimo"? Would the most brilliant and most successful officer of the early twentieth-century peacetime Navy be equally outstanding in war?

The die was cast and time would show. At midnight on Monday 3 August hostilities officially began. At daylight next morning Sir John Jellicoe, flying his flag in the *Iron Duke*, took the Grand Fleet into the North Sea from Scapa Flow.

John Rushworth Jellicoe came from seafaring stock. His father was a senior captain in the Royal Mail line and his mother's family included a number of officers who had served with distinction in the Royal Navy. Jacky was reared at Southampton amongst ships and sailors. He never had any doubts as to what he wished to be. On the flyleaf of one of his earliest school-books, written in a childish hand, appear these prophetic words "the property of Admiral Sir John Jellicoe." He was thirteen when he passed into the Navy and joined the *Britannia*, the old wooden line-of-battleship then moored in the estuary of the River Dart.

He was a little lad, only four feet six inches tall, but well-made and alert with exceptionally bright eyes, as quick and keen as a small fox-terrier. Captain Foley remembered him as "one of the cleverest cadets we ever had." He had an excellent brain, a retentive memory and a great desire to learn, though never labelled a "swot" by the other cadets, who found him equally enthusiastic at games or in practical work in small boats (of which he already had a fair knowledge) or aloft on the mast where sail drill was an important part of the curriculum. For seamanship was an easy first to navigation with general education "also ran." Engineering and mechanics were not taught in spite of the rapid mechanisation of the sea-going fleet. Discipline was strict in some directions, lax in others, the cadets being left pretty free to impose sanctions upon one another as they rose in seniority during the two years' course. It was a roughish life, but Jack, still four inches short of five feet when he left, weathered it successfully. He was an even-tempered lad, but never the type with whom liberties are taken. In the passing out examinations he was top of his term of thirty-eight.

At sea in the frigate *Newcastle* his training continued along the accepted lines, to make a smart seaman who could handle a ship under sail. In a long commission abroad he saw a lot of the world. Boylike he remembered the joys of getting ashore after weeks cooped up on board, often short of sleep and always indifferently fed. Guzzling cakes in Esmeralda's Confectionery at Gibraltar or custard apples at Madeira; playing cricket on all sorts of grounds (he had developed into a useful left-handed bowler), swimming in warm blue water, exploring strange places. He also remembered the thrill of being in a ship under sail—the silence, the leaning masts, the water streaming by and the satisfaction of mastering the complicated geometry of spars, rigging and canvas which drove her along.

His passion for learning was unabated, and in his examination in seamanship, taken on his eighteenth birthday, he obtained a first-class certificate having previously come out third of 106 midshipmen in mathematics, always a very strong subject. At nineteen he slightly lost his heart to the pretty daughter of the Swedish Ambassador to Turkey, a romance soon cut short, as sailor's romances so often are, by the disappearance of Constantinople below the horizon as the *Newcastle* sailed away.

Returning to England for the courses which Sub-Lieutenants undergo before becoming Lieutenants he did exceptionally well, getting a first in all three subjects—seamanship, navigation and gunnery. In his leisure time he played football, racquets and cricket; he was a bit above the average at all of them, and a very good shot with a rifle.

After another commission abroad (his heart was again slightly dented by a girl in Malta) he was selected to specialise in gunnery. A theoretical course, largely mathematics, at Greenwich was followed by practical instruction in the Gunnery School *Excellent* at Portsmouth. Jack Jellicoe showed very clearly that his brain-power was exceptional, passing out an easy head of his class and with a big margin over the marks necessary for a "first." In 1884 he was appointed to the junior staff of *Excellent*. Percy Scott was a senior staff officer, Jacky Fisher the Captain. The combination which was to revolutionise the gunnery efficiency of the fleet was together for the first time.

Fisher had already recognised that Lieutenant J. R. Jellicoe was something out of the ordinary. War with Russia was considered a certainty at about that time. In 1885 Fisher went to sea in a hurriedly organised squadron, selecting Jellicoe from all the staff officers of the Gunnery School to go with him.

The scare died down and Jellicoe returned to the normal run of appointments, which he filled with quiet efficiency. The Navy is, in the best sense of the words, a co-operative society. The basis of its training is to turn a collection of more or less selfish individuals into men who will put the interests of the ship before their own. But selflessness is the rarest of attributes in exceptionally clever young men. It was this quality, combined with unusual competence, which put Jellicoe in a special category. He was the ideal subordinate, highly thought of by his seniors and liked by his equals and juniors. Zealous, capable and cheerful he was a good messmate and a thoroughly capable young officer. An incident which occurred when he was serving in the *Colossus* in 1886 tells us quite a lot about Jellicoe at twenty-seven.

It was blowing a gale. *Colossus* was at anchor in Spithead and a very strong tide was running when a man fell overboard and was quickly swept away astern. Admiral Sir Cyprian Bridge, who was on the other side of the deck, ran across as Jellicoe jumped to the rescue.

He swam with extraordinary vigour, [says Bridge] breasting the waves continuously, and succeeded in reaching the man before he sank, and in keeping afloat until a boat picked them both up. The bluejacket was brought on board insensible, but soon recovered. Lieutenant Jellicoe smilingly received my congratulations and walked quickly to his cabin to put on dry clothes.

When Jacky Fisher was appointed Director of the newly formed Naval Ordnance Department at the Admiralty he asked for Jellicoe as one of his assistants. Fisher expected a lot and gave short shrift to those who disappointed him. Jellicoe proved a man after his own heart, and they became friends as well as colleagues. These were the years of very rapid technical development and Jellicoe was the sieve through whom new ideas for improvements in guns and ammunition were passed. Though always a quick worker he was often at his desk until 11 p.m., but he enjoyed working with Fisher, bursting with ideas and already a past master in getting what he wanted from the cumbersome Admiralty machine.

Promoted to Commander and due for a sea appointment he was specially asked for by Captain A. K. (Tug) Wilson of the *Sans Pareil*, a proof, if any was needed, that Jellicoe was a practical seaman and leader of men as well as a "back-room boy." So good was he in the exacting post of second-in-command of a large warship that the Admiral, Sir George Tryon, soon afterward had him transferred to the flagship, the battleship *Victoria*. "The penalty we pay for selecting the best men is that some Admiral is sure to walk off with him," wrote Wilson disgustedly.

"Malta Fever" was a scourge in the Mediterranean at that time, for no one had discovered that the infection came from drinking goat's milk. Jellicoe was laid up in his cabin, with a high temperature and really ill, when the *Victoria* and *Camperdown* had their notorious collision. Slipping a monkey-jacket over his pyjamas he made his way to his station by the main boat derrick. But power had already failed; listing rapidly the ship was on the point of capsizing. The doomed *Victoria* lurched violently to starboard, turned bottom up and sank, taking with her 358 of her crew of 649 officers and men. Weak as he was Jellicoe might have perished if he had not been helped by Midshipman Roberts-West. Except for a bout of rheumatism he was none the worse, for he had the gift, not very common in thoughtful men, of putting the irrevocable past behind him.

He continued his commission in the Mediterranean in the new flagship, the *Ramillies*. He was still a small man of less than middle height, lean, light and normally very active. Contemporary photographs fail to convey the impression he made on those about him. The very bright, intelligent, but kindly eyes, the ready sympathy which charmed those in close contact with him, the zest for work or play which brought him to the fore whatever the occasion.

There is no one more important to the well-being of a big ship than her Commander. *Ramillies* became a happy ship famous for her smartness, excelling in all the things held to matter most in those days; appearance, evolutions, sailing races, the fleet pulling regatta. No mention, be it noted, of any special prowess at shooting. Jellicoe, keen gunnery man as he was, seems to have been prepared, if not content, to take things as he found them. "All the Nelsonic virtues save one," wrote Jacky Fisher of Earl Jellicoe many years later. "He is totally lacking in the great gift of insubordination." "Saturated in discipline," was another Fisherism. As commander of a battleship his duty was to carry out policy, not to make it.

"Silent Jack" as he was sometimes called on the lower deck was without the touch of flamboyance which makes some officers known to the Fleet at large. In his own ship he came to be very much liked, for he had all the qualities by which officers are ultimately judged—knowledge of the job, scrupulous fairness, consistency and a genuine concern for his men's personal affairs. "He don't waste words," said one of the ratings who served with him, "but when he does speak he hits the mark every time." After three years in the *Ramillies* he crossed the Rubicon of naval life and was promoted to Captain. He was thirty-seven, and still a bachelor.

It was during his next appointment, to the Ordnance Committee at Woolwich, that he became friendly with the family of Sir Charles and Lady Cayzer. He stayed with them in Perthshire and got on very well with their second daughter Gwendoline. "The visit," he says in his not-so-lyrical style, "was one of the greatest pleasure." But a few months later he was on his way to China.

Except for a short period in Egypt as a Lieutenant, active service had so far not come Jellicoe's way, but in 1900, his third year on the station as a flag captain to Admiral Sir Edward Seymour, the unrest caused by the pillaging of Chinese territory by the Great Powers on the thin pretext of Treaties "freely" arrived at flared up in the Boxer Rising. The foreign community of Peking was besieged in the Legation quarter, in imminent danger of massacre. The nearest help was at Taku, where an International Squadron of British, French, German, Austrian, American, Italian and Japanese ships was at anchor. In the cold light of history the obtuseness of the diplomatic representatives of the great powers at Peking is almost unbelievable. When they at last woke up to the fact that the lives of all the foreign community were in deadly peril it was nearly too late. A landing party from the warships was hurriedly assembled and despatched at a few hours' notice. Seymour, the senior officer present was in charge, though hardly in full command, of a motley force of seven nationalities. With him, as Chief of Staff, was Captain John Jellicoe.

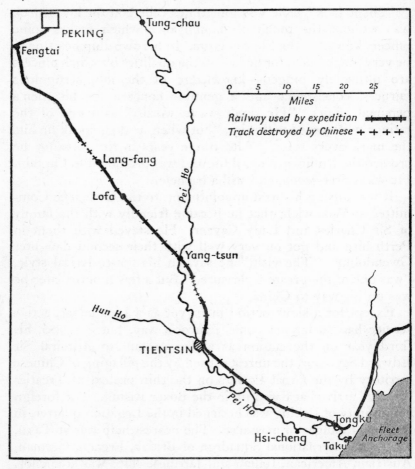

In four trains, the relieving force, repairing breaks in the line as it went along and fighting off sporadic resistance, penetrated within twenty-five miles of Peking, where it was brought to a halt by the state of the line and shortage of water. As the Boxers attacked in force it was learned that Tientsin in their rear was besieged and that the line behind them had been cut. A gallant if ill-advised attempt had ended in failure, and the column, to avoid annihilation, was forced to retreat by the river, for the trains were useless.

Jellicoe was his usual quiet, calm self; as imperturbable in action as at all other times. He had, said one of the French officers, "an astonishing gift of ubiquity. He seemed to be everywhere at once; *where* he should have been *when* he should have been." Mr Whittall, Reuter's correspondent with the expedition, fell completely under his spell. "A man to trust instinctively and to like from the beginning."

It was very nearly his obituary notice, for whilst the column was fighting its way back towards the coast Jellicoe was hit by a bullet on the left side of the chest and seriously wounded. One of the bluejackets cut away his tunic and shirt. A doctor came up and bandaged the wound, but told him he thought he was finished. Jellicoe made his will on a bit of paper and gave it to his coxswain—a simple document of six lines, astonishingly neatly written and clearly expressed and asking for remembrances to be given to his coxswain and boat's crew and servants "who have served me so faithfully," a typical act of thoughtfulness for others. He was put into a sampan to die, but fitness and determination pulled him through.

The man who returned to England after four years abroad had developed in a number of ways. He had proved himself just as good a leader when the bullets were flying as at other times, an important step in the development of any officer in the fighting services. He had gained a lot of useful experience of working with other nationalities. In particular he had been greatly struck by the efficiency and fighting qualities of the Germans, with whom he had considerable dealings when he returned to duty for the final stages of the campaign during which Peking was successfully relieved.

For the next decade his time was divided between appointments of constantly growing importance at the Admiralty and at sea. He renewed his visits to the Cayzer family and "came to the conclusions that my future happiness depended on my persuading Gwendoline to marry me"—a typical Jellicoeism and the prelude to a successful and very happy marriage which was celebrated in July 1901 at Holy Trinity, Sloane Street.

In 1904 Sir John Fisher became First Sea Lord. One of his

M

first acts was to gather round him the younger officers who
were to help him with the changes which transformed the
Navy during his period of office. Jellicoe, after serving as a
member of the Design Committee which decided on the
details of the *Dreadnought*, became Director of Naval Ordnance, the first D.N.O. to hold full responsibility for the design
and supply of guns and ammunition to the Navy; Percy Scott
was the Director of Target Practices. The bits of Jacky
Fisher's gigantic naval jigsaw puzzle, which depicted the fleet
which fought the 1914–18 war, were falling into place. Promoted to Rear-Admiral three years later Jellicoe went as
second-in-command to the Atlantic Fleet.

A year later Fisher wanted him back at the Admiralty.
Jellicoe was offered a seat on the Board as Third Sea Lord and
Controller. It was a key appointment, with several dreadnought battleships and cruisers coming into service each year,
guns improving and going up in size and torpedo craft both
surface and submarine developing apace. But the Liberal
Government then in power seemed to him to be more interested in economy than defence. Would they vote the money
to continue the expansion of the Fleet? It was not until
McKenna, the First Lord, had promised his unqualified support that Jellicoe accepted the post.

McKenna was as good as his word, backing up the naval
members of the Board by threatening his own resignation if
the 1909–10 programme was not approved. This battle was
won, but these were difficult years, with the great Beresford–
Fisher row coming to a head and Jacky Fisher's own position
threatened.

Jellicoe was not altogether satisfied with the capacity of our
heavy ships to withstand punishment. Whilst he was Controller he took some steps to improve the protection of capital
ships against heavy shell-fire. An experimental firing with live
ammunition using the old battleship *Edinburgh* as a target
raised serious doubts about the capabilities of our armour-
piercing shell. A few months before he again left the Admiralty
to take command of the Atlantic Fleet Jellicoe asked the

Ordnance Board to produce an armour-piercing shell which
would be fully effective when striking armour obliquely.
Later classes of capital ships had thicker armour and better
watertight subdivisions, but a great many ships had already
passed into service without these improvements, and the
matter of the shell proceeded on fatally leisurely lines.

It must be remembered that Jellicoe and his contemporaries
were without the basic engineering training which Fisher in
his genius had realised was necessary to the seamen of a
mechanical age. Even the cleverest of them were rather too
much in the hands of their technical advisers. Shipbuilder and
ship-user lacked a truly common language. Clearly Jellicoe
was not unduly disturbed; would that he had been. He was
regarded as a very successful Third Sea Lord. "No Controller
has been more popular," said *Engineering* when he eventually
returned to sea, "none has commanded greater respect."

It is unusual for such an excellent administrator to be
equally good afloat, but Jellicoe was outstanding. Quick in
coming to a decision, clear and precise in his orders, he never
fussed or seemed to worry. Cheerful, active and keen, he got
through work with great rapidity and took a full part in the
relaxations of his officers and men, pulling an oar in the
veterans' skiff in the regatta, sailing, playing racquets and
cricket, winning the officers' rifle-shooting competition at
500 yards and being a kind and charming host in his flagship.
Echoes of the great Fisher–Beresford storm were still rumbling
round the fleet. Jellicoe was one of Fisher's men, but none
suggested that he owed his rapid advancement, which had
passed him over the heads of a large number of older admirals,
to anything but his own ability. His appointment, late in 1911,
to command the Second Division of the reconstituted Home
Fleet indicated pretty clearly that he was now in the direct line
of succession to the Supreme Command afloat, but first he
returned once more to the Admiralty as Second Sea Lord.

Winston Churchill had been First Lord since 1911. Jellicoe
was always somewhat suspicious of politicians and he and
Churchill were horses of very different colours. Jellicoe's

actions were dictated by knowledge and experience. Everything he did was carefully planned, step following step in his meticulous, orderly mind. The brilliant Churchill with his astonishing gift of visualising the unknown would sometimes trust to his instinct. His ways were dictatorial and he had scant respect for the boundary between policy and executive action. "It did not take me long to find out," wrote Jellicoe, "that Mr Churchill, the First Lord, was very apt to express strong opinions upon purely technical matters; moreover, not being satisfied with expressing opinions, he tried to force his views on the Board." The gifts of advocacy which made Churchill such an asset to the Navy in putting its case to the Cabinet caused some resentment when he ran verbal rings round his much more knowledgeable colleagues in the Board Room. His habit of direct intervention in things outside his proper province and of leap-frogging the chain of command soon brought him into conflict with Jellicoe. Churchill, whose services to the Navy before the 1914–18 war can never be forgotten, was too much of an amateur sailor; Jellicoe perhaps too little of a politician.

In the summer of 1913 Jellicoe left the Admiralty for a few weeks to assume command of a fleet during manoeuvres designed to test the possibility of hostile landings on the east of England. So successful was he as the "enemy" that the manoeuvres were hurriedly stopped after three days for fear of putting ideas into German heads.

He was still at the Admiralty in 1914, though earmarked to go as second-in-command of the Channel Fleet in the summer before taking over from Callaghan at the end of the year. A few days before war was declared he was in the train on his way to join the Fleet at Scapa Flow when he learnt that he was to assume command forthwith. Jellicoe protested vigorously in a series of telegrams to the Admiralty, not from any lack of self confidence—all his life had been a preparation for this moment —but from a very genuine feeling of consideration for Sir George. But the First Lord was adamant. Only a much younger man could hope to carry the load. At fifty-five

Jellicoe took over the post of supreme responsibility of the 1914–18 war. "The only man," in Winston Churchill's well-known phrase, "who could lose the war in an afternoon."

After the drama and mounting tension of the pre-war years war itself came as something of an anti-climax, with both sides, fearful of unknown dangers, testing each other's strength. The Battle of the Heligoland Bight, described in a later chapter, in which the Germans lost three cruisers and a destroyer, made the High Seas Fleet more cautious than ever. The Grand Fleet, with a margin of superiority in dreadnoughts (27:18) which a single false move could easily upset, was far from being the decisively effective weapon it later became. Defeat at sea for the Germans would be a setback; for us a major disaster. Lose command of the sea and we would have lost the war; unable to send help to our allies on land, unable to defend our coast against invasion, or to maintain the tremendous flow of supplies from overseas on which the life of our island depends.

Jellicoe, assuming command on the very eve of war, had enormous difficulties with which to contend. He was not well known to the officers and men, many of whom were dismayed by the sudden departure of Sir George Callaghan. No one in the great fleet under his command had any experience of modern battle conditions—high-speed ships, long-range guns, the torpedo, wireless telegraphy, airships and aeroplanes introduced all sorts of unknown factors. The enemy was equally in the dark, but in their case a mistake would not be attended with such disastrous results. He had no properly protected base. At sea, screened by destroyers or steaming at high speed, the Fleet was reasonably secure from attacks by enemy submarines, but an extraordinary lack of foresight had failed to provide any of the strategically placed Scottish harbours with the guns, booms, nets and other permanent defences which would allow the Fleet to lie safely at anchor. There was nothing for it but to keep at sea, returning to harbour as infrequently as possible to complete with fuel and make good urgent defects, whilst work which should have been done years before at Rosyth, Cromarty and Scapa Flow was pushed forward. (A general map of the North Sea appears on pages 266 and 267.)

Summer turned into winter. The days shortened, the weather worsened. Defects accumulated. As Vice-Admiral Sir David Beatty, the commander of the battle-cruisers, put it: "The men can stand it, but the machine can't, and we must have a place where we can stop for four or five days every now and then to give the engineers a chance." The battleship *Audacious* was sunk by a mine. *Monarch* and *Conqueror* were badly damaged in a collision. With some of his ships out of action with defects the margin of superiority over the Germans was whittled away.

For the men of the Fleet it was hard and unrewarding work. At sea with no enemy in sight to take their minds off the inevitable discomforts of warships in bad weather; in harbour in some desolate place, guns manned because of the constant threat of enemy submarines, no chance of a run ashore to stretch their legs, hundreds of tons of coal to be taken on board and barely time to wash the all-pervading filth away before they were off to sea again. Even more serious than the growing list of defects was the impossibility of carrying out under reasonably safe conditions the constant practices with guns and torpedoes which are essential for full efficiency. As week followed week the Commander-in-Chief was aware that his ships were gradually losing their effectiveness.

It is a true measure of Jellicoe's greatness that none of these things had any effect on the confidence, very soon established, of his Fleet in the rightness of his leadership and of their own ability to defeat the enemy as soon as they were given the chance to get at him. Whatever might pass in the top secret telegrams between the *Iron Duke* and the Admiralty in which the dangers of the situation were coldly pointed out, the crews of the weather-worn ships had not the slightest doubt of their superiority over the foe. Grumble and curse as they sometimes did, their tails were well up. By subtle, unseen means the spirit with which the quiet, quick, clever little man in the *Iron Duke* infused those in daily contact with him spread to everyone in the flagship; from the flagship to each ship of the Fleet, from the Fleet via the ships detached for docking and repairs to those ashore. Jellicoe was the Grand Fleet; the Grand Fleet Jellicoe.

The direction of a fleet is visibly centralised in the person of its commander. He is a public figure, taking important decisions in the full view of those around him. He must live out much of his life and do a great deal of his work in front of an audience, watched, overheard; constantly if unconsciously measured in the balance. The tone of his voice, the look in his eye, everything he does and says is noted, gradually forming the picture which he eventually presents to the Fleet. Great reputations are very easily overthrown, which makes it all the more remarkable when they stand, grow, and keep on growing.

When the Fleet was at sea Jellicoe hardly ever left the bridge superstructure. On the upper bridge itself was a shelter where charts were laid out; immediately below this bridge was his cabin looking forward over the guns of "A" and "B" turrets to the bow; lower down, below the conning tower, was the war-room where movements of our own and enemy ships were constantly recorded.

The complicated business of handling a great fleet—twenty or more battleships with their attendant cruisers and destroyers —never appeared to give him the least trouble. In his clear and orderly mind half a hundred ships covering many square miles of sea were as exactly envisaged as a set of chessmen in a quiet room. Often when complicated movements were in progress he would himself send out the necessary messages to the signal staff from his bridge shelter; short and concise like his speech, written in his own neat hand and very rarely corrected. Whatever the circumstances Jellicoe knew exactly what he wanted, and how to order it.

In addition to the operational side an immense amount of administrative work had to be dealt with, in his sea cabin under the bridge or in his quarters aft when the Fleet was in harbour. Jellicoe would sit at his desk, quickly dealing with papers, quietly discussing a problem with a member of his staff, definite, unhurried, serene.

The furnishings of his quarters, like the man himself, were simple and unostentatious. His staff and his numerous visitors found him approachable and easy to deal with, with time for everything whatever the pressure of work. Whether discussing some trivial matter with one of his own personal retinue or high policy with his flag officers and captains his manner never varied; natural, courteous, giving his full attention to able-seaman or admiral. His most marked characteristic, the indescribable something which spread out from him, was a deep inner conviction. Faith in God. Faith in his country and the rightness of her cause. Faith in the men who manned his fleet. Faith in himself.

Later in the war, when Scapa Flow and Cromarty Firth had been made secure and the ships could spend more time in harbour, politicians and other distinguished visitors came to the Fleet. The long lines of anchored ships with their great guns and towering superstructures, lying on the grey water against the background of bleak hills, hundreds of men moving about their decks, was indeed an unforgettable sight, but the outstanding impression they received was of confidence. Confidence which sprang from the slight, agile figure of the Commander-in-Chief cheerfully bearing his load of solitary responsibility in the *Iron Duke*.

In October 1914 Jellicoe wrote a long letter to the Admiralty in which he gave his views on German tactics and a clear picture of his own policy, the policy he was to continue to follow throughout his time in command of the Grand Fleet.

The experience gained of German methods since the commencement of the war makes it possible and very desirable to consider the manner in which these methods are likely to be made use of tactically in a fleet action.

The Germans have shown that they rely to a very great extent on submarines, mines and torpedoes, and there can be no doubt whatever that they will endeavour to make the fullest use of these weapons in a fleet action, especially since they possess an actual superiority over us in these particular directions.

The C.-in-C. went on to discuss in some detail the general position in the North Sea. He next turned to what he called "the tactics of the actual battlefield" in which he then expected submarines to be used either with the scouting cruisers or in the rear or on the flank of the enemy battle fleet. Though Jellicoe wrote of submarines it is perfectly clear that he was laying down a principle equally applicable to other torpedo craft. The use of submarines with the battle fleet could be

countered by judicious handling of our battle fleet, but may, and probably will, involve a refusal to comply with the enemy's tactics by moving in the invited direction. If, for instance, the enemy battle fleet were to turn away from an advancing fleet, I should assume that the intention was to lead us over mines and submarines, *and should decline to be drawn*.[1]

I desire particularly to draw their Lordships' attention to this point, since it may be deemed a refusal of battle, and, indeed, might possibly result in failure to bring the enemy to action as soon as is expected or hoped.

Such a result would be absolutely repugnant to the feelings of all British naval officers and men, but with new and untried methods of warfare new tactics must be devised to meet them.

I feel that such tactics, if not understood, may bring odium upon me, but so long as I have the confidence of their Lordships I intend to pursue what is, in my considered opinion, the proper course to defeat and annihilate the enemy's battle fleet, without regard to uninstructed opinion or criticism.

Prophetic words! Their Lordships in their reply dated 7 November, gave their unqualified approval for these views and assured the Admiral of "their full confidence in your contemplated conduct of the Fleet in action."

This letter was written nineteen months before the battle of Jutland, but neither Jellicoe nor the Admiralty had amended this basic principle in the interval.

Waiting was weary work. At intervals the Grand Fleet would carry out sweeps into the southern North Sea, hoping to surprise the German High Seas Fleet on one of its occasional sorties. In January 1915 Beatty's battle-cruisers, working from Rosyth, intercepted a German scouting group near the Dogger

[1] My Italics.

Bank, sinking the heavy cruiser *Blücher* and severely damaging two battle-cruisers in a running action fought at high speed. But the battle fleet went on exercising, practising, trying out every likely manoeuvre, and never seeing anything of the enemy but an occasional submarine or Zeppelin. With the High Seas Fleet remaining inactive for the rest of the year, sweeps down the North Sea were varied with short cruises into the Atlantic, where tactics could be rehearsed without the distraction of submarine attack. Jellicoe was methodically perfecting the methods he would one day use in battle.

Interesting for the senior officers who understood what was going on, but it was deadly dull for most. Long hours at action stations with nothing in sight beyond the circle of their own ships but the tripod masts, funnels and upper works of the "enemy" hull down below the horizon; the great Atlantic swell rolling by, the destroyers bucketing along on either side; the smell and fug below decks in a battened-down ship; the shouting wind on deck; the waves which sometimes swept aboard the slowly rolling battleships as they wallowed along, turrets trained on the distant "foe." The return to harbour and the incessant coaling, coaling, coaling. Always —ing well coaling (sung to the hymn-tune "Holy, Holy, Holy . . .").

To keep 60,000 men fit, keen and happy whilst they waited for the battle which might never come was not an easy task. One month in three in Cromarty Firth was the nearest they ever got to civilised amenities. At Invergordon there were playing fields, a wet canteen, a shop or two, trains which had left the distant south only the day before, women walking in the street—a welcome change from the bare and empty hills of Scapa Flow. At Scapa Jellicoe did what he could to break the monotony. There were pulling regattas, when the weather and other circumstances allowed, a merchant ship converted into a theatre where those with acting talent could display their skill, a few football grounds of notable irregularity and even a rough golf course. Willing amateur labour worked wonders and the days, if not very full of incident, were fully occupied. The Fleet all things considered was happy enough, if frustrated.

1916 brought a change in the German high command and with it a change of policy. In April the German battle-cruisers made a tip-and-run raid on the East Anglian coast, bombarded Lowestoft for four minutes, dropped a few shells on Yarmouth and got away, though missing a chance to annihilate Tyrwhitt's light forces in a dawn encounter. Guessing that the German strategy was "divide and conquer" Jellicoe, using a British seaplane attack on the Zeppelin hangars at Tondern as a bait, cruised hopefully off the coast of Jutland ten days later. The Germans came out, but not within reach. Evidently a juicier lure must be used. Next time Jellicoe intended to send two light cruiser squadrons into the Kattegat on the eastern side of Denmark, whilst the Grand Fleet waited in the Skaggerak ready to pounce—a plan which was never carried out for the Germans, encouraged by the success of the Lowestoft raid, forestalled it with the preliminary moves for another sortie.

The presence of large numbers of U-boats in the North Sea was the first indication that something unusual was afoot. About noon on 30 May Jellicoe was informed by the Admiralty, whose intelligence on German movements was very good, that Scheer's High Seas Fleet might put to sea during the night. At 5.40 p.m. the Admiralty told Jellicoe to concentrate the Grand Fleet in a suitable position in the North Sea. Before midnight the battle fleet (24 battleships, 20 cruisers and 51 destroyers) from Scapa Flow and Cromarty and Beatty's battle-cruisers (6 battle-cruisers, 14 cruisers, 27 destroyers and a seaplane carrier) from Rosyth were at sea. Also with Jellicoe (*Iron Duke*) was the 3rd battle-cruiser squadron of three ships led by *Invincible*. With Beatty, his flag in the already famous *Lion*, was the 5th battle squadron of four fast battleships of the recently completed Queen Elizabeth class led by *Barham*.

Jellicoe was making for a point 90 miles west of the Naze. Beatty, after reaching a position 69 miles further south, would, if nothing had been sighted, turn north at 2 p.m. on 31 May and rendezvous with Jellicoe.

U-boats unsuccessfully attacked Beatty's force as it cleared

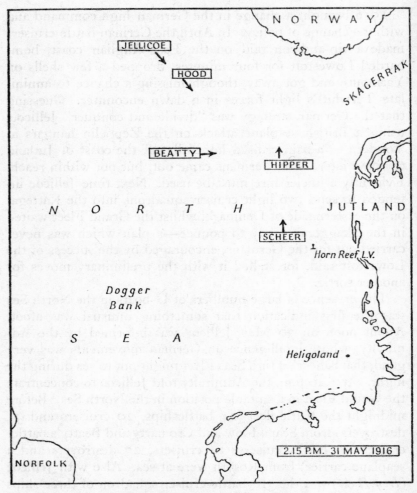

the coast. Other U-boats further north failed to intercept the battle fleet. More serious from the German point of view was the absence of adequate sighting reports. Scheer, in ignorance of the movements of the Grand Fleet, sailed his fleet (22 battleships, 5 battle-cruisers, 11 cruisers and 61 destroyers) from the Jade Roads during the small hours of 31 May. His course was somewhat west of north, off the coast of Jutland. He intended to send a scouting force ahead under Vice-Admiral

Hipper in the battle-cruisers to close the Norwegian coast near the Naze whilst he remained in the offing with his battle fleet. The scouting force was the bait with which he hoped to lure a detached force of British ships within reach of his battleship guns.

At 2 p.m. on 31 May a guard ship in the Jade Roads was transmitting on the German flagship's wave-length, leading the Admiralty to suppose that Scheer, who was keeping strict wireless silence, was still in harbour. Scheer knew that Beatty was at sea, but had no information about Jellicoe, whom he believed either to be in harbour or far to the north. Hipper with the scouting force was 52 miles ahead of Scheer and both German Admirals were steering north.

Beatty turned north to join Jellicoe as planned. The sea was calm with a light breeze from the south-east. Visibility was quite good, but there was nothing in sight. The great ships ploughed quietly along, surrounded by destroyers on the watch for submarines. Spread out ahead of them were the cruisers. Without radar or aircraft admirals had no other source of information of what lay beyond the limit of their view.

Twenty minutes later the cruiser *Galatea*, the easternmost of Beatty's scouts, saw a merchantman stopped and blowing off steam. Near her were two warships which looked like cruisers. A few minutes later *Galatea* saw something even more interesting; a great cloud of smoke on the horizon as from a fleet. The enemy was in sight! Beatty altered course to south-east to get between the Germans and their base and increased speed. Jellicoe, who was already steering in the right direction, also increased speed and ordered his ships to prepare for action. He was still over 60 miles away; there was not the slightest indication that the High Seas Fleet was ahead, but it was best to be prepared. The men of the Grand Fleet went, as they had often gone before, to their action stations; those off watch, who had been "getting their heads down" in the quiet of the afternoon, grumbling a little as they clattered up steel ladders or trotted along the decks. No doubt, as usual, it would prove to be a false alarm. The familiar routine of preparation went smoothly forward. Guns swung up and down. Bells tinkled. Orders were passed. Down below the engineers were raising steam for full speed, stoking the furnaces of the extra boilers whose fires had been banked. Smoke bellowed away astern as the battleships, in six parallel columns each of four ships, piled up bigger bow-waves as they gradually increased speed.

For nearly an hour there was no fresh news from below the horizon ahead. Then came further sighting reports. At 3.45 Beatty reported five enemy battle-cruisers steering south-east. Three minutes later our own battle-cruisers were in action, but of this Jellicoe was not at first aware.

He had already begun to suspect that the High Seas Fleet might be at sea. Beatty was some fifty miles away, more or less, for the exact accuracy of signalled positions is always a matter of conjecture. At 3.55 p.m., as he hurried south at full speed, Jellicoe learnt for the first time that the battle-cruisers were in action. At 4.15 p.m. he asked about the battleships of the 5th battle squadron. The *Barham*'s reply was highly satisfactory, "I am engaging the enemy." Beatty, with six battle-cruisers and four fast battleships, was apparently engaging five German battle-cruisers, but to make certain Jellicoe ordered *Invincible*'s battle-cruiser squadron, already some twenty miles ahead, to close the scene of action in support.

Time dragged slowly on without further news. But at 4.38 p.m. came the message which the Grand Fleet had waited for for nearly two years. The *Southampton*, one of Beatty's cruisers, had sighted the enemy battle fleet and Scheer was steering *north*.

"Fleet action is imminent," signalled the *Iron Duke*.

Beatty, with his battle-cruisers had engaged Hipper, without waiting for his fast battleships to close up in his support. In a furious running battle the *Indefatigable* had already been sunk, revealing for the first time the terrible weakness of our battle-cruisers, in which gun-power and speed had taken too much precedence over protection. Shortly afterwards the *Queen Mary*, following astern of the *Lion*, suffered a similar fate. The entry of the fast battleships into the battle redressed the balance, but only for a few minutes, for Hipper had now closed Scheer. Beatty, confronted by the whole of the High Seas Fleet, turned north towards Jellicoe.

None of this was known in the *Iron Duke*, for the *Lion*'s main wireless had been shot away some time before. At 6 p.m. the battle was coming up over the southern horizon ahead of the British battle fleet. Visibility, as is common in the North Sea, was patchy. At the moment it was limited to six or seven miles. From the murk came the continuous rumble of heavy gunfire, ahead and slightly to starboard of Jellicoe's ships, still advancing in six parallel columns. Suddenly the *Marlborough*, leading the westernmost column, saw the *Lion* emerging from the mist, crossing in front of the battle fleet from starboard to port.

Jellicoe's moment had come. He could still see nothing except certain of his own ships and had received very little positive information either about Beatty or the enemy. He was closing Scheer at forty miles an hour. He had to act now, and act correctly, disposing his battleships in the right place before Scheer emerged from the mist. There were many alternatives, but only one would be correct.

He was standing on the starboard side of the *Iron Duke*'s upper bridge looking in the direction from which he expected the enemy to appear. Below him the great guns were loaded and ready, but now there was silence—a tremble from the engines far below his feet; wind rattling a signal halyard. He had asked Beatty: "Where is the enemy Battle Fleet?" and was quietly waiting for the answer. He was dressed in an old blue raincoat rather tightly belted at his waist; an equally old Admiral's cap, its gold-leaf tarnished, was set very squarely on his head. Round his neck a white muffler. He was entirely composed, listening to the yeoman of signals calling out

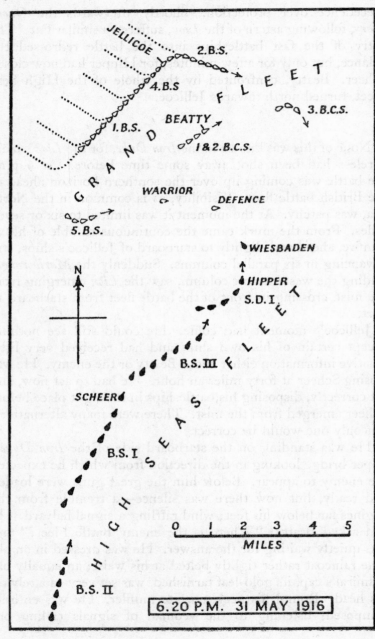

JELLICOE

2.B.S.

4.B.S

GRAND

I.B.S.   BEATTY

1 & 2.B.C.S.

FLEET

3.B.C.S.

WARRIOR   DEFENCE

5.B.S.

N

WIESBADEN

HIPPER

S.D.I

B.S.III

HIGH   SEAS   FLEET

SCHEER

B.S. I

B.S. II

0   1   2   3   4   5
MILES

6.20 P.M. 31 MAY 1916

Beatty's reply word by word as a searchlight flashed from the *Lion*. "HAVE — SIGHTED — ENEMY — BATTLE — FLEET — STOP — BEARING — SSW." His flag-captain[1] remembered how Jellicoe walked quickly across and bent over the slowly swinging card of the compass in the middle of the bridge. He had steel strips on his heels and his steps were sharp and distinctive. "I watched his keen, weather-beaten face with tremendous interest," says Dreyer, "wondering what he would do." For about twenty seconds Jellicoe stared at the compass, thinking. Then he lifted his head, breaking the silence with a crisp, clear order. "Hoist equal-speed pendants SE by E." It was the signal for deployment into line-of-battle.

Immediately the battleships began their manoeuvre from six columns in line abreast to a single line, the port column leading on SE by E, with the other ships falling in astern. There was still no sign of the enemy from the *Iron Duke*. Had Jellicoe correctly estimated what Scheer was doing?

Now things began to happen with great rapidity. Two heavy shells appeared from nowhere and cracked into the sea near the *Iron Duke*. Beatty's ships had vanished as they moved into position ahead of the Grand Fleet. A German cruiser solidified out of the greyness. *Iron Duke* quivered from stem to stern as her guns opened fire.

A moment later one of Jellicoe's own cruisers, the *Defence*, came under the concentrated fire of the German battleships, disintegrating in a great cloud of smoke and flame as she blew up and sank. A short pause, and out of the mist swam the silhouettes of three great ships, only half visible in the haze. Friend or foe? The range was only 12,000 yards, but it was at first impossible to be sure. Yes! They were *König* class battleships. *Iron Duke*'s guns blasted out at this new target. At last she was in action against the High Seas Fleet. It was 6.30 p.m.

The first encounter was of short duration. Five minutes later Scheer had turned about and vanished into the haze. Pursuing what he thought was a much weaker force he had

[1] Later Admiral Sir Frederick Dreyer.

N

suddenly been confronted by a line of great grey ships, flames
stabbing from them as they fired, stretching right across his
front; a very nasty surprise.

Jellicoe on the other hand was well content. The enemy
might retire westward, but to get back home he must turn east
again. In the lull he altered course towards the south, to place
his fleet squarely between Scheer and his base.

At 7 p.m. Beatty, who had taken position ahead of the Grand
Fleet, reported that the enemy was coming in again from the
west. Jellicoe turned his battleships three points to starboard
to close the range. Visibility was extremely variable with ships
appearing out of the mist, being fired on, and disappearing
again, but Jellicoe was once more in an excellent tactical
position, crossing the enemy's "T." The head of Scheer's
battle line came under the concentrated fire of the British
Fleet. Ordering his destroyers and battle-cruisers to attack to
cover his retirement Scheer once more made off to the westward.

Hipper's battle-cruisers, already damaged by Beatty's ships,
were now hit again and again by the British battle fleet.
Though forced to retire all of them got away—a wonderful
tribute to sound design.[1] The destroyers came on.

It was the moment Jellicoe had often foreseen. The enemy,
weaker in gun power, was relying on the torpedo. A flotilla of
destroyers supported by a cruiser was coming in on his starboard bow. Two of the battleships ahead of the *Iron Duke* had
already reported sighting a submarine. At 6.22 p.m. as their
secondary armament pounded at the oncoming German destroyers he swung the Grand Fleet to port, turning *away* from
the enemy, but remaining well-placed between Scheer and his
base. Torpedo tracks passed close to the battleships, but none
of them were hit. Gunfire dwindled and ceased as the German
ships vanished into the mist, made even more dense by a
smoke-screen laid by their destroyers. At 7.45 p.m. Jellicoe
turned back again, steering south-west. Beatty, ahead and to the
west, once more sighted the German battleships ten miles or so

[1] The *Lützow* sank several hours later.

away and apparently steering much the same course as Jellicoe. Hearing this Jellicoe turned the Grand Fleet on to a westerly course to close the enemy and at 8.23 p.m. Beatty was again in action for a short time. Shots were exchanged at long range, but the light was going (sunset was at 8 p.m.). In the gathering gloom, Scheer once more turned away.

Soon it would be dark. "Night action between heavy ships must always be very largely a matter of chance," Jellicoe had written earlier. It was a chance he was not prepared to take, as he felt he could achieve his object without doing so. The Germans were well to the westward and he was between Scheer and his base. All he had to do was to stay in this position until daylight, when he would certainly finish the matter. Scheer would try for home in the darkness. He would anticipate this movement by steaming south, the battle fleet in compact cruising formation with its destroyers astern to keep off the enemy flotillas which might again attack.

The men of the Grand Fleet remained at their action stations, taking a breather in relays on top of the gun-turrets and on deck. It was a dark night; nothing could be seen in the blackness ahead or on either beam. Astern, where the destroyers were massed, it was very different. At intervals the sky would be lit by the flashes of gunfire. Sometimes a huge explosion would flare up. Quite evidently things were not so quiet away to the northward. But no report came to Jellicoe to indicate it was anything but the expected attack by German destroyers. The Grand Fleet continued to steam south.

As dawn was breaking Jellicoe turned north, believing Scheer to be somewhere to the west, but there was no sign of the enemy. At 4.15 a.m. the Admiralty signalled that the High Seas Fleet was at the entrance to the Horns Reef swept channel. Somehow in the darkness Scheer had eluded him.

What had happened is now perfectly clear, but it was anything but clear at the time. Scheer, as Jellicoe thought he would, had steamed south during the night. On slightly converging courses the two fleets had moved through the darkness, invisible to one another, but drawing closer and closer together.

At 11 p.m. they had been so close that their positions plotted on
the same chart looked like one great fleet.

Scheer was steaming a little more slowly than Jellicoe.
Gradually he dropped astern. He believed that Jellicoe had
turned north some time before (and persisted in this belief for
many weeks after the battle). At about 10 p.m., thinking that
the coast was clear, he began to edge to the eastward, ran into
the assembled British destroyer flotilla and turned south again.
After a short interval he boldly tried again. Breaking his way
through the British light forces he managed to get clear away,
for the loss of one old battleship, three cruisers and two destroyers—a small price to pay in the circumstances. In a series
of short but violent night actions Jellicoe lost a cruiser and five
destroyers—epic encounters, which make stirring reading
even after all these years, but with one strange fact in common:
none of the many ships on the British side which sighted the
German battleships succeeded in getting this vital information
to their Commander-in-Chief. Some never even tried, assuming as they grappled with the enemy in the sudden glare of
searchlights and star-shells that what was so obvious to them
must be equally clear to the man many miles away. Amongst
the many lessons of Jutland this one stands out. It was a failure
of discipline. Over-discipline of the kind which allowed the
order which resulted in the sinking of the *Camperdown* by the
Victoria to pass unchallenged. Seniors knew best. Who am I
to draw attention to the obvious? Follow the flagship's movements. Years of over-centralisation had stifled initiative. One
is tempted to recall Jacky Fisher's opinion of Jellicoe, "Saturated in discipline." He had been altogether too successful in
impressing his personality on his fleet.

Until 1 p.m. on 1 June the Grand Fleet continued to patrol
west of the Horns Reef, but there was nothing to be seen but
the floating wreckage left behind by the battle. Next day
Jellicoe returned to harbour and that evening, with fuel and
ammunition replenished, reported his fleet ready for further
action.

A battle in which 250 vessels were engaged, which lasted

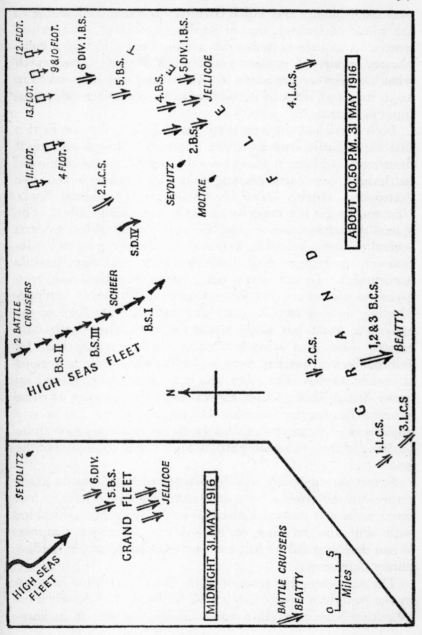

over twelve hours and which covered a sea area comparable to
the whole of Ireland, cannot be described in a few hundred
words. Adequate accounts fill a long book. It was a complicated affair. A student could stock a small library with
what has been written about it. An account which appeared in
1936 lists 191 titles in its bibliography, and other titles continue to appear.

Both fleets had suffered fairly heavy losses. On the British
side three battle-cruisers, three armoured cruisers and eight
destroyers had been sunk, against the German losses of one old
battleship, one battle-cruiser, four light cruisers and five
destroyers. British casualties totalled 6,945 against 2,921
German, by far the majority on both sides being killed. The
splendid construction of the German heavy ships enabled
several of them, including a modern battleship and two battle-
cruisers, to regain their harbours after receiving terrible
punishment. In our ships not enough attention had been
given to the effects of long-range hits by heavy armour-
piercing shell on or near their gun turrets. The flash of the
explosion could too easily reach the magazines, with fatal
results. Our own armour-piercing shells, as suspected by
Jellicoe five years earlier, were ineffective when striking armour
at certain angles. Far more hits (121 against 55) scored by
heavy British shells caused far less damage. Because of these
material factors the Germans claimed a victory, but it is a
queer sort of victory which leaves the strategic position quite
unchanged and your enemy still in undisputed command of the
sea.

Scheer acting boldly and decisively had succeeded in extricating himself from a very dangerous position. Jellicoe had
acted as he had trained himself to act, placing his battleships
with skill and refusing to be led into unknown dangers.
When darkness fell he had used his massed destroyer flotillas
purely defensively.

The very complete account of the battle published in 1936
by the American naval historian H. H. Frost, written when information from both sides was available, contains in its sum-

ming up these words: "Jellicoe executed a poor conception of war excellently." The conception of war to which the author refers is the impossibility of achieving spectacular results without running considerable risks. Another American, Vice-Admiral W. S. Sims, who later commanded the U.S. destroyer flotillas in European waters with so much distinction, puts it rather differently: "Jellicoe," he says,

knew, of course, the popular appeal of "damn the torpedoes, go ahead!" as well as he knew the risk of attempting to "achieve a Trafalgar under unfavourable battle conditions."

For the men of the Grand Fleet Jutland was a bitter disappointment, though their faith in themselves and in their Commander-in-Chief was unshaken. I speak knowingly for I was there, a sixteen-year-old midshipman, quite ignorant of most of the great matters involved, but closer than the mighty to the men of the lower deck.

Like everyone around me I had been filled with confidence (and was too young and foolish to be frightened). During the day, busy with my job in a gun-turret of the battleship *Canada*, I saw very little—the great ships of the battle fleet thrusting along in parallel lines before deployment; a glimpse of the battle-cruiser *Invincible*, broken like a stick, her two halves rearing strangely out of the sea.

What I remember best is the night. We had been told we could fall out for a short breather and I was on the roof of my turret as violent action flared up in the darkness to the northwest, passed astern across our wake and died away towards the east. Something tremendous was going on only a few miles away, but to our astonishment (it surprises me still) the battle fleet continued to steam to the southward. Not until the small hours did the Fleet reverse its course. We waited expectantly beside our loaded guns, but it was too late.

Fisher too was bitterly disappointed. A few days after the battle he wrote to both Jellicoe and Beatty. What he said to the C.-in-C. has not, to my knowledge, been disclosed. His letter to Beatty contains a version of one of his best known aphorisms. "Rashness in war is prudence, as prudence in war is criminal." He soon recovered his trust in Jellicoe (if he had ever lost it). When in November he heard a rumour that Beatty was taking over the Grand Fleet to allow Jellicoe to become First Sea Lord he wrote off at once; a strongly worded letter in which he almost ordered Sir John on no account to consent. "There is no one comparable to you to command the Fleet."

The rumour was quite correct. On 29 October 1916, Jellicoe had written to the Admiralty from the *Iron Duke*:

> There appears to be a serious danger that our losses in merchant ships . . . may by the early summer of 1917 have such a serious effect . . . as to force us into accepting peace terms, which the military position on the Continent would not justify and which would fall far short of our desires.

Grave words indeed. Jellicoe went on to discuss the relative failure of the anti-submarine campaign and to suggest changes —the formation of a committee of younger officers with a free hand to introduce new methods, a reorganised system of routing ships, the diversion of manpower to the shipbuilding industry and the possibility of taking destroyers from the Grand Fleet, even at the expense of immobilising some of its battleships.

A few days later he had been summoned to London to discuss these vital matters at a meeting of the War Cabinet. Later in November the First Lord (Balfour) suggested that Jellicoe should come to the Admiralty to tackle what was clearly the most pressing problem of the day himself. Believing that there was very little hope of the Grand Fleet being given another chance of engaging the High Seas Fleet Jellicoe accepted "with the greatest possible reluctance." He had no illusions about the difficulties of his new task. After bearing what Baldwin later described as "the greatest single responsibility on any man in the war" for nearly two and a half years he had been called in at the eleventh hour to do what should have been done months before.

In February 1917 the Germans started to wage unrestricted warfare against merchant ships. Losses which were already averaging around 150,000 tons a month rose very rapidly; 353,478 tons in March, 545,282 tons[1] in April—an appalling total which could not possibly be sustained. Jellicoe submitted a memorandum "The Submarine Menace and the Food Supply" which coldly set out the highly unpalatable facts. Defeat stared us in the face.

Jellicoe had been tackling his great task with his usual quiet efficiency. He had found the existing Admiralty organisation quite inadequate and had made some sweeping changes. Good foundations had been laid, but it would, as he was anxiously aware, be weeks or even months before concrete results were apparent. He was being strongly pressed to extend the convoy system, but believed it was at present impossible to do so because of the shortage of escorts. Time was needed, but time had already run exceedingly short. It was, perhaps, the moment for bold and dramatic decisions, but that was never Jellicoe's way.

Jellicoe's task, already difficult enough, was greatly complicated by his relations with the War Cabinet, particularly the Prime Minister, Lloyd George. Jellicoe was a very gifted man, but he was not a politician. With Sir Edward Carson, the new First Lord, he was quite at home. Carson believed in allowing full scope to his naval advisers and had complete trust in Jellicoe. Not so Lloyd George. Jellicoe was unable (a serious disability in the Chief of the Naval Staff) to "put himself across" to the Prime Minister to whom his studiously accurate statements of cold truth gave the impression of pessimism. His habit of refusing to promise anything he was not sure he could do appeared, to a worried, overworked man anxious for reassurance, to be defeatist. "They go about with gloomy mien and despondent hearts," wrote Lloyd George of

[1] These figures are for British shipping alone. Total losses from all causes were 503,800 tons in March and 881,000 in April, *Merchant Ship Losses*, H.M.S.O., 1919; *The German Submarine War*, by R. H. Gibson and Maurice Prendergast, Constable, 1931.

his naval advisers. "Their reports are full of despair. It is clear that they think the case is now hopeless." He did not realise how much had been done since Jellicoe arrived at the Admiralty, a misunderstanding for which the First Sea Lord's inability to state his own case was partly to blame.

Lloyd George was convinced that Jellicoe and his Board were hobbled by out-of-date notions. "When you are confronted with a situation for which there is no precedent and where therefore experience does not count as much as inventiveness, audacity and celerity of decision . . . the able but unimaginative expert is a public danger." Jellicoe, who liked to try the ground before putting down his feet, was never at his best when suddenly confronted with a revolutionary project. He detested arguing. The sort of verbal fireworks in which the Prime Minister delighted made him angry. When angry he became silent; his mouth would shut like a trap and he could look exceedingly grim. Lloyd George who liked to have around him optimistic, obviously brilliant men, failed to appreciate Jellicoe's sterling qualities. Thomas Jones, one of Lloyd George's secretaries, writes that the Prime Minister would "sometimes rally and chaff the Admiral across the table and bid him sweep the seas with his telescope to discover, if he could, some dove of hope or promise above the waves, some gleam of sunshine in the pitiless storm." Lloyd George was a Celt; Jellicoe as English as they are made. It is an old conflict.

In April 1917 the Prime Minister took the extraordinary step of personally visiting the Admiralty, taking the head of the table at a Board meeting. He had correctly made up his mind that the solution lay in an immediate extension of the convoy system. Incorrectly he had also assumed that the Admiralty, in the person of the First Sea Lord Sir John Jellicoe and backed by the First Lord Sir Edward Carson, were opposed to convoys. In fact the entry of the United States into the war earlier in the month had entirely transformed the chief objection—shortage of escorts. At the meeting Lloyd George was informed of what was being done and what was contemplated. "The Higher Admirals," he wrote, "had at last been persuaded by the 'Convoyers' not perhaps to take action, but to try action." It was a gross understatement of the facts, though, in the light of subsequent experience, it must be admitted that Jellicoe had over-estimated such subsidiary difficulties as the supposed inability of merchant ships, used to sailing alone, to move in close formation. Lloyd George went back to Downing Street with the firm intention of getting rid of both Carson and Jellicoe and replacing them with men of his own choosing. Lord Beaverbrook in his book calls it "a brave decision." It was certainly a very risky one. But in the early summer it received support from an unexpected quarter, Field Marshal Sir Douglas Haig.

In the spring of 1917 Sir Eric Geddes, an ex-director of the North Eastern Railway, who had done very good work in France in reorganising the transport system for the Army, had been installed at the Admiralty as Controller of Shipping. In the early summer Geddes informed Haig of his conviction that the Admiralty was in the hands of "a number of incompetent sailors." Haig who had met Jellicoe two or three times and had not been impressed passed this information on to the Prime Minister. At breakfast on 26 June Lloyd George, Haig and Geddes "discussed the state of the Admiralty." In July Carson unwillingly consented to be kicked upstairs into the War Cabinet, where he continued to voice his absolute trust in Jellicoe. Sir Eric Geddes became First Lord.

It could hardly be expected that the change would be a happy one. Jellicoe, who had not been greatly impressed by Geddes' efficiency as Controller, resented his immediate assumption of dictatorial powers, his autocratic and peremptory manner and his way of treating the Sea Lords as inferiors rather than colleagues. The Prime Minister, with his avowed intention of having someone at the Admiralty "who was accustomed to force his will on his subordinates," was heavily on Geddes' side. On Christmas Eve, five months after Geddes became First Lord, Jellicoe found a short letter on his desk bluntly stating that a change of First Sea Lord was desirable.

Lloyd George has stated that "a persistence of a few more weeks in (the Admiralty's) refusal to listen to advice from outside would have meant irretrievable ruin for the Allies." The chart of merchant tonnage sunk coldly gives the lie to this misstatement showing how losses, after touching a peak of 545,282 (881,000)[1] tons in April 1917 steadily fell away for the remainder of the year and had been reduced to 173,560 (239,200) tons in November. When Jellicoe left the Admiralty in December the work he had begun twelve months before had had time to take effect. Rapid and spectacular results were always impossible. Lord Beaverbrook in *Men and Power* gives the credit to Geddes. "By November 1917, figures for Allied shipping losses gave testimony to [Geddes'] success in action . . . From the disastrous days when Britain's survival hung in the balance on the seas, the position had been wholly retrieved." Jellicoe had been at the Admiralty since December 1916 and was still First Sea Lord. Sir Eric Geddes became First Lord in July 1917, when the gross tons sunk had already been reduced to 364,858 (557,900) tons and were falling rapidly. The facts speak for themselves.

The Bishop of London met Sir John walking on the Embankment shortly after he had received the note dismissing him from the Admiralty. Jellicoe was his usual calm, courteous self. "This is the first time, Bishop," he said, "I've been sacked in my life."

A strange curtain-line for the most brilliant naval officer of his time, but not the finale.

Jellicoe's acceptance of hard knocks, of which he had more than his share, was almost saint-like. He was an extraordinarily selfless man. This, and the stable background of a happy family life, brought him safely through a very bitter time.

But life had its compensations. In April 1918 his only son was born. The story is that Sir John ran along the passage off which his four daughters were sleeping calling: "Out of your beds, girls, and down on your knees. Thank God you've got a brother."

---

[1] Total losses in brackets. The British losses are the smaller figure.

He had been offered, and had refused, the Plymouth command, but immediately after the armistice he accepted a Government request to lead a mission to India, Australia, New Zealand and Canada to discuss the naval defence of the Commonwealth. The warmth of his reception, particularly in the Antipodes, showed very clearly that this great and gentle man was perhaps more truly appreciated outside his own country than at home.

In 1920 at the personal request of the Prime Minister, W. F. Massey, Lord Jellicoe (he was raised to the peerage in 1917) was appointed by King George V as Governor-General of New Zealand, a post he filled for four years with great success.

Whilst he was abroad the official Admiralty "Narrative" of the Battle of Jutland was at last published: a long and very complicated document almost incomprehensible to the general public, but including a preface which contained statements of what was assumed to be in the minds of Jellicoe and other officers, and criticism of action subsequently taken. The "Narrative," or rather its preface, hurriedly swallowed and only partly digested by the press, gave the unfortunate impression that the part played by the main Battle Fleet was comparatively unimportant and suggested that Jellicoe was more concerned in saving his own ships than in defeating the enemy—just the sort of thing which always makes the headlines.

Jellicoe, the man who hated publicity, was again front page news. As on every previous occasion he refused to join in the controversies which raged about his name, only entering the lists when imputations were made against some of the officers who had served under his command. For himself he was prepared to accept the judgment of history. He had given his best; he believed that the record would eventually prove that the great trust placed in him in 1914, 1915 and 1916 in the Grand Fleet and 1917 at the Admiralty had never been betrayed.

Returning to England shortly before his sixty-fifth birthday he continued to give his time to the public service as Vice-

President and later President of the British Legion; simple, courteous and efficient, answering hundreds of letters in his own hand and making those who came to the Legion for help feel that it was a personal matter, hand grasping hand and not the cold competency of a great machine. At seventy he was still working hard, but finding time for sport; leading a team of Admirals into the field to play cricket against the Pangbourne cadets; shooting at Bisley. He died in 1935. "His death," wrote the Archbishop of Canterbury, "was like his life, calm, peaceful and well-ordered."

BEATTY
1871-1936

The Nelson Touch

I FIRST went to sea in 1915, in the battleship *Canada*, newly commissioned and just completing in a Tyneside shipyard. On our way to join the Grand Fleet at Scapa Flow we called at Rosyth Dockyard in the Firth of Forth. I shall never forget my first view of Beatty's battle-cruisers, lying at anchor above the great bridge.

It was typical Firth of Forth weather, foggy and cold. As the *Canada* passed under the bridge the battle-cruisers swam into view, gradually solidifying out of the murk which partly obscured the shore on either hand; *Lion, Queen Mary, Princess Royal* and *Tiger*, the ships of the First Battle-Cruiser Squadron, long and powerful, built for speed, heavily armed and already proved in battle. We drew closer. As we passed the *Lion* bugles sounded the still. Standing stiffly to attention with my division I had my first view of this famous ship. The damage she had received in the battle of the Dogger Bank six months before been repaired, but we still saw, or thought we saw, dents in her armour. On her foremast the flag of Vice-Admiral Sir David Beatty hung limply down, for there was not a breath of wind. Smoke drifted upwards from her great funnels to mingle with the mist overhead.

Later, landing at Hawes pier, I had my first glimpse of Sir David himself, a stocky, jaunty figure, striding along and leaping lightly into his barge. Away went the boat, quickly gathering speed. Spray flew over the bowmen standing like statues in front of the casing carrying the man whose name was already a legend; D.S.O. as a lieutenant, Captain at twenty-nine, Admiral before he was forty.

I was still serving in the Grand Fleet when Beatty succeeded Jellicoe as Commander-in-Chief in December 1916. The bitter disappointment of Jutland, in which we had been in action for two brief periods, was still in our minds. After months of intense preparation and weary waiting we had at last opened fire on the enemy, but somehow he had escaped us. We midshipmen did not understand how this could have happened. Like everyone else in the Grand Fleet we had complete confidence in our chief, Admiral Sir John Jellicoe, but we had a feeling that perhaps he had been too cautious. If fate was kind we would be given another chance, and then the complete victory which had eluded us on 31 May 1916 would be ours. The doubts (soon to be resolved) of our seniors that the new Commander-in-Chief would upset rather than build on the splendid foundation laid by Jellicoe were not for the likes of us. To the confidence already instilled by Jellicoe something new had been added; the strength given to every member of a fighting force whose policy is offensive rather than defensive.

But the battle we hoped for was not to be. The only time we ever saw the High Seas Fleet again was when its ships, led by the little cruiser *Cardiff*, steamed tamely into the Firth of Forth to surrender on 21 November 1918, a victory without savour.

Was Beatty, as many had believed, the greatest British sea commander since Nelson? Or was he, as others declared, only a very lucky man whom fortune had favoured with extraordinary opportunities, though denying him the most wished for chance of all?

David Beatty was country bred. He was born near Nantwich, Cheshire, in 1871, but both his parents were Irish. His mother, the beautiful Kathleen Sadleir, came from County Meath. Generations of Beattys had lived in County Wexford; a family of fearless men usually to be found on the back of a horse in their spare moments. David's grandfather was

Admiral of the Fleet Earl Beatty, Viscount Borodale of Wexford, Baron
Beatty of the North Sea and of Brooksby, PC, GCB, OM, GCVO, DSO

Master of Foxhounds for forty years. His father began to hunt before he was ten years old, a hard-riding squire who took to breeding 'chasers later in life. His elder brother Charles rode in the Grand National, was recommended for the V.C. in the South African War and died of wounds in Flanders in 1918. His younger brother William Vandeleur (Vandy) served as a soldier when the country was at war and trained horses at Newmarket at other times. George, who died in 1915, was well known as a steeplechase rider and David's only sister Kathleen (Mrs Courage) rode as straight and as fearlessly as her brothers. They were a happy, hard-riding family who enjoyed risking their necks and played a merry part in the activities of their country life.

David's great-grandfather had fought at Waterloo. None of the Beattys or Sadleirs are known to have been in the Navy, but David was determined to go to sea. Though just as fond of horses as the rest of his family he was different in other respects —more thoughtful and more imaginative. Perhaps for this reason he was his mother's favourite. With her backing and with the easy consent of his father David was entered at Burney's Naval Academy at Gosport when he was twelve years old to be "crammed" for the examination for a naval cadetship. Ninety-nine candidates presented themselves to the Civil Service Commissioners and thirty-two were selected. David Beatty passed tenth into the *Britannia* for two years' training in the old wooden line-of-battleship moored in the River Dart. With 1,235 marks out of a possible 1,700 he had done quite well, which is much to the credit of Burney's Academy, for he was never very clever with his books.

The *Britannia* had advanced a little, but not much, since Jellicoe was there twelve years earlier. Natural science, drawing, English and French were taught as well as seamanship, navigation and gunnery; even a little engineering had thrust its oily nose into the curriculum.

David was a small lad, lightly built and not very strong, but a good boxer and a determined Rugby footballer. He enjoyed the *Britannia*, did not take life too seriously and was

o

frequently in trouble for minor misdemeanours under the general heading of "skylarking." But he managed to pass out twelfth of the twenty-five surviving cadets—a good lot of boys no less than six of whom were to reach flag rank.

Beatty was appointed to a ship in China, but his mother, ambitious for her favourite son, thought this too far away and too obscure a post. She went up to London and saw Lord Charles Beresford. Charmed by Mrs Beatty's beauty Lord Charles put in a word in the right quarter and Beatty joined the flagship of H.R.H. the Duke of Edinburgh in the Mediterranean Fleet. The *Alexandra*, an iron-armoured battleship with muzzle-loading guns, though really a steamship, was fully-rigged. Smartness aloft was still the measure of efficiency. Complicated exercises at sea produced ship-handlers of a high order, but little else was done to prepare the Fleet for battle.

As a midshipman Beatty was unexceptional, no better and no worse than his messmates. Ashore there were plenty of opportunities for riding. Horses were his chief preoccupation outside working hours. He did well as an amateur jockey on Malta's Marsa racecourse. Being a good-looking, well-mannered lad he was popular with the family of the Commander-in-Chief, children of much his own age who shared his passion for horses. The eldest girl, Princess Marie, was the future Queen of Rumania. "Beatty," she wrote many years later in her memoirs, "was my special friend." Boxing was another relaxation. Coached by the *Alexandra*'s boatswain he became useful with the gloves, quick and courageous. His two years on the Mediterranean station were rounded off with a few months in the masted corvette *Ruby* for intensive seamanship training followed by an examination in which he was awarded a second-class certificate.

Returning to England as an acting sub-lieutenant he went to the Royal Naval College at Greenwich for the usual six months' study of theoretical subjects—mathematics, applied mechanics, astronomy, meteorology, physics, chemistry, naval architecture and naval history—a formidable list made even less appetising to a gay young man by the attractions of London only seven

miles away. Beatty had a good brain, but he was more interested in the lesser lights of the West End stage than in the
college curriculum and passed his final examinations with
some difficulty; a first-class certificate in torpedo but "seconds"
in seamanship, gunnery and pilotage and a "third" in navigation. Like many another Sub at Greenwich with a taste for the
fleshpots and not much private means he was often broke, but
he enjoyed himself and had some splendid leaves at home (his
parents had now moved to Rugby) particularly in the hunting
season.

Returning to sea in the battleship *Nile* he was selected to
serve in the Royal Yacht *Victoria and Albert* for her summer
cruise—a coveted distinction, for the "Loyal Rotters" were
much envied. Promoted to Lieutenant he sampled a very
different sort of life, when he went as a watchkeeper to the
corvette *Ruby*. His Captain was a bit of a "hard case" of the
old blue-water school. The ship was old and small and long
passages made under sail were no sinecure, but Beatty preferred the rough, independent life to walking the quarterdeck
of a big ship with a telescope under his arm as one of her
watchkeeping lieutenants. This was to follow, in the battleship *Camperdown*, which he joined a few months after she had
rammed and sunk the *Victoria* (in which Commander John
Jellicoe had been serving as executive officer).

In 1896 Beatty was in another battleship, the *Trafalgar*.
He was twenty-five; a competent, well-set-up young man who
rode a horse better than most, had more than his share of good
looks and was a bit of a dandy. Rather thoughtful and reserved,
liked, without being extravagantly popular, a good average
officer who seemed destined for a good average career. One of
those who enjoyed his company and thought quite a lot of
him was the executive officer of the *Trafalgar*, Commander
Stanley Colville.

It was ten years since the murder of Gordon at Khartoum.
The Sudan was still controlled by rebel tribesmen, but a strong
Anglo-Egyptian force was being assembled under the Sirdar,
General Kitchener, to restore the Khedive's sovereignty. It

would be a River War, advancing up the Nile, and a flotilla of
gunboats would support the Army. Colville, appointed in
command, selected David Beatty to go with him. It was the
turning point in Beatty's career. (See map, page 45.)

In September 1896 most of the flotilla had passed the Second
and Third Cataracts and was assembled below Hafir, strongly
held by the dervishes under the Khalifa who had occupied the
whole province of Dongola. The railway, which was being
pushed rapidly forward, had reached Kosheh where an improvised dockyard was assembling three more river gunboats,
sent in sections from England. But Kitchener would not wait.
On he went with three older craft, *Tamai* (Colville), *Metemmeh*
and *Abu Klea* (Beatty)—stern-wheelers about ninety feet long,
armed with a gun forward and two machine-guns in the upper
battery.

The Army was advancing along the right bank, but Hafir
was on the opposite side of the river whose channel was about
six hundred yards wide. Unless the gunboats could silence the
enemy fire it would be impossible for the troops to cross over,
or even to advance close enough to support the flotilla. The
Arab artillery was well served and a brisk engagement began,
watched by hundreds of soldiers at the moment powerless to
assist.

Tamai, *Metemmeh* and *Abu Klea*, their stern wheels churning
round, wood smoke pouring from their funnels, advanced
slowly against the current until they were off the town. It was
point-blank range for the guns on both sides and many hits
were scored. Heavy rifle-fire raked the gunboats' decks. In
the *Tamai*, leading the line, two men were killed and a dozen
wounded, including Colville whose wrist was shattered.
Metemmeh had also suffered several hits. A shell struck the
Abu Klea at the water-line and came to rest in the magazine.
Beatty, under fire for the first time but perfectly cool, picked
it up and threw it overboard. The *Tamai* dropped back out of
range, followed later by the *Metemmeh*. A great shout went
up from the Arabs in Hafir, but Beatty's holed and leaking
Abu Klea held on. The other two gunboats returned in sup-

port. With Colville out of action Beatty had succeeded to the command. He decided on a daring manoeuvre. The gunboats though unsuccessful in silencing the enemy's fire had reduced it sufficiently to enable the Sirdar to move artillery and infantry into position opposite the town. Helped by this covering fire Beatty led his little flotilla upstream past Hafir. Thirty-five miles further south was Dongola. His plan was to cut the enemy communications, forcing them to withdraw from Hafir. It was successful. As Beatty bombarded Dongola the Arabs fell back north along the bank. Kitchener, crossing the river, captured Hafir. A few days later the Army had advanced in sufficient strength to take Dongola, but the bluejackets from the gunboats were the first to enter the town. The Arabs continued to retire upstream harassed by fire from the gunboats which followed them as far as the Fourth Cataract where the Sirdar, his lines of communication dangerously extended, called off the pursuit.

"I cannot speak too highly of this officer's behaviour," Kitchener wrote of Beatty in his despatches. Beatty was sent to England for some well-earned leave, awarded the D.S.O. and noted in the Admiralty records for early promotion. He had shown quite unusual qualities of leadership, courage and dash; quickness to seize an opportunity and a cool appreciation of what was possible. A triumphant return was marred by the fact that his mother, to whom he was devoted, had died during the campaign.

In July 1897 he was again lent to the Egyptian Government at the special request of the Sirdar. The gunboat flotilla assembled below the Fourth Cataract. Keppel, who had served with Beresford in the *Safieh*, was in command. Attempts to pass the cataract when the river was still too low began disastrously. Beatty's *Hafir* capsized in mid-stream with the loss of three of the fifteen men on board. Beatty was pulled out of the river near exhaustion, having lost everything except the clothes he stood up in, but quite undaunted.

Ten days later the Nile had risen. More men were available on the hauling ropes and the gunboats were passed up successfully. It was the prelude to a long and strenuous campaign. From the end of September 1897 until the capture of Khartoum ten months later the gunboats were constantly in action, reconnoitring the river ahead of the Army, engaging enemy positions on the banks, bringing up troops and supplies and acting as mobile artillery. Beatty, under fire several days a week, revelled in the danger and more than lived up to the reputation he had earned the year before. Lieutenant Walter Cowan[1] describes seeing his friend and his gunboat *Fateh*, "her funnel riddled with shot, and holes in her side where shell had hit her. He looked supremely happy against this battle-scarred background . . . Even at that age [twenty-six] and with that splendid lot of soldiers, he was with no show of arrogance a natural king of his company."

He was indeed supremely happy, seeking out every opportunity for action. When the Battle of Atbara was fought Beatty, his gunboat being temporarily out of it, landed in charge of a rocket detachment of bluejackets and took part in the final assault. In his diary he described how, when all the rockets were expended,

I left a guard, and with the remainder joined in the firing-line, who were advancing with a rush the last short distance, yelling for all they were worth which, in conjunction with the bands and pipes, made an astonishing noise . . . It was during the last 100 yards that most of our casualties occurred, and they fell pretty thick, the enemy holding out until we got within 20 yards of them . . . We marched back to Omdelia everybody tired but delighted.

After the battle of Omdurman which brought the campaign to its victorious close, Beatty was ordered to salvage a gunboat which had been in enemy hands. It was the *Safieh*, the same little ship in which Lord Charles Beresford had fought so gallantly during the abortive attempt to relieve Gordon. Mr Benbow's patch was still doing duty on her boiler!

There is a certain similarity between the careers of Beresford and Beatty though the parallel must not be carried too far. Both were Irishmen; both were fond of a horse and good living.

[1] Later Admiral Sir Walter Cowan.

Both revelled in action and were at their best when the bullets were flying.

In his despatch of September 1898 the Sirdar made very favourable reference to the work of Commander Colin Keppel's gunboats. Amongst the honours awarded for the campaign was an Admiralty notice promoting David Beatty D.S.O. to Commander. He had spent less than half the average time as a lieutenant and passed over the heads of 395 of his brother officers.

Lucky Beatty! Lucky, certainly, to be alive. For the rest, it was, of course, very much more than luck. He had had his chance, and taken full advantage of it. Week after week and month after month he had shown himself to be a first-class fighting man. Danger never flustered him; on the contrary it seemed to clarify and stimulate his mind. His rapid decisions in moments of stress were due to his having anticipated every likely situation and never being taken wholly by surprise. The lessons he learnt on the Nile were to stand to him for the rest of his life, and he had served under a great commander, whose carefully laid plans boldly and decisively acted upon had brought their rewards. Kitchener of Khartoum was the greatest contemporary influence on Beatty of the North Sea.

1898 was indeed a decisive year. In the hunting-field young Commander Beatty met, and fell in love with, a beautiful American woman, Ethel Tree. Mrs Tree was the daughter of the millionaire Marshall Field. Both she and her husband spent a lot of their time in England. There was one small son, but the marriage was not a happy one. Beatty and Mrs Tree were strongly attracted to one another, though not even their closest friends suspected it. Early next year Beatty was appointed as executive officer of the battleship *Barfleur* in China, under his old Commander, now Captain Stanley Colville. For six months after he had left home David and Ethel wrote to one another, until Beatty heard that she was constantly being seen in the company of another man. Disdainfully, but very sadly, he left her further letters unanswered.

Beatty had arrived in China as the Boxer Rising boiled over

with the attack on the Foreign Legations in Peking. The British Commander-in-Chief, Admiral Sir Edward Seymour, with Jellicoe as his chief of staff, was ashore attempting their relief. In his absence the command afloat had devolved on Rear-Admiral James Bruce in the *Barfleur*. Bruce now sent a detachment of 150 bluejackets and marines under Beatty to reinforce the Allied garrison at Tientsin. (See map, page 176.)

It was very different from the River War, so skilfully conducted by Kitchener. This was an international affair, difficult to control, and the early stages of the campaign saw a good deal of bungling and confusion. Regular Chinese troops in very large numbers had joined the Boxers; the Allied forces were in a dangerous situation and there was plenty of fighting, with heavy casualties on both sides. Nine days after going ashore Beatty was twice wounded, in the left arm just below the shoulder and in the left wrist, but was out of hospital three days later with his arm in a sling "rather weak from loss of blood but otherwise all right." He continued to take a major part in the fighting for another month though suffering a good deal of pain from his wounds, the effects of which lingered on for years. For six weeks fighting was almost continuous, with the Allies heavily outnumbered until strong relief forces eventually arrived.

Captain E. H. Bayley, R.N., the Senior British Naval officer in Tientsin, wrote to Beatty after the lifting of the siege, repeating

what I hope you will find my official letters have always stated, my belief that you are one of the best and most loyal supporters that any man could wish to have in trying times, or I believe, in any others . . . Your personal gallantry and disregard for danger need no remarks. They are known to all . . . but perhaps no one has noticed more than I have, your endurance of suffering patiently when you might well have rested, because you would not put any work on others, or wanted to lighten someone else's burden. I can never forget it . . .

Beatty, in his journal, describes his experiences in some detail in a matter-of-fact way which takes his own contribution for granted. There is no doubt that he enjoyed the fighting, but he felt the loss of comrades killed at his side very deeply. "The joys and wild delight of conflicts followed by the ever-lasting bitter regrets." His months of active service on the Nile had given him confidence and experience. We sense again his extraordinary coolness under fire and gift for making the right decision and his wonderful qualities of leadership. An entry in his journal speaks for itself:

I found gun and limber stuck, with the gun's crew and escort taking shelter amongst the ruined houses from a perfect hail of bullets and shell-fire that swept the street . . . Another minute and the limber boxes would be blown up, and it was the *work of a second*[1] to get the gun's crew out and retire the gun.

The gun and its crew were saved, but Beatty's A.D.C., Mid-shipman Esdaile, was mortally wounded.

It was a merciful Providence that caused us to go and see what was going on, otherwise there would have been a catastrophe and a lost gun. But at what a price! My best midshipman knocked over . . . It was the worst I have had, and I can never forget it.

His personal safety was something he simply didn't think about. "Beatty had no fear," wrote a brother officer, Captain C. C. Walcott, "or better still, nobody ever knew if he had any."

But he was not reckless, only running risks which he believed necessary. It was particularly galling for a man of his temperament to be reproved by a General (of whose competence he had a low opinion) for suggesting that a force he was commanding should seek shelter when caught in an open position by enfilading fire. Beatty received "a very unnecessary rude message" to remain where he was until he received orders to move—"downright crass stupidity" which cost a number of valuable lives. The order to take cover was eventually given and the wounded men had either to be abandoned or brought in under conditions which led to the award of a V.C. to Midshipman Guy. Many thought that Beatty himself, directing operations with his arm in a sling, was at least as

---

[1] My italics.

gallant. Guy himself remembers how Beatty was "an absolute inspiration" to them all "so cool and collected and absolutely fearless," telling Guy, who wanted to take his place at the handle of a stretcher, to "get the hell out of it."

When the list of honours and awards for the campaign was published, all who had served with him were delighted to see that Commander David Beatty, D.S.O., had been specially promoted to Captain. He was only twenty-nine, thirteen years younger than the average age at which officers reached that rank and had jumped over the heads of 218 other Commanders.

His wounds were still troubling him and when he returned to England he went into a nursing home for an operation. Three weeks after being discharged and strictly against the doctor's orders, he was in the hunting field.

He was on the top of the world, for he was again seeing Ethel Tree, whom he had never ceased to love (and never did). Though only twenty-five she had been living apart from her husband for nearly two years, without any judicial separation. Now Ethel had discovered that she was as much in love with the proud and elusive Beatty as he with her. She would never return to her husband, who eventually consented to sue for a divorce on the grounds of desertion. There was no question of Beatty being the co-respondent; indeed he had seen her only infrequently, in the hunting field and other public places. The private lives of a millionaire's daughter and the youngest Captain in the Royal Navy would have been front pages news even in 1900. But there was no scandal, and when they were quietly married everyone except a very few relatives was amazed.

Lucky Beatty had done it again   He now had a rich and beautiful wife, a hunting-box at Brooksby in Leicestershire, Grantully Castle in Scotland, Hanover Lodge in London and the steam yacht *Sheelah*. Young, charming, good-looking and well-heeled, the Beattys were very popular. For two years they lived a gay, extravagant life, for Beatty, still partly incapacitated by his old wounds, was unemployed. But in 1902 he was appointed to the cruiser *Juno*, first in the Home Fleet under the redoubtable "Tug" Wilson and then in the Mediterranean where Lord Charles Beresford was Commander-in-Chief. When the *Juno* paid off he took over the cruiser *Arrogant* and later the *Suffolk*.

It was, on the whole, a happy time. The Beattys were very much in love. Malta was gay; Ethel content. Beatty enjoyed being in command, though often exasperated by the attitude of his much older brother Captains. War would come one of these days and little, as he believed, was being done to prepare for it. He was a long-sighted, imaginative man who felt very strongly that the enormous changes in strategy and tactics called for by new and revolutionary ships and weapons were not being sufficiently studied, and that developments in material were not being matched by progress in its use. Beresford, whose long battle for a Naval Staff had been defeated by successive Boards of the Admiralty, was on his side, but most of the other flag officers and captains were unimpressed. The progressive minority was largely made up of those who followed Jacky Fisher—men, as Beatty believed, who were more concerned with forging the weapon than with wielding it. Beatty was prepared to leave material to the technicians. His study was *war*.

As a Captain he was efficient, strict and rather ruthless; respected, but not extravagantly popular, though men were proud to serve under him and his ships did well. His youth and wealth caused a certain amount of jealousy. It was all very well to have such independent ways if you had the Marshall Field millions at your back. Ever since the Nile he had been the sort of man about whom legends are retailed, more or less founded on fact, but losing nothing in the telling. On one occasion *Suffolk*'s machinery was damaged through Beatty ignoring the advice of his Chief Engineer. Ethel (so ran the story) was believed to have exclaimed: "What—court-martial my David? I'll buy them a new ship!" His friendship with the Commander-in-Chief was noted and sourly commented upon, but no one could deny that the *Suffolk* was clean, smart, happy and efficient.

Three years at sea were followed by a year on half-pay and his only shore appointment until he reached flag rank, as Naval Adviser to the Army Council. In 1908 he was back at sea in command of the battleship *Queen* in the Atlantic Fleet. Fisher had been four years at the Admiralty; material progress was considerable, but there was still no Naval Staff, in the accepted sense and the study of war was neglected. The tactical problems which the new weapons, particularly the torpedo and modern guns of much greater range, had introduced, were not being worked out. Ships had been concentrated in home waters to meet the rapidly growing menace of German sea power, but the leadership afloat was lagging behind. A proper doctrine of how great fleets should be handled in action was lacking. Beatty, increasingly convinced of the inevitability of war, was worried. Selected to lead twelve hundred bluejackets through the streets of the City of London, when the fleet was anchored off Southend, he made a grave speech at the Mansion House, replying to the toast of ".the Navy."

Never in the history of the world has there been so overpowering a preparation for war. The time must be drawing very close when the efficiency of the Navy will be put to the test.

His vision of the future was often astonishing clear. Five years before the war he wrote to his wife:

When the blow falls we shall be unprepared, suffer many losses, and lose many lives and valuable assets . . . out of the debris we shall dig our way to a successful issue.

He feared the singleness of purpose of the Germans, contrasting it with dissensions between the Fisher and Beresford factions which were weakening his own Service—quarrels in which he refused to be involved though personally friendly with Beresford, and admiring much that Fisher was trying to do, though not his methods.

The Atlantic Fleet was often based on such remote places as Berehaven and there were long separations from Ethel, whose social activities kept her very busy doing the right thing at the right time. She had always acted as she pleased and was not prepared to alter her habits. The long battle between Ethel and the Navy was beginning; the Navy always won, but Beatty was the chief casualty. He missed her very much. Being so much younger than his fellow-captains made him rather a lonely figure. He had always discussed his problems with her. She was intelligent, good about people, and had inherited some of her millionaire father's flair. He would take long walks ashore, returning on board to write to her about his work, about themselves—revealing letters which show a man utterly devoted to the Service, passionately fond of his wife and much more human than the popular conception of a heroic but slightly forbidding figure. A dance was given for the fleet at Queenstown where "we bumped and banged away with glorious creatures we've never seen before and never shall see again." The scents of the land were carried by the offshore breeze as they steamed past Flamborough Head, "a great bluff that sticks out into the sea like the nose of a shark . . . very solid and homely."

With all his preoccupations with a complicated life ashore Beatty loved the sea:

Then we steamed into the fog . . . could see nothing, hear nothing except the wash of water on the bow, and I sat on the rail of the bridge and opened my lungs and swallowed long draughts of damp, soft, pure, warm air . . . [one of his officers] thought I was mad because I said what a nice night it was. And I pictured you in stuffy London surrounded by a polluted atmosphere and the crowds of hunters of excitement which is principally composed of doing something which others don't do and consequently the enjoyment lies in making one's friends envious, isn't it?

Ethel's replies were irregular and brief, sometimes by telegram. She would send him flowers from the South of France which arrived "poor sweet things, crushed and mostly dead." She was too busy to tell him the sort of intimate details he wanted to know, but only very occasionally did this rather intolerant man show even a trace of impatience. "Well, I fear that, if there is no news to be obtained at Ascot during Ascot week, there is not much chance for Oban" on a Scottish Sabbath.

He was worried that their marriage was drifting on to the rocks because of these long separations, yet when the *Queen* had to spend Christmas at Gibraltar Ethel made no attempt to join him. He wrote her a long, rather humble letter: "if only you are happy and contented, so am I, but I fear I am making a hash of it somehow."

It was just as well that he had, at under thirty-nine, reached the top of the Captains' list and would be relieved in January.

A Special Order in Council was necessary before he could be promoted to Rear-Admiral as he had been at sea only three years and five months as a Captain, largely because of the en-forced period on half-pay due to his China wounds. On 1 January 1910 he became the youngest flag officer in the British Navy for over a hundred years, though Rodney at thirty-one and Albemarle, thirty-seven, had been younger still. For two years he was on half-pay, refusing a junior flag appointment to the Atlantic Fleet offered by the First Lord—a refusal which was generally believed to put paid to his chances of further employment. Evidently, said his critics, this meteoric young man was more concerned in living the life of a rich socialite than in serving his country. But Beatty had a deep confidence in his own destiny. "The stormiest, most exciting and success-ful that ever was seen" which a fortune teller had promised some years before would surely be his. He had felt in his bones that the post he had been offered was not the right one. Some-thing else would turn up.

The year after Beatty was promoted Winston Churchill be-came First Lord of the Admiralty. What he had heard of Beatty had not been much to that officer's advantage. "He had got on too fast. He had many interests on shore. His heart, it was said, was not wholly in the Service." They met, and Churchill decided immediately to "disregard this unfortunate advice" and make Beatty his Naval Secretary. Churchill had come to the Admiralty with his "mind full of the dangers of war." In Beatty he had found a proven fighting man who was not blinded by detail. "He did not think of material as an end in itself, but only as a means. He thought of war problems in their unity by land, sea and air." For over a year they worked together in harmony, increasingly convinced that at any moment war with Germany might come. There was a short break in 1912, when Beatty took over a Cruiser Squadron for the manoeuvres. In March 1913 when the command of the Battle-Cruiser Squadron became vacant Churchill "had no doubts whatever" in offering the forty-one year old Rear-Admiral this post, second only in importance to that of C.-in-C., passing him over the heads of many of his seniors.

Beatty accepted with alacrity, but his first actions were typical. His flagship the *Lion* was refitting at Plymouth. He visited her briefly, satisfied himself that his flag captain, Chatfield,[1] had everything very much under control and went off on leave to Monte Carlo, returning in the middle of the night (by taxi from London) a few hours before the Squadron was due to sail. It was neither recklessnes nor irresponsibility which made him act like this, but the belief, which many hold but which few are strong enough to live up to, that capable men produce the best results with the minimum of interference, and that his job was to think and plan ahead, not to fill his mind with details.

Once on board he lost no time in moulding his force to his ideas. Ships capable of steaming at 28 knots were still exercising and manoeuvring at half that speed or less. Guns with a range of nearly ten miles did target practice at a few thousand yards. With the co-operation of the Commander-in-Chief, Sir George Callaghan, but in the face of considerable opposition from the Admiralty (where Wilson had relieved Fisher), he insisted on manoeuvring at 24 knots in close order and firing at 16,000 yards and high speed. The combination of vibration and long range showed up serious defects in the range finders, defects which unfortunately had not been rectified two years later.

The battle-cruisers were the fastest and most powerfully

[1] Later Admiral of the Fleet Lord Chatfield.

armed ships in the world, but their functions had never been properly defined. This Beatty proceeded to do, preparing a paper which accurately anticipated requirements of the coming war.

In long walks ashore with his flag captain, he would continually discuss the problems war would bring. "Confident in his own judgment," wrote Lord Chatfield who served with him until 1918, "he was able by careful mental preparation to decide rapidly on his next step without hesitation or visible anxiety."

He took great pains to know and be known by the men of his squadron, frequently visiting other ships from the *Lion* and explaining his views to his Captains.

Ethel continued to lead her own life, though sometimes arriving in the *Sheelah* at harbours where the battle-cruisers were lying. A letter, unusually sharp in tone, takes her severely to task for trying to persuade Prince Louis of Battenberg, the First Sea Lord, and Winston Churchill to send the Battle-Cruiser Squadron to a place which suited her for Whitsun. When they were separated he wrote to her daily, sometimes a little bitterly:

Your wire of yesterday just received. Well, love, you might be a little more communicative. It's only twopence a word. Give me a shillingsworth—and say how the weather is. It brightens me up for instance to know the weather is fine.

In July 1914 he was awarded the K.C.B. in the Birthday Honours.

On 2 August the Fleet had passed up the North Sea and was on its war station at Scapa Flow.

"Keep a strong heart, dear one," he wrote to his wife, "you have much trouble, trial and tribulation before you."

A few days after war was declared, he found time to send Ethel the names and addresses of four young men in the *Lion* who were engaged to be married asking her to write to them. During the next few years she was to use her considerable abilities to great effect in the service of the men of the Fleet and their wives and dependants.

But the action which everyone had expected to follow the outbreak of war did not come. "This waiting is the deuce," wrote Beatty. He did not have to wait very long.

On 27 August 1914 Beatty, with the battle-cruisers *Lion*, *Princess Royal* and *Queen Mary* and six light cruisers under Commodore Goodenough, sailed from Scapa Flow. At 5 a.m. on 26 January he rendezvoused with two more battle-cruisers, the *New Zealand* (Rear-Admiral Moore) and *Invincible*.

The Admiralty was conducting operations in the Heligoland Bight, using light forces from Harwich: cruisers and destroyers under Commodore Tyrwhitt and submarines under Commodore Keyes. Tyrwhitt was to close Heligoland at 8 a.m. and sweep westward, hoping to mop up German patrols. The submarines, after acting as a bait, would intercept ships which escaped the drag-net or came out in support. Carried out on the enemy's front doorstep, it was a sufficiently daring plan.

At dawn on 28 January some of Tyrwhitt's ships mistook Goodenough's cruisers for the enemy and nearly opened fire on them. Staff work had been ragged, and neither Tyrwhitt nor Keyes had been told that Beatty's ships would be out in support.

An hour before the westward sweep was to begin, Tyrwhitt sighted some German destroyers, chased them to the eastward to within sight of Heligoland and was heavily engaged by German cruisers hurrying to their assistance. In an inconclusive action, broken off when the enemy disappeared into the mist, Tyrwhitt's own ship, the light cruiser *Arethusa*, was badly damaged.

The westward sweep began, one German destroyer being sunk, but Keyes now sighted Goodenough, reported him as "enemy cruisers" and brought Tyrwhitt hurrying back in support. It was after 11 a.m. before Tyrwhitt again turned west. He had been in the Bight for over four hours, the crippled *Arethusa* could only steam at slow speed and his force was still close to Heligoland, with other German bases on its flank. Three definitely hostile cruisers now appeared. Others were on the way. Tyrwhitt was in a very tight spot.

P

Beatty, some thirty miles north-west of Tyrwhitt, had received very little information about what was going on in the mist ahead. Radio sighting reports indicated a large number of enemy ships, but he correctly deduced that some of our forces were mistaking friend for foe. He had broken wireless silence to give his own position and had ordered Goodenough to find and support Tyrwhitt, from whom he had heard nothing since 8 a.m., and who must be in trouble. To the surprise of some of his staff he did not immediately move in himself, refusing to be drawn in what might be a wrong direction. At 11.25 a.m. he at last heard from Tyrwhitt, only twenty-six miles from Heligoland and hard-pressed by German cruisers.

"The situation," as he wrote in his report, "seemed to me extremely critical."

He at once decided to take the battle-cruisers at full speed to the eastward, accepting the danger of hazarding his great ships in a position where enemy submarines were likely—he had already sighted three—and our own submarines were unaware of his presence. He might encounter strong German forces issuing from the River Jade, only twenty-five miles south of Tyrwhitt's reported position, but if he was quick enough he could probably forestall them. Within five minutes the battle-cruisers, led by the *Lion*, were working up to full speed. Black smoke billowed from their funnels as their crews hurried to action stations and loaded the great guns. On the flagship's bridge Beatty, calm and concise, but elated at the thought of battle, swept the misty horizon for his first sight of the enemy.

At 12.15 p.m. gunfire could be heard. Flashes stabbed the mist and shortly afterwards Tyrwhitt's ships loomed up ahead. A destroyer officer described how the battle-cruisers came tearing out of the murk "in lovely procession, like elephants" to save the day. Long tongues of flame and clouds of cordite smoke enveloped the great, grey ships as their turrets fired. Of the four German cruisers in sight, *Köln* was soon a blazing wreck; three salvoes disposed of *Ariadne*; *Strasburg* and *Stral-*

sund managed to make off into the mist. Beatty turned in a wide circle, finished off the *Köln* and gave the order to retire.

It was a satisfactory finish to a day which, but for Beatty, might have ended disastrously. All our ships returned safely to harbour. The Germans lost three cruisers and a destroyer and over a thousand officers and men, and the fact that British heavy ships had ventured so close to their fleet bases caused the Kaiser to issue an order that risks were not to be taken without his approval; instructions which handicapped the High Seas Fleet for several months.

"In an emergency," wrote Admiral Chatfield, "you will act as you have trained yourself to act."

In battle, as in games, *timing* is all important. Beatty had acted at exactly the right moment, making a bold stroke and withdrawing before he could be overwhelmed. He had fully upheld the reputation won in Egypt and China as a fearless fighting man. He had also proved that he possessed the no less important characteristic of being able to divine, from incomplete and often inaccurate information, what was happening.

Without this peculiar gift [wrote Wolseley in his *Life of Marlborough*] no campaign can be directed with success. To realise what is going on beyond the range of human vision is one of the problems which perpetually confronts the Commander . . . From a minute and close study of the possible, he [must be] able to calculate the probable.

Those who stood with Beatty on the bridge of the *Lion* had noted that when the guns began to speak he became even more than himself; thoughts clarified and vision sharpened by the danger. If anything was needed to confirm their complete confidence in their chief he had given it to them.

Until the end of the year the enemy fleet was inactive, but submarines took a considerable toll. Opinion which had at first inclined to regard these new weapons as useful only for coast defence, swung to the opposite extreme and began to credit them with extraordinary powers. (The same thing happened with the air in the 1939-45 war.) Fisher returned to the Admiralty as First Sea Lord. Beatty's Squadron was weakened by the despatch of three of his battle-cruisers against raiders on the high seas. *Invincible* and *Inflexible* were unquestionably the decisive factor in Sturdee's victory over von Spee's cruiser squadron in the Battle of the Falkland Islands, but in mid-December the Germans, taking advantage of the comparative weakness of the North Sea battle-cruiser force, decided on a sortie. On 15 December von Hipper's scouting force bombarded Hartlepool and Scarborough. The weather was bad, with low visibility and a very rough sea. Beatty, with four battle-cruisers, supported by Admiral Warrender's Second Battle Squadron of six ships, was between Hipper and his base. The opposing battle-cruisers passed very close to one another in the mist and fire was exchanged between one of Beatty's scouting cruisers and a German light cruiser. The writer Filson Young, serving on the staff in the *Lion* as a Lieutenant, R.N.V.R., tells how Beatty, behind whom he was standing, saw the flash of gunfire in the swirling mist ahead, turned and pressed his hand on Young's shoulder with the eager words: "We've got them!"

But it was not to be. With visibility sometimes less than two miles, contact was lost and the Germans escaped. Beatty was bitterly disappointed. "I can't bear to write about it," he told Ethel, "and I can think of nothing else."

To give better protection to the east coast the Admiralty moved the battle-cruisers from Scapa Flow to Rosyth; nearer the enemy bases, but without a safe exercising area where practices could be carried out.

On 23 January Beatty with *Lion, Princess Royal, New Zealand* and *Indomitable* and the brand-new *Tiger* was in the Firth of Forth. As darkness fell the great ships were lying peacefully moored above the bridge. Next morning the anchorage was empty.

The Admiralty, whose intelligence was excellent, had warned him that Hipper was coming out again. Since dawn Beatty had been on the bridge of the *Lion*. Commodore Tyrwhitt's cruisers and destroyers from Harwich were to rendezvous with him at 7.15 a.m. As contact was made one of Tyrwhitt's cruisers reported that she was in action with the

enemy. It was Hipper! Correctly deducing that he was confronted by superior forces, the German Admiral turned about
and made off at high speed.

But the British position was highly favourable. It was a
clear, calm winter's day with maximum visibility. Hipper with
Seydlitz, *Moltke*, *Derfflinger* and *Blücher*, a light cruiser
squadron and a flotilla of destroyers, was one hundred and
fifty miles from home. He was handicapped by the presence
of the armoured cruiser *Blücher* whose maximum speed was
only twenty-four knots. Making his dispositions for the chase
Beatty went below to have his breakfast.

Returning to the bridge he gave the order for 27, 28 and
finally 29 knots. This was a knot faster than the maximum
speed of his fastest battle-cruiser, but it would encourage the
stokers, working like demons far below. Smoke billowed away
over foaming wakes as Beatty gradually overhauled the enemy.
Lion, *Tiger* and *Princess Royal* drew ahead of the older and
slower *New Zealand* and *Indomitable*. Ranging shots were exchanged. Shortly after 9 a.m. *Lion* crossed the target. Battle
had been joined.

It was a strange scene as the two fleets tore along, forcing
their way through the calm sea. Speed and effort everywhere,
but the distance between the opposing ships, still nearly ten
miles, reduced only at walking pace. Columns of spray, masthead high, rose around them from shells falling short or over.
Sometimes a dull flash proclaimed a hit.

At 9.45 a.m. the *Blücher* was dropping back. Beatty had
slightly reduced speed to allow *New Zealand* and *Indomitable*
to come up, but Hipper was still over a hundred miles from
home. This time he really had "got them."

The enemy had been concentrating his fire on the *Lion*
which had been hit several times, putting one of her four main
turrets out of action and doing other damage. After an hour's
engagement at long range the *Blücher* had fallen some distance
astern of the German battle-cruisers and was obviously suffering severely. *Seydlitz* had both after turrets out of action;
Derfflinger was on fire. But in this first action between heavy

ships the British fire was hampered by something which peace-time exercises had failed to reveal. The speed at which the battle-cruisers were steaming into the wind (on their engaged bow) hurled sheets of spray and tons of solid water from enemy "shorts" over their decks, obscuring the gunlayers' view and reducing the rate of fire. Only the brand-new *Tiger* was fitted with a director [1] (above the spray-level), and she had not had the necessary practice to do good shooting. But the day was still young, there was plenty of time. Beatty was in his element, watching the distant enemy and calmly giving his orders, quite indifferent to the pandemonium around him—the blast and smoke-clouds from the *Lion*'s great guns, the enemy shells crashing aboard or deluging the decks, the spray which soaked him to the skin and periodically hid the smudge along the horizon peppered with stabs of flame which was Hipper's battle line. Filson Young, watching it all with his trained civilian eye, wrote later that Beatty and his flag-captain Chatfield, "enjoyed this performance more than I have ever seen anything enjoyed by anyone—a child-like blandness of demeanour which I had at no other time observed in either of them, but which had nothing whatever of insanity in it."

After nearly two hours' fighting the *Blücher* had hauled out of the enemy line with a heavy list, on fire and obviously done for. Two of the German battle-cruisers were still concentrating on the *Lion*, which now received so violent a blow that many thought she had been torpedoed. A heavy shell striking below the water-line had driven in an armour plate, puncturing the port main feed tank and putting half her engines out of action. Making water rapidly, listing to port and gradually slowing down *Lion* could no longer retain her place in the line. At this juncture a submarine was reported on the dis-engaged bow. Beatty turned his ships sharply to port. *Lion* was now listing ten degrees. Her speed was down to 15 knots and all electrical power had failed. With radio out of action Beatty, using the only signal halyards which had not been shot

[1] See *Scott*, page 162.

away, tried to transfer the command to Rear-Admiral Moore in the *New Zealand*. Nelson's "Engage the enemy more closely" had been removed from the book, so he hoisted "Attack the enemy's rear." This signal was flying at the same time as his "Course N.E." "This would have cut the enemy battle-cruisers off from the *Blücher* should they turn to support her, as I anticipated they would. Should they leave her to her fate our ships could have again turned to a parallel course" wrote Beatty in his report on the action.

Moore, who had seen no submarine, did not know why Beatty had turned to port. The severely damaged *Blücher* bore North-east at the time. As the wounded *Lion* dropped out of the hunt Beatty was mortified to see all his remaining battle-cruisers leave Hipper to escape and make for the already doomed armoured cruiser. A destroyer was called alongside the *Lion*. Beatty leapt aboard, hoping to overtake and hoist his flag in the *Princess Royal*. Grimy stokers taking a breather on the *Lion*'s upper deck raised a cheer. "Well done, David," shouted one of them, "finish 'em off!"

"The scene when he left the ship was something beyond words," wrote Beatty's flag-lieutenant, Ralph Seymour, to his mother a few days later.

The men came up from below to see the Admiral leave, and the sight of him seemed to send them off their heads . . . *Lion* was one huge grandstand of cheering men, but she looked rather a sad sight heeled over to port with a good many holes in her side.

But it was too late. Hipper had escaped. Moore continued to carry out what he believed to be his orders. What Beatty would have done if their positions had been reversed is not in doubt.

The *Blücher*, fighting bravely to the end, was sunk. The disabled *Lion* was brought back to harbour, but the crippling blow which for a time had seemed so certain was not delivered. The press made much of the "victory" of the Dogger Bank, but Beatty was bitterly disappointed. In his despatch he accepted full responsibility for the failure to follow up and destroy the enemy, avoiding even an implied criticism of Moore. Privately he must have agreed with Jacky Fisher:

> I've already written to tell you that you're splendid, [said the First Sea Lord,] but I cannot understand . . . why *Tiger* and *Princess Royal* absolutely unharmed did not go and finish off *Derfflinger* and *Seydlitz* . . . It's quite terrible to me that they should have been allowed to go free at noon. What possible explanation is there? What excuse have we to offer?

The *Lion* was repaired. The battle-cruisers, reinforced by additional ships, were at pains to make use of the experience gained in this first battle between modern ships. Unfortunately for the British the most important lesson of the Dogger Bank was only available to the Germans. *Seydlitz* had been nearly destroyed by a fire which ignited the ready-use ammunition in both the after turrets, killed over a hundred men and severely threatened the magazines. Warned by this experience, the Germans modified all their heavy ships to prevent flash from spreading in this way. The British, without this terrible object lesson, continued unaware of the danger.

Beatty was forty-four; a handsome, active, youthful-looking man who carried responsibility without visible effort. Everything about him was highly individual; his uniform with its slightly horsy cut, six buttons on his monkey jacket instead of the usual eight, a very broad peak to the cap he wore at the well-known Beatty tilt.[1] At first glance the keen strong face was a little grim and haughty, an impression soon removed by his frank speech ("half the ills in the world would vanish if people spoke their minds"), lively eyes and a personal magnetism almost as tangible as a visible aura. Powerful, broad-shouldered, lithe, he looked a fighter; poised and ready, wary, thoughtful; calculating rather than impetuous. Clearly a man who could be relentless and did not suffer fools gladly, but you would know where you stood with him.

He had the power of all great leaders of making others wish to do his will, fired by his own confidence that what he wanted

---

[1] His biographer, Rear-Admiral Chalmers, explains the tilt was due to a formation of the head.

was right. The admiration and respect of his staff was evident, their loyalty absolute. They would have followed him anywhere, but there was something a little lonely about the man himself.

He believed that no man can think really straight or shoulder great responsibilities unless he is physically fit. In harbour he landed every morning before breakfast, pulling himself ashore in a skiff if the tide allowed, for a brisk walk. Dealing with paper-work during the forenoon he usually remained on his feet, standing at a high desk, rapidly picking out the essential; letters and papers quickly finding their way into two trays marked OUT and BALDERDASH. Visitors and office business were dealt with until the early afternoon when he would land and drive to Aberdour House six miles from Rosyth where Ethel and his two small sons, David and Peter, were living. After some hard sets of tennis, a round of golf or a long walk he would be back on board at 7 p.m. He always changed for dinner, a leisurely meal eaten with his staff or with guests. This was a time for relaxation. If there was a cinema show on board he would attend it, remaining to the end of the programme even when, as was quite often the case, the squadron was getting under way to slip out to sea in the dark. From August 1914 to November 1918 he slept on board his ship every night.

He made a point of being known in other ships of his fleet, attending such functions as boxing matches and concert parties. Often he would conclude the proceedings with a brief, sailor-like talk, giving his men his views and firing them with his own conviction that the constant practices, weary waiting and arduous sweeps over an empty sea would one day be rewarded in victorious battle.

His wife had thrown herself whole-heartedly into the work of converting the *Sheelah* to a hospital ship, turning Brooksby Hall into a convalescent home, and providing canteens for the men of the battle-cruiser force. She was an able woman of strong character who knew how to get things done, but she quickly tired of any activity. She resented seeing so little of her husband and his preoccupation with his work. Relations between them became somewhat strained. The comparative inactivity and the effort of always appearing confident that the longed-for battle would come, when he felt in his heart of hearts it was less and less likely, were telling on Beatty at that time. He wanted Ethel to be happy and contented and did his best to help her, when she might so well have been helping him.

You see in the past, [he wrote to her] you have spoilt me horribly and given me so much love and sympathy that it is difficult to realise I must do without it or without so much of it. It is unfortunate (for me) that it should come at a time when we can do with so much more.

Ethel thought him selfish and self-centred. She was an intelligent woman, but jealousy of the Navy blinded her. Why couldn't he be gay and light-hearted? He tried to explain his feelings and those of his men.

If you think what the fact of being immediately ready for battle means in mind and spirit as well as in organisation and detail, you will realise it is not a frame of mind or condition of life that one wants to dwell in longer than can be helped.

1915 ended quietly in the North Sea, but with the new year came a change. The events leading to the Battle of Jutland have already been described. When one of Beatty's scouting cruisers reported hostile ships in sight Beatty immediately set a course to get between them and their base. Soon afterwards the German battle-cruisers were discerned on the horizon. It was his old adversary Hipper.

Beatty in the *Lion* had with him *Princess Royal*, *Queen Mary*, *Tiger*, *New Zealand* and *Indefatigable*. Hipper was in the *Lützow* with *Derfflinger*, *Seydlitz*, *Moltke* and *Van der Tann*. Neither admiral was aware that his opponent was supported by a battle fleet in the offing and when Hipper turned (to fall back on Scheer) Beatty assumed that he was making off, as he had always done before. Without waiting for the Fifth Battle Squadron of four fast battleships which was ten miles on his port quarter to catch up, Beatty at once closed Scheer and engaged him in battle. The presence of the Fifth Battle

Squadron would, of course, have given him an overwhelming superiority over Hipper, but past experience had shown him how easily a few wasted minutes could result in the escape of his enemy. He had full confidence in his own ships. The enemy battle-cruisers were difficult to see against a misty horizon whereas his own ships would be silhouetted against the clear western sky, but this was a tactical disadvantage which must be accepted.

A furious action ensued, with both squadrons steaming at high speed. The German shooting was good and hits were scored almost immediately, though the first few shells which struck the *Lion* had no notable effect. Twelve minutes after the opening of the battle the range was down to 14,000 yards and both sides were heavily engaged. It was now that a shell penetrated the roof of *Lion*'s midship turret, killed nearly all the crew and set fire to the ready-use cordite charges. Only the extraordinary courage of Major F. W. J. Harvey, R.M.L.I., who gasped out an order to flood the magazine as he lay mortally wounded saved the ship from destruction. A few minutes later *Indefatigable*, last ship of the line, was suddenly enveloped in a huge cloud of smoke through which she could clearly be discerned as she rolled right over and sank. At almost the same moment the *Lion* suffered a number of hits which put her radio out of action and started several fires. The Fifth Battle Squadron now joined in the fight, but three minutes later the *Queen Mary*, third ship in the British line, suffered the same fate as *Indefatigable*; a gush of flame, an enormous column of smoke crowned by a mushroom head and the great ship was gone, so suddenly that the *Tiger*, the next astern, passed through the wreckage.

During this tremendous half-hour Beatty had been on the unprotected bridge, calmly giving his orders. Captain Chatfield was standing beside him. Something made them both look round at the very moment when the *Queen Mary* was destroyed. "There seems," said Beatty as he turned away from that awesome spectacle to continue his direction of the battle, "to be something wrong with our bloody ships today."

He was outwardly as calm as ever when the tremendous news came through a few minutes later that Commander Goodenough in one of the scouting cruisers had sighted the German battle fleet. Beatty altered course at once towards the position where Scheer had been reported, holding on until he saw across the horizon ahead the forest of masts and funnels of the High Seas Fleet. Then and not till then he turned sixteen points, ostensibly in full retreat, but really to draw Scheer to Jellicoe.

"In an emergency you will act as you have trained yourself to act." It has been argued by his detractors that Beatty "lost" the battle-cruiser action on 31 May because two of his ships were destroyed on the run south. It would be fairer to say that he coolly and calmly carried out his intentions and continued to follow a definite plan when faced with a wholly unexpected weakness of material. With *Indefatigable* and *Queen Mary* sunk and *Lion* only narrowly avoiding a similar fate he held on until he had confirmed Goodenough's report, and then fell back on Jellicoe in good order. On the run north he continued to engage Hipper's battle-cruisers.

The function of the battle-cruisers was to force back the enemy cruisers, locate the enemy's main fleet, keep in touch and make sure that our own main fleet was not uncovered too soon. This Beatty did. As a result Scheer's High Seas Fleet found itself suddenly confronted by the battleships of the Grand Fleet. In the concluding stages of the daylight action, when Jellicoe had lost touch with Scheer after the German torpedo attack, it was Beatty's battle-cruisers, which had seen *Invincible* follow *Indefatigable* and *Queen Mary* to destruction, which closed the German battleships and fired the last shots of the main battle as darkness fell.

Beatty's biographer, Rear-Admiral W. S. Chalmers, gives us a moving postscript. It was the afternoon of 1 June. That morning *Lion* had buried her hundred dead at sea. Now she was returning to Rosyth. The battered decks seemed strangely quiet after the turmoil of the evening before. Beatty, greatly moved by the burial service, had gone back to the bridge. Now he walked slowly into the chart house where Chalmers was working, settled himself on the settee and closed his eyes. It was twenty-four hours since the battle began and he must have been deadly tired. "Unable to hide his disappointment at the result of the battle," writes Chalmers, "he repeated in a weary voice, 'There is something wrong with our ships;' then opening his eyes and looking at [me] he added, 'And something wrong with our system.' Having thus unburdened himself he fell asleep."

When Jellicoe was called to the Admiralty in November 1916 Beatty succeeded to the command of the Grand Fleet. All eyes were upon him. Some said he would destroy the organisation that Jellicoe had so painstakingly built up. Others delightedly averred that now we should at last see action, with Beatty trailing his coat across the North Sea, the Germans following after to be caught and destroyed. In the event both factions were wrong. Beatty, who fully appreciated Jellicoe's administrative genius, rapidly won the confidence of the Grand Fleet's officers and men. He was equally alive to the limitations of the strategic situation with its utterly disproportionate risks. He was now the "only man who could lose the war in an afternoon." He was quick to try and remove what he believed was "wrong with our system": the too rigid and too centralised control which hampered initiative, prevented opportunities being seized and gave rise to a defensive rather than an offensive outlook. "Battle orders" became "Battle Instructions"—a clear statement of basic principles rather than a detailed guide. Their theme was clear: attack when you can; accept some risk; *never* lose contact with the enemy.

The great Jutland controversy had already begun, though Beatty took no part in it. Jutland for him, as he wrote to his wife, was "one of the saddest days of my life, on which I lost so many old and trusted comrades. That terrible day when we might have accomplished so much."

He continued to speak and act as if he was convinced that

there would be another chance, upholding and encouraging his great fleet in the long months of waiting and preparation. His confidence seemed so genuine that it was infectious though we know through his letters that he was increasingly aware that the task for which his whole life had so fittingly prepared him would never come his way. "Fate is not over-generous in the matter of giving opportunities and if you miss one you will never get another."

The lines on his face were deeper, his eyes graver, but outwardly he was very little changed. His tremendous fleet, reinforced by an American battle-squadron under Admiral Rodman, was the most powerful the world has ever seen. To keep so many thousand men happy and contented was no easy task. When the Fourth of July came round he sent Rodman to the other side of the Flow to celebrate. "I told them to do what they liked. What they *can* do it is hard to say." Rodman and his men became firm friends of Beatty and their "comrades of the mist."[1]

The dramatic surrender of the German High Sea Fleet, decisive as it might be, was a day of muted triumph. Four days after the Armistice in November 1918 Admiral Muerer came to Rosyth in the cruiser *Königsberg* to receive Beatty's instructions. It was night when Muerer was brought on board the *Queen Elizabeth*. Lights blazed down on top of the gangways and illuminated the way across the quarter-deck to the hatch leading below to Beatty's day-cabin. Everything else was in inky blackness, but the gleam of the fixed bayonets of the Marine guard was just visible. Fog shrouded the Firth, making the darkness thick and palpable.

Muerer was received in silence, led below and formally invited to sit down in the middle of the long dining table opposite Beatty. Between them stood Beatty's bronze lion.

"I have never seen him to better advantage," wrote Commander Seymour, with Beatty throughout the war. "He was courteous in the extreme and firm as a rock. He discussed

---

[1] The name of the post-war association between British and American sailors of the Grand Fleet.

details of the British and German Fleets without once referring
to a paper, although the British and German staffs were constantly looking up details." Muerer "the most deathly ashy
colour I have ever seen" could sometimes scarcely speak.

Beatty admitted afterwards that he could not resist a twinge
of compassion for another sailor in such a pass.

"When it came to signing the documents," he wrote to a
friend, "I thought he would collapse." Muerer returned to
the *Königsberg* through the silent, foggy darkness. Beatty
withdrew to his other cabin "and was nearly sick."

Six days later the High Seas Fleet, led by the British cruiser
Cardiff, steamed between the advancing lines of Beatty's ships.
The once-proud German battle-cruisers which had fought so
well were dirty. Unkempt men lounged about their decks. In
perfect formation the Grand Fleet swung round to escort them
to their anchorage in the Firth of Forth. It was over.

Back in harbour Captain Chatfield reported to Beatty that
the *Queen Elizabeth*'s ship's company were assembled on the
quarterdeck. Would he speak to them? Beatty complied very
briefly. It had been a painful if dramatic day. He turned to go
below, but with one foot on the gangway he paused, cocked his
eye, smiled and said:

"Didn't I tell you they would have to come out?"

Later a signal was made by the *Queen Elizabeth*:

"The German flag will be hauled down at sunset today and
not hoisted again without permission."

Beatty's great services to his country were well recognised.
He was promoted to Admiral of the Fleet, created an Earl and
awarded £100,000. Other honours flowed in from at home and
abroad; the Order of Merit, Honorary degrees, the freedom of
great cities. Ever since he was quite a young man he had been
accustomed to public adulation and he took it all in his stride.
He was deeply concerned about the future of the Navy. "Now
that the fighting is over," he had written to the American
Admiral Rodman, "the talking will begin." Much of this
talk was of a coming era when great navies would no longer be
needed and the cost of maintaining them could be saved.

Beatty, convinced that the future of his country depended on her retaining command of the sea, opposed this view. He was equally determined that the pay and conditions of the men of the Navy, long overdue for revision, should be brought more in line with those ruling in industry. In speeches made up and down the country, as he visited the cities which wished to honour him, he continually stressed both these points.

His flag was struck in the *Queen Elizabeth* in April 1919. Beatty went off on leave, his first holiday for nearly five years. The Admiralty had finally persuaded the Treasury to increase naval pay and in September 1919 Beatty again made history by attending a banquet given at Portsmouth Guildhall by the men of the lower deck, sitting between a chief writer and a petty officer. In November, at the age of forty-eight, he became First Sea Lord.

Great fighting men are only rarely great administrators. Beatty was a good organiser who trusted and cleverly guided his subordinates and had complete confidence in his own judgment. Comparative youth and physical fitness, which he was at pains to preserve, enabled him to carry the burdens of his high office for the very long period of over seven years. It would be idle to pretend that all the arrangements made during his time at the Admiralty were ideal, but the work he did between 1919 and 1927 was of inestimable value to the Navy. For Beatty proved to be a statesman.

In the wider field of national policy the problems he had to tackle were of great complexity; their solution of the most far-reaching results. The Washington Conference of 1921 limited the size of navies, giving Britain parity with the United States in capital ships. This could be accepted, but Britain with her world-wide responsibilities must be in a special class when it came to cruisers and smaller vessels. It fell to Beatty to educate the successive Governments in power at Westminster during his long period of office with the necessity of continuing to spend large sums on the Navy which they, beset by the social problems of the post-war world, wished to divert elsewhere. Beatty was greatly helped by his tremendous prestige with ordinary men and women of all classes and political parties. Though not a politician he had shrewd political sense, recognising that ultimate power rested in the people, who must always feel it was *their* wishes which were being met. But Britain is ruled by the Cabinet and it was Beatty's influence over successive Prime Ministers, Chancellors of the Exchequer and First Lords of the Admiralty which ensured success. Completely without awe for the great, clear and concise in his expositions, equable, forceful and with a nice touch of humour he got his way, not by intrigue, but by the strength of his character and the soundness of his views. Sir Maurice Hankey, Secretary to the Cabinet and of the Committee of Imperial Defence, wrote in 1927:

"You are the only First Sea Lord I have known in my twenty-six years experience who could really talk on even terms to the highest Cabinet Ministers and stand up to them in argument."

"All power corrupts." What was it that saved Beatty from that slow but deadly deterioration so often concomitant with reaching the top of the tree; wisdom gradually eclipsed by egoism? The answer may well lie in the extraordinary dual life he was forced to lead.

For his beloved wife was now a very sick woman, sick in the cruellest and most distressing of all ways; sick in mind. During practically the whole of Beatty's time at the Admiralty Ethel Beatty was suffering from a nervous breakdown. As is usual in that terrible disease she had her ups and downs, sometimes returning for a short time to normal health, but never for long. All too little is known about the causes and cure of mental illness in 1961. Forty years ago even the best of doctors were virtually helpless and there was less understanding by healthy people of a complaint, control of which is as much beyond the powers of the sufferer as the mending of broken bones. Beatty loved his wife. His care for her was unremitting. Night after night, after a long and tiring day, he would read to her when she could not sleep. He would sacrifice everything on her behalf, except his work. What he

Q

found difficult to understand was her insistence that he should abandon the Admiralty and go with her on her ceaseless journeyings abroad in search of a peace she would never find for long.

"I am a public man," he wrote to her, "and I have a right to ask you to do all you can to make yourself well, so that you can be of assistance to me in my life."

Poor Lady Beatty. It was beyond her powers to "make herself well," but perhaps she was of more assistance to her husband in his battle to save what he could of the Navy than either of them knew. The tremendous emotional struggle kept Beatty a humble man at heart, constantly aware of things beyond his control. With Ethel so often away he took her place with their two sons. "It is hard work being Daddy and Mummy to two boys," but it brought him down to simple things.

Beatty left the Admiralty in 1927. Five years later Ethel died. He loved her to the end, and there were some happy times when the family was together and Ethel's illness momentarily less severe. When she had gone he could "forget all the difficulties and only remember the sweetness of her."

At sixty-one Beatty was still remarkably young in body and mind: hunting four or five days a week; still living dangerously. He was for his age and weight one of the best and boldest horsemen in the "shires." His unmistakable face and sturdy figure and the way he cocked his eye and cracked a joke were as well-known as his habit of usually being somewhere pretty near the head of the hunt. With only his own well-being at stake he took more risks than ever and had a number of heavy falls; a serious one in 1933 when a kick in the face laid him low for several months. ("Hit on the jaw by a horse which wasn't wearing gloves and I did not 'pass out,' " was Beatty's comment.) Two years later, still suffering from the after effects of his hunting accidents, he caught influenza and was in bed on the morning of Jellicoe's funeral. Beatty insisted on getting up and taking his place as a pall bearer for the long procession through the streets of London, though no doubt feeling as ill as he looked. "His face might have been carved out of grey, hard stone," reported one of the newspapers. Within three months he was again disobeying doctor's orders to walk behind the coffin of King George V. "Not only my King, but my friend."

He died a few weeks later of a heart attack at the age of sixty-five. Rallying just before the end he said to his eldest son:

"I could ride from the Prince of Wales to Coplow now. Good-night, Sonny."

TYRWHITT

1870-1951

Commodore (T)[1]

ALL the careful apparatus of selection—examinations, confidential reports, promotion boards—is only moderately successful in forecasting who will succeed in war. The favourite sometimes wins, but it is often a new name which becomes a household word. "The true war leaders of the Navy had already emerged from the ranks of peace-time merit," wrote Winston Churchill on leaving the Admiralty in May 1915. Beatty, Keyes and Tyrwhitt head his list. History confirmed this early judgment. The first shot of the war at sea was fired by a destroyer of Tyrwhitt's Harwich Force. Led by their Com. (T) the light cruisers and destroyers under his command were more continuously in action with the enemy than any other ships. To have served under Tyrwhitt in World War I was to have been in the forefront of the fight.

Reginald Yorke Tyrwhitt was born in 1870. His father became the Vicar of St Mary Magdalen, Oxford, and some of his family were still living there fifty years later. Oxford was his "home town," but Tyrwhitt was essentially a countryman. His mother came from Yorkshire and young Reggie often stayed with his uncle at Beverley Hall—a second home to him as a boy.

He was a nice little boy, vigorous and high-spirited, but at the Dragon School where his serious education began he was not a scholastic success. "Dear Mr Tyrwhitt," wrote the head-

---

[1] Commodore Torpedo-Craft, and the name, usually abbreviated to Com. T, by which Tyrwhitt was invariably known in his own force, even when he became an Admiral.

master to his father when Reggie was transferred to Burney's
Naval Academy at Gosport to be "crammed" for the Naval
entrance examination, "your son Reggie is no good and will
come to a hard end." Even Burney's only succeeded in getting
him into the Navy at the third attempt, thirtieth of the thirty-
one successful entrants. In the training ship *Britannia* he did
better, passing out twenty-first two years later. His book-work
was undistinguished, but he was made a cadet captain, an early
indication of his powers of leadership, and he was very happy.
He went off to sea as a midshipman in the flagship of the
Mediterranean Fleet, the battleship *Alexandra*, where Beatty
was to join him two years later.

The life suited him admirably and he was very content,
visiting nearly every port in the Mediterranean and enjoying
himself enormously in spite "of a very limited cash account."
Lack of money was endemic to most of the midshipmen, but
it rarely prevented them from taking full advantage of any
opportunity which presented itself.

During one of her periodical cruises the *Alexandra* came to
Jaffa. Leave was granted to officers wishing to visit Jerusalem.
Tyrwhitt managed to "touch" his father for the £5 fee demanded by the enterprising local representative of Thomas
Cook and Son for the hire of a horse for the return journey and
accommodation in the Holy City. With seventy-nine other
officers he set off, arrived at his destination, "without incident
except loss of skin on certain parts of my anatomy" and spent
three days seeing the sights and being "for some reason" tat-
tooed with the Jerusalem Cross. The return journey was to be
made through the night, but when young Tyrwhitt went to
fetch his horse at 6 p.m. someone had already taken it. With
the Fleet due to sail at 12.30 p.m. on the following day the
situation was serious. He was alone, no one in the vicinity
understood a word of English, he had no money, and it was
forty miles to Jaffa. There was nothing for it but to
walk, so off he went. No one else seemed to be on the road,
and it was now quite dark. After about an hour a dim light
showed up ahead—a wayside inn outside which fifteen horses

were tethered. Voices and laughter came from the open door. One horse was somewhat separated from the others. Cautiously Tyrwhitt untied it, led the beast for a couple of hundred yards, mounted and galloped away. The horse was a good one and the pursuit, if any, was outdistanced, but he was a little disturbed to find that the beast he had commandeered was a cavalry horse evidently belonging to an officer. Shortly afterwards he picked up the rearguard of the rest of the party and halted with them at Ramleh, planning to resume the journey two hours later. It was still only 4.30 a.m. and young Tyrwhitt had had a busy night. Finding a quiet corner he went to sleep. He was tired, but content. At 6.30 a.m. the cavalcade moved away. Tyrwhitt slept on. At 8 a.m. "I woke. There was a deathly silence. Not a soul about." The cavalry horse had disappeared and in its place was a sorry nag, dead lame. He was still sixteen miles from Jaffa and again he had to walk, arriving at the landing place as the last boat was leaving. The Commander of the *Alexandra* to whom his absence had been reported promptly stopped his leave for the remainder of the cruise. Luckily for Tyrwhitt the Commander-in-Chief, H.R.H. the Duke of Edinburgh, was so amused by the whole incident that the punishment was rescinded. The horse young Tyrwhitt had made off with was the charger of the officer in command of the Duke's cavalry escort.

This incident has been recounted at some length because it gives a very good picture of Midshipman R. Y. Tyrwhitt, evidently a young gentleman of considerable resource.

After three years in the *Alexandra* Tyrwhitt was appointed to the little corvette *Calypso* in the training squadron. The captain was a martinet, the food was bad, the ships went almost everywhere under sail and life was hard, but he took it all in his stride, enjoyed the work aloft, and passed his examination in seamanship after eighteen months spent almost continuously at sea. The usual shore courses for Sub-Lieutenants followed, Tyrwhitt scraped through his examination with a second-class certificate for seamanship and torpedo and "thirds" for navigation, gunnery and pilotage. It might be remarked at this point that the only "first" scored by the three most successful younger commanders in World War I (Beatty, Keyes and Tyrwhitt) was the first's "one" in torpedo. In spite of his lack of distinction academically he was clearly thought to be an excellent young officer, for after a spell in the sailing brig *Pilot* he was selected, with Beatty, to join the Royal Yacht *Victoria and Albert* for Queen Victoria's summer cruise. Promoted to Lieutenant at the end of the season he went abroad once more in the fully rigged corvette *Cleopatra* to the North America and West Indies Station. It was during this very happy commission that he proved what he could do in an independent command.

Each fishing season a torpedo-boat was commissioned to patrol 150 miles of the west coast of Newfoundland visiting the canning factories and watching local interests. H.M.T.B. 78, one of the very first torpedo-craft ever built, had never been intended for the work she was now required to perform. She was 69 feet long, 8 feet in beam and accommodation for the crew of an officer and eight ratings was strictly limited:

The cabin which was so low that I could not stand up in it had three benches on which the Coxswain, Artificer and myself slept, the Leading Stoker and Stoker occupied the stokehold and the two A.B.'s and signal boy squeezed down under the forecastle. All our stores were kept in the cabin so there was not too much space when we were all on board.

There was however a wooden hut ashore used as headquarters and known as "Admiralty House," "one large room and a cupboard which I occupied, the crew using the other room for all purposes." Patrolling that rocky and often uncharted coast in this ancient craft was no sinecure. "My ship was . . . totally inadequate for the service she was used for, but the hardships we endured at sea were amply made up by the sport we enjoyed in our spare time." There were rivers full of fish, game in the woods; a hired cow provided milk and butter. T.B. 78 had many adventures. Once she lay for nearly two hours with her machinery broken down, kept off some cliffs only by the backwash of the waves, whilst the engine-room hands, working under unbelievably difficult conditions, fitted a spare eccentric strap. On another occasion she struck an uncharted rock and broke her propeller-shaft. Propeller and shaft were recovered by Tyrwhitt "personally diving for them, and I may mention that the water in the month of May was very little above freezing point."

It was an unpleasant dilemma. The nearest telegraph office was thirty miles away; no roads or even tracks existed, as all normal communication was by sea. Local opinion considered the journey through the virgin forest with several fairly big rivers to be crossed extremely dangerous. Ten miles a day was the recognised rate of travel and there was a strong probability of getting lost in the woods. Nevertheless Tyrwhitt decided to take the telegram asking for assistance himself. "Out of pure bravado I told them that I intended to start at daylight the next morning and that I should be back on the following evening." Off he went at dawn "and soon realised what I was in for. There was not a sign of a track and I was obliged to keep close to the sea coast to keep my direction." For fifteen hours, practically without stopping, he struggled along; wading through rivers up to his waist, plunging through bogs and forcing his way through the undergrowth. Darkness had fallen when he reached the telegraph station where he was kindly received by the man in charge. "I have forgotten his name, but I shall never forget his welcome . . . He sent off my telegram, fed me, gave me his bed, called me at 4 a.m. . . . and sent me off in good fettle." The return journey was completed by 9 p.m. that night. "I was desperately tired, but was kept going by the determination to show those Newfoundlanders who pride themselves on their walking powers that other people can walk too."

In addition to his other duties this young man of twenty-three acted as magistrate in the frequent disputes between Newfoundland and French fishermen. "Unexpectedly I never had the least trouble; both parties invariably accepted my decision on the many squabbles I had to adjudicate." Tyrwhitt takes it all very much as a matter of course, but the disasters which might have overtaken a less forceful character are easy

Admiral of the Fleet Sir Reginald Yorke Tyrwhitt, Bart,
GCB, DSO, as Commodore 'T', 1918

to imagine. His services whilst in command of T.B. No. 78 were recognised by a letter expressing the satisfaction of the Lord Commissioners of the Admiralty—a very unusual distinction for so junior an officer.

Later in her commission *Calypso* was sent to the Mosquito Coast of Central America where Tyrwhitt had his first taste of active service. At this time the Mosquito Indians who lived in the coastal belt were independent. Neighbouring Nicaragua coveted their territory which she had made frequent efforts to annex. Early in 1894 a force of about 200 Nicaraguans seized the coast's only seaport, Bluefields. The news of this coup eventually filtered through to the outer world and *Calypso* was sent to Bluefields to watch over foreign interests. She found the situation more serious than had been anticipated. There was, of course, no radio in those days and the only way of seeking instructions was through the telegraph office at Colon, 350 miles away. Leaving her senior Lieutenant with three boats and fifty men to keep the peace, *Calypso* sailed away again. With luck she would be back in a week. Tyrwhitt, who was in the landing party, described what happened in a long letter to his brother Beauchamp.

The Nicaraguans had been quiet enough whilst *Calypso* was in the offing, but the day after she left they tried to assassinate the Chief of the Mosquitoes, "just 21 years of age and rather a nice fellow," who sought sanctuary with the naval party, camped on an island in the lagoon. *Calypso* returned with orders to disband the Nicaraguan troops, if possible without bloodshed. It was not a very formidable undertaking, "a poorer and more starved looking lot of scoundrels," says Tyrwhitt, "I never saw. They do not run to uniform, none of them have boots and a few don't wear trousers." But the ship had once again to leave and there was further and more serious trouble in which two men were killed. The naval landing party put the town under martial law, forbade the carrying of arms and closed the liquor shops, "pretty hard work, as we have to be on the job day and night." Tyrwhitt himself "had the pleasure of disarming the remainder of the Nicaraguan army.

. . . I collared 200 rifles and 35,000 rounds of ammunition."
Keeping the peace and searching for arms kept the landing
party busy. In the intervals they amused themselves fishing
for sharks and alligators in the lagoon. One night they hooked
a very large alligator. Ten men managed to haul it ashore,
"but as soon as it got on the beach it went for them open
mouthed. They all ran," says Tyrwhitt disgustedly, "and the
beast got off."

Not a very serious military operation, but a situation requiring initiative, firmness and tact. Tyrwhitt took it all very
coolly. Search parties for arms, usually taking place at night,
were "rather exciting." A man collared single-handed after a
chase through the bush "not very deadly."

His next appointment was to a real destroyer, the type of
craft with which his name was to be associated for many years.
The *Hart* was a little ship less than half the size of the smallest
destroyer of World War Two. In those days torpedo craft
were designed to operate at night, relying on their small size
and high speed to approach unobserved and get away. Every
effort was made to reduce their silhouette by cutting all upper
works to a minimum. The bridge was an open platform a few
feet above the flush-deck, encircled with light rails which gave
no protection from the weather. To be on deck in anything
of a sea was uncomfortable and hazardous. The *Hart* was on
passage from Queenstown to Berehaven when orders were
given for the six destroyers in company to race. It was blowing
hard with a stiff Atlantic sea.

Hart was second, [wrote Tyrwhitt to his sister] a quarter of a mile
behind the first boat, the others nowhere . . . At times I really think we
were absolutely under water fore and aft. A good deal of damage was
done; half the bridge was washed away (luckily I was standing on the
other half) . . . I got washed off my feet and was banged against an iron
stanchion, which knocked the stuffing out of me. My left thigh is about
twice its proper size and I am in bed . . . I was lucky to get off so easily
and not go overboard.

Destroyers in those days were something of a law unto themselves and often acted independently; "as long as we put in the

requisite number of hours under weigh no one seemed to care
a hoot where we went or what we did." There followed three
"idle but very happy years" as First Lieutenant of the despatch
vessel *Surprise*, acting as C.-in-C.'s yacht in the Mediterranean. A naval officer's life at the turn of the century has been
described, not altogether inaccurately, as one long holiday.
"But the Navy," says Tyrwhitt, "was just beginning to realise
that guns were supplied for a definite purpose, that of hitting
the enemy." Percy Scott was the captain of the cruiser *Scylla*.
Prize firing was instituted and a more realistic attitude was
gradually taking shape. The *Surprise* was not much affected
until late 1899 when the Fashoda scare led to ships in reserve
being hurriedly put into commission. Her crew was turned
over to the *Orion*, an old ship armed with four eleven-inch
muzzle-loading guns. Sir John Fisher who had recently
arrived on the station as C.-in-C. came on board to inspect progress. He seemed quite satisfied, but as he went over the side
he ordered the all-round anti-torpedo nets to be rigged on the
following day. The heavy steel nets had been stored away for
ten years, but somehow the job was done, Tyrwhitt making
"quite a nice little packet" from the adverse bets of brother
officers.

His next appointment was to the cruiser *Indefatigable*, again
on the North American and West Indies Station. She was an
old ship and, like all the rest of the squadron except the flagship, not of "the least use from the fighting point of view."
It was a critical period for Tyrwhitt, who would come up for
promotion to Commander in about three years' time. His past
record was a good one, but his selection would depend to a
great extent on his success as executive officer, in particular
the reports of the annual Admiral's inspection. His captain,
F. Campbell, was a difficult man (commonly known as F.F. or
Fretful Freddie), but Tyrwhitt always got the best out of any
ship's company and he soon had the old *Indefatigable* looking
like a well-kept yacht. His efforts to maintain her in this highly
desirable state received several rude checks. In 1902 his ship
was hurriedly despatched to Martinique for rescue work after

the appalling disaster of the eruption of Mont Pellé which wiped out the town of St Pierre. A second eruption took place whilst *Indefatigable* was anchored off the remains of the town, covering the cruiser with ash to a depth of several inches; for some weeks she was employed carrying stores and trying to help the survivors. Tyrwhitt described a minor eruption he witnessed in a letter to his sister Polly. His style is as usual very matter-of-fact.

I was never in such a funk in my life. We were ten miles from the volcano and the cloud of stuff which came out was over us in less than five minutes. It looked like a seething mass of brains and lightning. We were deluged with stones about the size of a 6d piece and then dust. Otherwise no damage . . . I hope we have finished with eruptions. . . . I am quite fed up with them.

Later that year *Indefatigable* was going up the St Lawrence at night when a local pilot ran her ashore. Seriously damaged she was docked at Quebec. Tyrwhitt was disgusted: "we were in tip top order and now of course everything has gone to blazes," but a few months later he was writing

we had a great reputation in the Fleet before we had our accident for cleanliness and smartness and although it's me as says it we were far and away the smartest ship on the station in every way. Unfortunately everything went back terribly after nearly four months in dock but we are pretty well all right now and I will bet my commission that we get a thundering good report.

This letter was to Miss Angela Corbally, for something far more important even than Inspection Reports had happened to Lieutenant Reginald Yorke Tyrwhitt.

Angey Corbally was staying with her friend Lady Moloney whose husband Sir Alfred was the Governor of Trinidad. *Indefatigable* came into harbour. Tyrwhitt attended a party at Government House. The young people only met five more times, but before *Indefatigable* sailed away to Tobago Angey and Reggie were engaged.

At first sight it seemed rather out of character. Though not at all a cautious man, particularly where physical dangers were involved, he was far from being impetuous. He was quietly

determined to rise in his profession, and a wife was a handicap
rather than an asset in those days of long commissions abroad.
Yet from the moment he saw Angey standing in a window at
Government House he was determined to marry her if she
would have him. *Indefatigable* was ordered away sooner than
had been expected. Tyrwhitt "fired by the knowledge it was
then or perhaps never" proposed and was accepted. It was
nearly a year before they met again, but neither's judgment
had been at fault and the marriage was a very happy one.

His messmates were very much surprised: "I told . . . our
Paymaster, as I thought he knew, but he nearly threw a fit."

It was a struggle for this extremely reserved man to express
his feelings in the long letters which he wrote to Angey, mostly
telling her of his doings on board and ashore.

Don't think because I am very undemonstrative that I don't think
of you every moment of the day. I don't think you have been out of
my thoughts for 5 mins since I first met you . . . I have no conversa-
tional powers and no parlour tricks . . . I really don't know what I have
got, except the dearest girl in the world.

They had seen so little of each other that he tried to tell her
more about himself.

"I told you I had a bad temper and so I have." In fact
he was explosive rather than bad-tempered, but Angey's influence had smoothed him down. After a trying morning at
General Drill during which Fretful Freddie had been "enough
to drive a saint mad" F.F. was apparently "flabbergasted at
my being so mild."

He was extraordinarily frank. "The mail had arrived when
we returned on board [from a ball] but I was too tired to read
your letter." This was from a party at which there was

one lady nearly as black as my boots, but she was extremely pretty
and most immaculately turned out. I wanted to dance with her, but her
card was full up.

Indeed in some respects he treated his obviously beloved
Angey as he would have treated another man. It was perhaps
the highest compliment of all.

Trouble again blew up in Venezuela and the *Indefatigable*
was sent to patrol the coast. It was dull work. "I am sorry
to say there is not the least chance of our being shot at." It
looked as if their return to England after three years abroad
would be delayed. "We are all as cross as bears." Preparations
for the wedding were well in hand. "What *are* you going to do
with Six Bridesmaids . . . but I am quite resigned. It is your
show, so do your worst."

In the end all went well. Tyrwhitt was promoted to Commander, at the age of thirty-two, sent home and duly married.

From 1903 until 1919 Tyrwhitt served almost continuously
in the smaller types of war vessel, commanding a number of
destroyers and, on promotion to Captain in 1908, scouts, light
cruisers and destroyer flotillas. In 1913 he was appointed
Commodore of the Home Fleet Torpedo Craft, Commodore
(T). Until he went to Gibraltar in 1920 his only shore appointment in thirty-five years was a few months at the newly established War College in 1909. After the Spithead Review in 1914
Tyrwhitt, flying his broad pennant in the light cruiser *Attentive*,
sailed for Harwich with two flotillas of destroyers. The "Harwich Force" had been constituted. What sort of man had
Tyrwhitt become?

In a crowd of strangers you would certainly notice his tall,
well set-up figure (he had played rugger for the Navy and
looked it). His face, with bushy black eyebrows overhanging
deep-set penetrating eyes, a firm mouth and rather prominent
chin, was a striking one. It was something of a shock to discover that above those splendid beetling brows was a perfectly
bald head. He was a man who listened closely, speaking little,
but very much to the point; as firm as a rock, but far from
stolid; a man of action, quick to make up his mind and clear in
his decisions. Even to those who knew him he was a formidable figure, if essentially gentle and just. When angry, or
wishing to appear so, the great eyebrows would draw together,
transforming a kindly face into a ferocious mask. On the
lower deck he was known as a driver who expected a great deal
and saw that he got it. He kept his ship's companies on their

toes and his standards were high. On the other hand his rule, though firm, was remarkably free from petty restrictions; a hard taskmaster, but generous with leave. He loved his own home and was the devoted father of three small children, but he was a dedicated man. For Tyrwhitt there was no conflict between duty and his own interests.

He was a seaman through and through. Great commanders have come increasingly to be identified with administration as well as command, some of them spending more time at a desk than on the bridge. Tyrwhitt was in the direct line of descent from the sea captains of the eighteenth century, a clear-headed, exceedingly competent and utterly fearless fighting man. What he lacked was the fault of the system—a knowledge of how best to apply modern weapons to the science of war. He was to prove a quick learner, but the process would have been expedited if the Admiralty itself had had explicit plans of how the tremendous weapon which Fisher had forged was to be used.

Just before war was declared he wrote to his sister Kitty.

. . . . Steam is ready, ships are stripped, and everything not required has been landed . . . It seemed dreadful to think of it at first, but now I am only longing for this desperate *waiting* to be over and to begin business. I can't see how we can fail to defeat Germany afloat, but there will probably be many losses and much destruction first . . .

The Harwich Force was responsible for preventing enemy vessels passing unobserved and unattacked through what is sometimes known as the Hoofden or Flanders Bight—an area bounded by the English, Netherlands and German coasts, and by an arbitrary line drawn across the North Sea at the 54th parallel—say Flamborough Head to the south of the River Elbe. This rough triangle of shallow sea is liberally sprinkled with sandbanks. Mist, fog and strong tides added to the hazards of close proximity to enemy bases. Harwich was well placed, closer to Germany than any other suitable harbour, covering the mouth of the Thames and on the flank of enemy forces moving against the east coast. The day after war was declared the Harwich Force was in action, intercepting and sinking the minelayer *Königin Louise*. For over four years they were at it without a pause, in action far more often than any other naval force and suffering correspondingly heavy casualties. Throughout this period Tyrwhitt remained in command, a command which he exercised from the bridge of his flagship during all important operations, and they were very numerous. No other naval officer held an equally responsible position in such an active fighting command for the whole war. It says a lot for his constitution and self-control that he finished the war in comparatively good health, though he had had no leave for over four years except for three weeks taken by order early in 1918.

It is quite impossible to follow the doings of the Harwich Force in any sort of detail. The Battle of the Heligoland Bight has already been mentioned on pages 225–7. It was Tyrwhitt's first engagement and very nearly his last. He had hoisted his flag in the *Arethusa* only two days before, "a brand new ship with a brand new crew . . . everything about her new and untried." Her first action, with the German cruiser *Frauenlob*, lasted for thirty-five minutes. It was fiercely contested, at a range which was sometimes as little as 4,000 yards. "I can only wonder that everyone on the upper deck was not killed," wrote Tyrwhitt to his sister. "The air seemed thick with bursting shells and the sea was alive with splashes from shells and splinters."

The signal officer, Lieutenant Westmacott, who was standing at his side

had just pointed out that we were on fire when he was killed instantaneously . . . I could not say exactly what my feelings were all the time, but I don't think I ever thought of the danger nor do I think anyone on board did. I was very agreeably surprised as I was under the impression that the first time everyone bobbed their heads when shells flew over them, etc., but it was not the case.

All but one of *Arethusa*'s guns were disabled, both her torpedo tubes were shot to bits, the upper works were "very much knocked about" and eight of fifteen hits low down had penetrated her side. Some of the guns were made serviceable before *Arethusa* was in action again an hour later, but her machinery had been damaged reducing her speed. In spite of this Tyrwhitt had no hesitation in turning back when Keyes radioed for help and was soon in action for the third time, with the German cruiser *Mainz*. "My engines, or rather boilers, were extremely groggy and our maximum speed had dropped from 28 to 7 knots." A fourth German cruiser, one of a number sent out from Heligoland, now appeared and the position was extremely critical. It was at this point that Beatty's battle-cruisers came tearing out of the mist and overwhelmed the German cruisers, sinking two and putting the others to flight. At nightfall *Arethusa*'s machinery gave out altogether when she was still only fifty miles from the German coast, but she was successfully towed back to Sheerness.

What might have been a British reverse had been turned into a British success in which three enemy cruisers and a destroyer were sunk. Our own light forces had been gallantly handled, though their gun and torpedo-fire had not proved particularly effective. Unfortunately in the flush of victory far too little attention was paid to their serious shortcomings.

The effects of this action were considerable in both navies. The Germans were badly shaken. As already mentioned they decided to adopt a more cautious policy which hampered the effectiveness of their naval forces for several months. The British on the other hand returned with their tails well up from their first serious brush with the unknown. They had proved that they could remain for several hours in the immediate proximity of powerful German bases in waters which should have been easily dominated by the enemy, inflict considerable losses and withdraw without the loss of a single ship. The effect on their morale was profound, and lasting.

Amongst the many duties of the Harwich Force was the difficult task of doing what they could to minimise the effects of enemy tip-and-run raids on the east coast by getting in contact with the attacking force and reporting their movements until the Grand Fleet, hurrying down from the north, could intervene. The first of these German raids took place early in

R

November; minelaying destroyers covered by German battle-cruisers with the High Seas Fleet in support. Scapa Flow had not yet been made into a safe base and the Grand Fleet was in Lough Swilly and no encounter took place. On 16 December, when Beatty so narrowly missed bringing the Germans to action after their attack on the Yorkshire coast, the weather was so bad that the destroyers had to be sent back to harbour and again the enemy slipped away. At the end of January the Harwich Force was more fortunate, taking part in the Battle of the Dogger Bank with Beatty's battle-cruisers. It was one of Tyrwhitt's cruisers which first sighted and engaged the enemy, torpedoes from the *Arethusa* gave the *Blücher* her *coup de grâce*, but the light force were never heavily engaged on that day though they had a grandstand view of the battle. By one of war's paradoxes the Admiralty's plan was almost too success-ful, British and German forces meeting at exactly the time and place forecast. Tyrwhitt described his part in the battle in a letter to his sister Polly.

Really it was a most unfortunate day for me and mine as the possi-bilities were vast and yet I was never able to take advantage of them. It all came of being punctual! I will never be in time again for anything. If I had been ten minutes late on arriving at the end of a 200 mile run at 23 knots in a fog, the Germans would have passed to westward of us and could not have escaped without fighting. As it was we sighted each other before dawn, they being to the eastward and turned at once and bolted. We all chased and when it was light I was on the [engaged] side of [our] battle-cruisers and could not get to the off side without losing ground.

Arethusa picked up 130 survivors from the *Blücher*. As one of them was being hauled over the side by a stout British stoker he said, "Hullo, Nobby, fancy meeting you here." Before the war they had been next-door neighbours in Hull!

Four weeks earlier Tyrwhitt had been engaged in the first of a long series of air–sea operations against the enemy. Aircraft were brought within striking distance of the coast and picked up again by ships of the Harwich Force—an operation of great historical interest because it marked the beginning of a new era in naval warfare.

The early efforts were almost unbelievably primitive. Three converted channel steamers in which seaplanes could be carried were attached to the Harwich Force. There was, of course, no question of flying on or off a ship in those days and the aircraft used were slow, unreliable and of very limited endurance. In dead calm weather they could be hoisted out; they would then rise off the water if they were lucky, trundle away on their mission and return (perhaps) after a considerable interval. The ships had to stop to hoist them out, remain in the vicinity and again stop to pick them up.

The first of these raids took place on Christmas Day 1914. Tyrwhitt with two cruisers and eight destroyers brought the three aircraft ships within twelve miles of Heligoland before dawn. At first light nine seaplanes were hoisted out, seven of which took to the air as the cruisers and destroyers made a circular screen. Conditions were favourable with good visibility and a calm sea, but over the land it was misty and most of the targets could not be found. Two of the seaplanes did, however, succeed in reaching the Schillig Roads, where ten heavy units of the High Seas Fleet were lying. In the meantime Tyrwhitt had been attacked by German seaplanes and a Zeppelin. No hits were scored on the ships, but it was the first occasion on which warships had been attacked from the air. Many had believed that aircraft would be much more formidable than proved then to be the case. At the height of the engagement their fears were further stilled by a signal from Com. T.: "I wish you all a very happy Christmas." Three of our seaplanes returned and were picked up and the aircrews of three more were rescued by submarines and another craft. For some extraordinary reason no surface force interfered and Tyrwhitt, after waiting for over four hours in the immediate vicinity of Heligoland, returned safely to Harwich.

Tyrwhitt, writing to his sister Polly a few days after Christmas, shows another side of his character.

We were discovered at 4 a.m. by some small craft who reported our approach by wireless. We were then three hours from the position it had been arranged to let the seaplanes start from. This spot was only one hour from Heligoland and easily within three hours of where we knew the fleet, or part of it, to be lying. My force was a very slight one and one battle cruiser would have dispersed us in daylight, so I felt I was running a risk of severe disaster by going on and I very nearly made up my mind to retire altogether before it was too late. You must know that the ships which carry the seaplanes are unarmed and very slow. However, while I was considering the question, the star I told you about suddenly bobbed up. It was the biggest star I have ever seen and we all thought it was a fire balloon or a zeppelin with some extraordinary searchlight. Well the long and short of it was that it was Venus coming out of the fog. But it put the heart into me and I had no more misgivings. It was not for nearly an hour after that we were sure it was a star, and I am equally sure it was sent to cheer us up!

He was a man of simple but profound religious faith. There was no doubt in his mind that his cause was just. The star which shone for him that Christmas Day was a visible portent of his beliefs.

The immediate military results of this first seaborne air raid were not important, but the Cuxhaven Raid opened the way to a new conception of sea warfare. It was Tyrwhitt the "Salt Horse," who never claimed to be a technician, who at once grasped the possibilities and persisted, in spite of repeated setbacks, with their development. Throughout the war the Harwich Force engaged in many similar operations using different types of aircraft—seaplanes which had to be placed in the water, seaplanes which could take off from a ship and finally land planes, from ships and from flat-decked lighters towed at high speed.

The Harwich Force came directly under the operational control of the Admiralty and Tyrwhitt found himself—a new experience—working with those at or close to Cabinet level.

If anyone had suggested two months ago that I should shortly be travelling by special train with Winston Churchill and the War Staff to attend a Council of War "somewhere" in the North of Scotland, they would have been locked up. It is extraordinary how the pendulum has gone up and I only hope that I shall not be found out too soon! Winston Churchill is extremely nice to me, and I like him for himself very much. He is just a boy and a born fighter . . . Barring his political views I like him immensely.

The liking was mutual. Tyrwhitt was a silent man, but when he opened his mouth he carried conviction; quietly confident in his own ability, long-headed, full of horse sense but open to new ideas. Morally as well as physically courageous he could always be relied upon to speak his mind. On this particular occasion he came out very firmly against

two very distinguished Admirals whose proposals were the equivalent of the death-warrant of a very large number of officers and men, beside being impossible and displaying considerable ignorance of the defences of Germany. It was not pleasant as it was not easy, nor entirely diplo- matic to disagree with people who are old enough to be my father, but . . . I was not going to agree to murdering half my command.

Tyrwhitt carried his point.
The return journey to London and Harwich had a queer Buchanish flavour. During the long drive by motor car from Inverness they had passed a large house in the middle of a deer forest with a high tower on which a searchlight appeared to be mounted—a strange phenomenon which they decided to investigate.

We arrived at 11 p.m. pitch dark and pouring with rain. The party consisted of Winston Churchill, a certain admiral, Commodore Keyes . . . and self. We had previously armed ourselves with revolvers and marched up to the front door. The house, a very big one, was brilliantly lit . . . and evidently contained many people. The owner was sent for and he admitted the searchlight being in position and spun an obviously untrue story . . . besides being very much annoyed by our demand. We . . . ordered its instant removal . . . I don't think our plans were altogether dignified, but it was impossible to choke W. Churchill off. He was . . . delighted at the possibility of a scrap.

Equally delighted, as is clear, were R. Keyes and R. Tyr- whitt.
His friendship with Winston Churchill continued. When the Government was reconstructed in May 1915 Tyrwhitt

wrote to the outgoing First Lord. In his reply Churchill says
how sorry he is to be losing touch with the Navy

and most of all . . . to work no longer with the men I knew and trusted,
amongst whom in first rank is yourself. Your letter is therefore a special
pleasure to me and your good opinion of very great value.

"Incessant in all weathers" in the words of the official historian, Sir Julian Corbett, was the work of the Harwich Force
—covering minelayers in the Heligoland Bight, escorting air-
craft-carrying ships close to the enemy coast, patrolling the
coast of Flanders, often acting as a bait in endeavours to draw
the High Seas Fleet in reach of the Grand Fleet and being in
the front rank of the defences of the east coast.

German propaganda and public interest in her doings combined to make Tyrwhitt's *Arethusa* as well-known as *Ark Royal*
in the 1939–45 war. After a number of very narrow escapes
she struck a mine off Harwich in February 1916 and was sunk.
Loss of life was fortunately small, but Tyrwhitt was very dis-
stressed to lose his ship and extremely angry when the Admiralty ordered a Court Martial.

I am told merely a matter of form [he wrote to his brother Beauchamp]
but I believe it is due to the gentlemen who are always seeking for a
scapegoat. Damn them. I would dearly like to give them my views on
the subject and think I could open their eyes for them.

The trial was to be held at Chatham and Tyrwhitt arranged
to meet his wife, who was still living in Hampshire and whom
he had hardly seen since the beginning of the war, in London
on his way back to Harwich. "You will provide tickets for
'Tonight's the Night' or 'A Little Bit of Fluff' and we shall I
hope have time for a wee bite of dinner and then go and have
a good laugh."

The Court Martial was cancelled and the night in town
never took place, but shortly afterwards Mrs Tyrwhitt came to
live nearby. Like many others Tyrwhitt had thought that the
war would be a short one and had strongly discouraged officers
and men from having their wives and families in the vicinity.
This rule was now relaxed. The Tyrwhitts had rented a farm-

house within a few minutes of the harbour where he would be able to spend a few hours during the afternoon when his ship was in port. "Mrs Com. T" would dispense tea "from a huge tea pot . . . and remember we all like large cups."

The life of the commander of a detached force is a lonely one and he was delighted to have his beloved Angey within reach, though still invariably returning to dine and sleep on board where he amused himself making miniature furniture in the company of his cat Nigger "the joy of my existence." (One day the cat, a black one, ate some white heather sent to him by an unknown admirer. "Is that good or bad luck?" wrote Tyrwhitt to sister Polly.) For Mrs Tyrwhitt and the other wives being so close at hand was a mixed blessing. The ships of the Harwich Force were never at more than three hours' notice for steam. When the frequent warnings of enemy activity were received sirens would wail out from all the ships in harbour bringing their crews hurrying on board. Cruisers and destroyers slipped out to sea, leaving anxious womenfolk waiting and watching for their return. From 1916 onwards the sense of being in the front line was further emphasised by frequent Zeppelin raids.

Within a week of Mrs Tyrwhitt's arrival her husband, flying his flag in the cruiser *Conquest*, was engaged in a particularly tricky operation.

Admiral Scheer had planned an elaborate raid to coincide with the Irish Rising of Easter 1916, and involving the whole of the High Seas Fleet. Admiral Boedicker's battle-cruisers supported by cruisers and destroyers were to bombard Lowestoft and Yarmouth, with the battleships in support fifty miles to the eastward. Soon after noon on 24 April all Scheer's ships had sailed.

The Admiralty knew that something big was in the wind, but believed that a more damaging blow than the shelling of coastal resorts might be contemplated. Attacks on the shipping in the Downs and the mouth of the Thames or on the heavy Channel traffic across the Straits of Dover were envisaged.

The timing of the German operation was not known and the

Grand Fleet, which had only returned to its harbours on the morning of 24 April from an abortive sweep in the North Sea, was busily engaged in completing with fuel. At about 4 p.m., when Scheer was well on his way, Jellicoe in Scapa Flow and Beatty at Rosyth were told by the Admiralty that the High Seas Fleet was out. All the heavy ships were still coaling, but could have been ready to sail around 7 p.m. Instead they were brought to two hours' notice. Not until 7.15 p.m. did the Admiralty order "raise steam and sail". They had intercepted and decoded a German signal giving a clear indication of the German intentions between 5 and 6 p.m., but did not pass this information to Jellicoe and Beatty until 8 p.m. All in all there was considerable delay, and it was nearly midnight before the British Battle Fleet was clear of its harbours and hurrying south in the teeth of a southerly gale. Beatty had reported that he could be ready to sail at 9 p.m., but it was 10.50 p.m. before he sailed from Rosyth. Scheer was now north of Terschelling steering south-west with the Scouting Group under Admiral Boedicker ahead of him. Our heavy ships, hampered by a strong head sea, were far away to the northward. Except for the light forces from Harwich (three light cruisers and eighteen destroyers) and some small local defence forces the east coast was wide open.

Tyrwhitt had orders to take up a position between Southwold and the Hook of Holland, with a line of submarines, over which he was to endeavour to draw the enemy, to the southward. The exact direction of the German blow was not known when he was told to sail the Harwich Force, but just before he left harbour at 12.30 a.m. on 25 April the Admiralty sent him the position, course and speed of Boedicker's battle-cruisers. As Tyrwhitt cleared the mouth of the Orwell and set a course for the Sunk Light vessel he plotted this information on the chart. It was at once clear that the Germans would pass the position originally assigned to him before he could get there. He made up his mind to ignore orders which could no longer serve. In the words of the official naval historian "with the fearless independence of judgement characteristic of his high qualities of command he decided to act on his own responsibility." Believing that the Germans were making for Lowestoft, Tyrwhitt turned north at 1.50 a.m., to place his little force at the point of attack. He could not hope to drive them off, but "he might at least entice them to chase him and draw the fire on himself."

At half-past two the ships of the Harwich Force went to action stations. Here it was a clear, calm night with a bright moon promising an early dawn. Surprise was essential for a successful torpedo attack, and conditions would be far from favourable when they arrived off Lowestoft. On the open decks men peered over the dark sea towards the north and east for signs of the enemy.

At half-past three the eastern sky was lightening. The southerly breeze was from astern. It was comparatively warm and very quiet, except for the water rustling by.

At 3.48 a.m. it was nearly daylight. Suddenly lookouts in the cruiser *Penelope* sighted the dim shapes of strange ships about three miles away. Almost at the same moment *Conquest* distinguished the silhouette of at least half a dozen cruisers surrounded by destroyers broad on the starboard beam. Tyrwhitt "steered a parallel course and awaited events." Ahead were more ships—four or five battle-cruisers followed by destroyers, moving towards the dim line of coast where the unsuspecting people of Lowestoft and Yarmouth slept in their beds.

Tyrwhitt had been given no information about the movements of the Grand Fleet, but he was pretty sure that these were hostile ships. Yet it was almost day and they must have seen him. He turned sharply to port as though to escape. "I endeavoured to lead the enemy to the southward with the intention of drawing them away from Lowestoft."

At first the strange cruisers seemed to come on, but as *Conquest* was radioing the position, course and speed of the ships she had seen to Jellicoe and Beatty flashes of heavy gunfire stabbed out as the German battle-cruisers, not to be dissuaded from their object, began to shell Lowestoft. At the same time

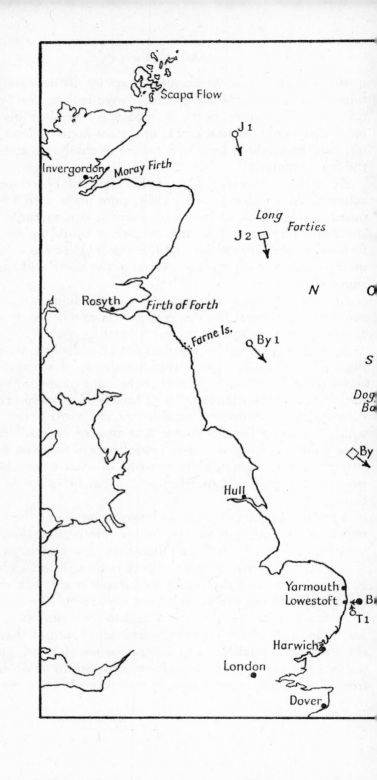

Scapa Flow

J 1

Invergordon • Moray Firth

Long Forties

J 2

Rosyth • Firth of Forth

N   O

Farne Is.

By 1

S

Dog
Ba

◇By

Hull

Yarmouth •
Lowestoft ◦── • B
        T 1

Harwich •

London •

Dover •

NORWAY

The Naze

Skagerrak

DENMARK

T H

A

Horn's Reef L.V.

Heligoland

Kiel

Terschelling

Wilhelmshaven
Borkum
Jade R.
Cuxhaven
Bremerhaven

S1
S2

Br2

Emden

2

of
nd

25 APRIL 1916

J1, By1, S1 etc...positions at 3.30 a.m.
J2, By2, S2 " " " 8.30 a.m.

J....Jellicoe with Grand Fleet
By...Beatty   "   Battle Cruiser Fleet
T....Tyrwhitt "   Harwich Force
S....Scheer   "   High Seas Fleet
Br...Boedicker "   Battle Cruiser Fleet

the German cruisers were seen to turn away. Tyrwhitt swung towards the coast to give himself more sea-room from the British minefield to the eastward and then turned north "to tempt them again."[1]

After bombarding Lowestoft for a few minutes Boedicker also turned north for Yarmouth, but his cruisers altered course to south-east. As soon as they were within range *Conquest*, *Cleopatra* and *Penelope* opened fire with their six-inch guns (each had two) on *Rostock* and *Elbing*, who turned about and fell back on the rest of their squadron. Reinforced by four more cruisers they again swung south-east, exchanging shots with Tyrwhitt's cruisers at long range. The German battle-cruisers had opened up on Yarmouth, but seeing gunfire astern Boedicker now hurried back to support his cruisers.

Tyrwhitt had deliberately placed himself in a position of great danger with the coast to port, six hostile cruisers on his starboard bow and battle-cruisers ahead. As soon as he saw the great ships bearing down on him he turned sharply about and made off at full speed. The battle-cruisers were beyond the effective range of his guns and torpedoes, but they were only 15,000 yards away, very much too close for comfort. As he ordered the destroyers to scatter astern and make smoke, salvoes of heavy shells cracked into the sea all around him.

For the next few minutes it was touch and go. The British light cruisers were frequently straddled. *Conquest* was hit by several twelve-inch shells which caused a serious fire and over forty casualties. "Shorts" and "overs" deluged the decks with water and spray. The destroyer *Laertes* had a boiler-room damaged, but both she and *Conquest* kept going.

It was fortunate that Boedicker though presented with a chance to pursue and destroy a much weaker British force was more concerned in getting away from the coast. Very prematurely as it seems he broke off the action and turned east. It might have been the Battle of the Heligoland Bight in reverse, but Boedicker was not Beatty.

[1] He was sighted by the German cruisers, mistaken for some of their own ships and then correctly reported to Boedicker as British.

By the time Tyrwhitt had called off his own smoke-screen the Germans were out of sight. After making emergency repairs to the *Conquest* he turned north-east after them. At 8.30 a.m. he again sighted smoke ahead, "a great cloud, as though from a fleet," but was recalled by the Admiralty. *Penelope* had her rudder blown off by a U-boat on the way back, but all ships returned to harbour.

Tyrwhitt's spirited intervention had not saved Lowestoft from bombardment, but it had reduced the time during which the town was under fire whilst Yarmouth had escaped almost scot-free. His skilful and gallant action was recognised by the Mayor of Lowestoft, who wrote to the Admiralty expressing

the high appreciation of the inhabitants of this Borough of the splendid way in which . . . the enemy ships, though in greatly superior force, were engaged by the British Squadron. The Council is convinced that, but for this plucky intervention at a critical moment, the Town would have suffered much greater destruction of property and loss of life.

Tyrwhitt, acting on his own initiative, had done his best, but the German raiding force had escaped. Beatty was disgusted, particularly with the system at the Admiralty which combined the evils of tight tactical control of the use of our ships and the lack of a plan to co-ordinate the movements of different units. In a long letter to Jellicoe, written after a talk with Tyrwhitt on 18 May, Beatty expressed himself very forcibly.

The Chief of the War Staff has priceless information given to him which he sits on until it is too late for the Sea Forces to take action with any possibility of achieving a decisive result . . . The 24 April was an object lesson which makes me weep when I think of it. There was absolutely no reason why every unit could not have been on the move $3\frac{1}{2}$ hours before it was! . . . Commodore T and the Harwich Force had no idea where I was, or when I might be expected or where I was going to. I had no idea of anything appertaining to the Harwich Force . . .

The opportunities of inflicting damage were priceless; they were thrown away and may never occur again.

Commodore T could have brought off a torpedo attack, our Submarines could have been in the right place at daylight. The Battle Cruisers and indeed the whole Grand Fleet could have been $3\frac{1}{2}$ hours further south . . . The raid would never have taken place or if it had the raiders would have been severely punished which would have produced a feeling of security in the country that would have strengthened the confidence in our Sea Power and produced a moral effect of supreme value to the nation—instead of the feeling of insecurity that actually exists and the continual questioning of what the Navy is doing.

As it is the result is not fair to the Nation, is not fair to the Navy, and is not fair to you . . . I cannot put all this into a Service letter, but I urge upon you my dear Commander-in-Chief to stop this perfectly hopeless way of muddling on.

Beatty's fears were realised. The "feeling of insecurity" which was evident after the unpunished Lowestoft raid came out like a rash in the press. The Cabinet was worried and the Admiralty hastened to increase their *defensive* arrangements. The next major sortie of the German Fleet five weeks later led to the Battle of Jutland, but the Harwich Force, although officially a part of the Grand Fleet flotillas in a Fleet action, was retained in harbour long after it was perfectly clear that there was no threat to the east coast towns.

Tyrwhitt, without any special information other than the usual short notice for steam, had been on the alert since 27 May. On the afternoon of 31 May he went ashore, knowing he could be back on board in a few minutes. He was digging in his garden when his flagship intercepted a signal from Beatty to Jellicoe: "I am in action with enemy battle-cruisers." Still no orders from the Admiralty, but half an hour later the Harwich Force was under way, briefly signalling Whitehall "I am proceeding to sea." They had reached the Cork Light vessel off the mouth of the Orwell and were setting a course towards the scene of the fighting when they were peremptorily ordered to return to base and await orders, instructions Tyrwhitt could not ignore by pleading, as on 24 April, that circumstances which the Admiralty had had no time to digest had overtaken his instructions. To rub salt into an already smarting wound he heard a few days later from Jellicoe's Chief of Staff that his judgment had been perfectly correct and that the presence of the Harwich Flotillas with the Grand Fleet on the morning after the battle might have made all the difference.

I wish you had been allowed to come to us on 1 June, [wrote Admiral Madden.] Our trouble at daylight was low visibility 3 miles and our T.B.D.'s much scattered after the night attacks, it was impossible to stand into Horn's Reef until the Fleet was screened and our T.B.D.'s did not turn up until 9 a.m., then too late; had you come to us I think only three undamaged ships would have escaped; as it was some that barely floated were dragged in behind the minefields.

Jellicoe fought one great battle, Beatty three; in the interval they watched, waited and prepared. Tyrwhitt's engagements with the enemy were very numerous and though mostly on a much smaller scale, involved a continuous strain which lasted almost without a break for more than four years. There was no comparatively "safe" area in the waters constantly ploughed by the Harwich Force. The Heligoland Bight should by right have been dominated by the enemy. The Flanders Bight, though nearer home, was within very easy reach of German bases. The policy of the Open Blockade with our heavy ships based well to the north at Rosyth, Cromarty and Scapa Flow left the southern North Sea as a sort of no man's land with only the Harwich Force and local defence forces immediately available to counter an enemy threat. Distances from the Bight to the German main fleet base were much shorter than from our own Scottish bases, and until help arrived from the north strong enemy forces were opposed only by our light craft. But the enemy never succeeded in denying us access to the Heligoland Bight or preventing mercantile traffic from moving in the Flanders Bight where the "Beef Trip" between Holland and the Thames was a regular run; 520 eastbound and 511 westbound ships in 1917 of which only 6 were lost. The Harwich Force and the Dover Patrol between them ensured that the sea-routes between England and France were not interfered with, and it was the Harwich Force and local defence flotilla to the north which protected mercantile traffic moving up and down the east coast. On the offensive side over thirty minefields were laid in the Heligoland Bight and large numbers of air–sea operations conducted against Germany and Flanders. The Harwich Force grew in size and carried increased responsibilities as the war went on. With some of its ships always at sea on its multifarious duties it was impossible for Tyrwhitt to be present in person on all occasions, but even when he was not there it was his spirit which animated and dominated the activities of his little ships, the spirit expressed in the orders he issued immediately before the war: "The general attitude is to be offensive to anything that can be attacked with a reasonable chance of success." Casualties in both ships and men were heavy, but officers and men of the Harwich Force, far from being dismayed, took a tremendous pride in belonging to a part of the Navy where conditions were particularly difficult and dangerous. When ships were lost their crews would volunteer for further service in the Force, largely because it meant further service under Com. T, a man whose personal qualities they respected, whose skill and judgment they admired and who never let them down.

Tyrwhitt's successes did not pass unrecognized. He was awarded a c.b. in 1914, decorated with the d.s.o. in 1915 and made a k.c.b. (an unusual honour for a Captain) in July 1917. He continued to hold the temporary and non-substantive rank of Commodore, but in 1917 a section of the press, acting without the least encouragement from Tyrwhitt, began to agitate for a change in the rule that promotion to Rear-Admiral is by seniority only. "The reform which is most badly needed in the British Navy is . . . promotion by selection in the higher ranks" said the *Daily Mail* (28 May 1917). A correspondent to *The Times* was more explicit. "Outstanding merit compelled to wait while the wheels of time grind the senior men out of the way." The exploits of the Harwich Force had caught the popular imagination, and Tyrwhitt's name was frequently mentioned. "He has done splendid work in the war, but he cannot become a Rear-Admiral until more than sixty captains above him are either promoted, retired or dead" (*Daily Mail*). In October a retired naval commander asked a question in the House of Commons about the rule for promotion to Rear-Admiral, mentioning Tyrwhitt by name. Tyrwhitt was furious. "Am having trouble with one Carlyon Bel-

lairs," he wrote to his sister Polly. He went to the Admiralty
"to arrange the Bellairs business . . . very unpleasant, but
necessary." A week later Bellairs was again on his feet, this
time to announce that he had received the following letter
from Sir Reginald Tyrwhitt:

Dear Commander Bellairs,
  I should be grateful if, in future, you will refrain from taking a
personal interest in my professional career. I am perfectly content to
leave my advancement, etc., in the hands of my superior officers, who
have risen by merit to the positions they hold at the Admiralty.

  The agitation must have bubbled on under the surface, for
in January 1918 Tyrwhitt "had a surprise packet . . . They
suddenly made me an Admiral." "Acting," it is true, but
an unprecedented step. "I believe I am the first captain to
be made an Admiral out of his turn within the memory of
man."
  Tyrwhitt was the least ambitious of men, but he took a very
natural pleasure, in the strict privacy of his own family, in the
honours which came his way. Much too objectively-minded
to be unaware of work well done, he still seemed metaphorically
to pinch himself when tangible proof of his fame were given.
He had been at sea when the first investiture he should have
attended was held, but was "sent for by the King and had over
20 minutes all on my lone. He was more than charming and
gave me my C.B. without any ceremony which was particularly nice." "Fancy me having lunch with the King," was his
comment on a Royal visit to Harwich.
  His wife, though quite ambitious on her husband's part, was
equally free from pomposity. "Isn't it ripping Reggie a K
while still a Captain," she wrote to Polly Tyrwhitt in May
1917. The letter gives an idea of the genuine pleasure his
honours gave to the Navy at large.

  Such hundreds of friends—everyone seems as pleased as we are ourselves and last week we went together to a lecture and as soon as R
appeared on the scene they gave him a delicious cheering—I am making
an effort to live up to his reflected glory! He is really delighted to have
something that I share in.

8

Though constitutionally very strong and careful to try and keep fit he was beginning to feel the strain. Early in 1918 he admitted to feeling "not very well." His friend the celebrated surgeon Sir Alfred Fripp, one of the King's physicians, came to stay at Harwich and spent a night on board. Perhaps he put in a word in the right quarter, for in February Tyrwhitt was sent for by the First Lord and ordered to take his first and only leave of the war. The Tyrwhitts were lent a house in the Border Country where he could spend all day beside a river (he was a keen and very skilful fisherman) and try to forget the war. It did him "no end of good," wrote Lady Tyrwhitt, "and got rid of that horrid strained look that used to worry me so." For four consecutive weeks he did not go to sea "but I expect he'll go for a blow through before long," adds his wife resignedly. It must have been very satisfactory to Tyrwhitt that on a subsequent "blow through" one of the sea–air devices which he had sponsored had a very lucky break when a little fighter aircraft taking off from a lighter towed by a destroyer at thirty knots succeeded in shooting down a Zeppelin which had been attracted to the scene by a mock battle staged by some of his ships—a fanciful plan fraught with endless difficulties which worked like a charm. He gave the pilot, Lieutenant Culley, R.A.F., aged eighteen and a half, a cigarette-case engraved "Hymn 227, verse 7."

> Oh! Happy band of pilgrims
> Look upward to the skies
> Where such a light affliction
> Shall win so great a prize.

In October came the week of extreme tension when it was fully expected that the German Fleet would make its last desperate sortie. In November it was over. A few months later he hauled down his flag after one of the longest spells of continuous command on record.

All great leaders are trusted by their officers and men; some are regarded with genuine affection; very rarely indeed this affection is so deep as to warrant being called love.

Nelson's famous words at Spithead before Trafalgar: "I had their huzzas before. I have their hearts now," can fairly be applied to Tyrwhitt. The personal esteem in which "Com. T" was held by the Harwich Force was extraordinary; he was the finest man they had ever met. As a crew of senior officers pulled him ashore in his galley the crews of his ships—cruisers, destroyers and battered little minesweepers—lined the rails and wished him God-speed, a spontaneous demonstration of trust and affection which had no parallel in this century. He was still only an acting-Rear-Admiral and had yet to celebrate his forty-ninth birthday.

He had been singled out for the very unusual distinction of a Baronetcy, participated in the cash awards made to a selected few of the leaders of the Services and received the thanks of both Houses of Parliament. It is strange that such an outstanding leader was almost without personal ambition. Now he seemed to have no desire to remain in the limelight, forming policy and shaping what was to come. King George V, who had taken a liking for this courteous, outspoken and very competent sailor, suggested that he should be appointed to the Royal Yacht, a good stepping-stone to higher things. Tyrwhitt, though greatly flattered and pleased, was anxious to get right away and spend a few years in some appointment where he could have a rest and enjoy a less exacting life with his wife and three young children. The First Sea Lord explained the matter to the King and Tyrwhitt was invited to York Cottage, Sandringham, where he had "a long talk with H.M. about the Yacht and I told him plump and plain *our* troubles. He was perfectly charming about it."

There is no doubt that travelling by special train is quite comfy . . . I . . . arrived here at 9 ocl and was shewn straight into the dining-room. The King was alone except for Godfrey. We had coffee and talked for about half an hour and then I was taken to the drawing room and presented to the Queen, Princess Mary, Lady Mary Trefusis and a French lady whose name I have not yet discovered. It was not as bad as I expected. I remained with them until 11 ocl all by my lones and kept up a conversation of sorts. The Queen is really charming but shy like me! Then to bed, where I had not enough bedclothes. I was frozen.

Next day the Royal Party went partridge shooting, Tyrwhitt did not do so very badly . . . It was freezing hard all day and was bitterly cold but I managed to exist. Several Lords, etc. appeared and were all very pleasant . . . We had a tophole lunch . . .

Next morning he found Brekker rather a trying meal as the King's Parrot took a violent fancy to me and insisted on sitting on my shoulder . . . I being the only guest always have to sit next to the Queen. She is not v talkative but I manage to blurt out a remark now and then . . .

The house is quite small, but as usual I have great difficulty in the geography . . . I am just able to find my room now. Dinner is the next ordeal but I expect if I get quickly on to the second glass of Bubbly my tongue will become looser and things may hum a bit . . . I'd love to have you here, it would all interest you so much. It really is very wonderful and I sometimes wonder if I am dreaming.

Tyrwhitt was appointed as Flag Officer, Gibraltar, where he spent two happy years. Though temperamentally very different the Tyrwhitts were devoted to one another. He was very English, she as Irish as they are made. The Navy was his life, but she was not at all "naval minded." In small ways they were equally dissimilar. Punctuality was a fetish to the Admiral, but meant nothing to his wife. "Fancy your being in time for your own party," he wrote to her when he was away. "What did it feel like?" The blend of their temperaments produced a very happy marriage, though Lady Tyrwhitt was sometimes irritated by her husband's lack of ambition.

Tyrwhitt was essentially a man of action and a commander of men; independent and extremely competent he did any job entrusted to him exceptionally well. Though he was very ready to shoulder responsibility any form of self-seeking or intrigue was entirely foreign to his character. He seemed to have no wish eventually to join the "establishment"—to be at the centre of things and to direct present and future policy. Gibraltar was an easy post, but he proved his true capabilities a few years later when he became Commander-in-Chief China.

The China Station was considered of secondary importance

to the Atlantic and Mediterranean Fleets, but his arrival in
Hongkong in December 1926 coincided with the development
of a first-class political crisis.

Since the fall of the Manchu Dynasty in 1912 China had
been in a state of civil war with rival warlords fighting and
bargaining for possession of the country. In 1926 the Nationalists, followers of Sun Yat-Sen whose headquarters were at
Canton, were in the ascendant. Their armies, led by General
Chiang Kai-Shek, had advanced north as far as the River
Yangtze and might be strong enough eventually to obtain
control of the whole of China. Troops commanded by General
Chiang Kai-Shek entered Hankow in September. North and
east of the Cantonese were the Northerners, a loose conglomer-
ation headed by Sun Chang Tsolin, whose capital was Peking,
supported by Sun Chuan-Fang, who still controlled the lower
Yangtze, and Chang Tsun-Chang, in Shantung. The Cantonese, though better disciplined and better led than the
Northerners, were divided into two elements, both radical and
anti-foreign, but differing sharply in their views as to the
method of achieving a united country in which the British and
other foreigners would no longer enjoy the special privileges
which past treaties had imposed on China for many years. On
the right, led by General Chiang Kai-Shek, were the moderates
who aimed at conquest of the country, uniting all China and
then restoring the rights lost to Foreign Powers by negotiation.
On the left were the communist elements with their Russian
advisers headed by General Borodin, who intended to embroil
Foreign Governments at once, compelling them to surrender
their rights and privileges. It was this faction which spurred
on the mob to overrun the British Concession at Hankow in
January 1927.

Tyrwhitt decided to proceed at once to Shanghai and Han-
kow, leaving Lady Tyrwhitt at Hongkong. He arrived at
Shanghai on 10 January and was soon in consultation with the
British Consul-General, Sir Sidney Barton—a very experienced
and competent man who was to become a firm friend. From
Barton and others he obtained first-hand news and the views

of the Municipal Council, the governing and administrative body responsible, under an international agreement with China, for the International Settlements—nerve-centre of the very considerable commercial interests in China. Three days later he was on his way up the great Yangtze River to Hankow after sending to the Admiralty for transmission to the Government an appreciation of the situation which proved remarkably accurate. He pointed out that the Cantonese Army might be expected to reach Shanghai within thirty days, that the Defence Force of local volunteers was entirely inadequate to protect the International Settlements and that unless very substantial reinforcements were sent immediately Shanghai would follow the fate of Hankow.

I consider that a fully equipped Division, repeat Division, is urgently required for the defence of Shanghai and that moreover it should be dispatched with the least possible delay. Urgency of situation calls for immediate action and delay may be disastrous . . . the presence of the strong British force in Shanghai would without doubt encourage our allies to follow suit.

The alternative was evacuation, either peacefully or under fire. Tyrwhitt pointed out that the Consul-General of Shanghai (who was in entire agreement with his proposals) considered that evacuation would prove physically impossible in practice

"I have never had such problems to deal with before and the war was child's play to this sort of thing," he wrote to his wife "Why did we ever leave our happy home?"

Whatever his private feelings he was his usual calm, competent self, quickly absorbing what was going on, making up his mind about what must be done and stating his opinion in forthright terms. In Hankow the Cantonese authorities had undertaken to restore order and "protect" the Concession. In fact they were in full control and likely to remain so unless dislodged by force. Mr Owen O'Malley had arrived from the British Legation in Peking and was endeavouring to come to terms with Mr Chen, of the Cantonese Foreign Office. After interviewing people all day and walking round the Concession in uniform Tyrwhitt returned to Shanghai and sent a further very candid appreciation to the Admiralty. "Please God they will act on it. Time is so vital," he wrote to his wife.

Tyrwhitt's forthright telegrams had created a considerable stir at home where the Cabinet was urgently considering what action should be taken. Tyrwhitt waited impatiently at Shanghai whilst the Cantonese armies came closer to the helpless city. Although British interests predominated in Shanghai the Foreign Settlements were International and the other powers concerned had not yet been persuaded that concerted action was essential. The American Admiral had orders not to fight. The French with their own Concession adjoining the International Concession were secretive; the Japanese intent on furthering their own interests. Tyrwhitt pegged away, patient, determined, courteous, ploughing a straight course which gradually drew the others into his wake, but sure that the immediate action necessary to protect Shanghai would have to be taken by Britain alone. There were endless conferences and meetings and much paper-work to be dealt with, but he kept himself fit by playing squash with Kit Caslon his flag-lieutenant and taking long walks around the racecourse. He had his carpenter's bench fitted up near his cabin and sometimes found relief from the anxieties and irritations of the day by making some of his exquisite miniature furniture. Calm and confidence radiated from him, though the British Minister had expressed his opinion that an attack on Shanghai could be expected very soon.

The British Government had, in fact, acted with quite amazing promptitude. For once it was not a question of too little or too late. On 27 January troops from India were embarking at Bombay. Next day six battalions from England left Southampton—a very remarkable performance by the Defence Ministries and the Board of Trade. The first arrivals at Shanghai were expected in mid-February, but Tyrwhitt was worried, not without cause, that the Chen–O'Malley talks at Hankow might include some agreement which would prevent their landing. O'Malley, as he had written to his wife, was "a very nice person, "but" very much of a diplomat."

There is no doubt that Tyrwhitt's outspoken telegrams were a deciding factor in helping the British Government to make the correct but very difficult decision to "go it alone." Luckily they felt that their principal military adviser on the spot was a man whom they could trust, sharing the views expressed by Winston Churchill in the House of Commons, that he was "one of the most determined, most cool and sober-minded officers in the Navy." Time was the essence of the problem and it was clear that anything in the nature of an effective International Force would never be agreed to, assembled and dispatched until far too late.

In the great sprawling city itself communist and nationalist sympathisers were stirring up trouble. At the end of January a general strike was called for several days. When it is remembered that the International and French settlements which had to be protected covered an area eleven miles long and up to two miles wide, with a population of about a million of whom only 36,000 were foreigners, and in which all the vital services depended upon Chinese labour, the magnitude of the task of protecting it from troops from without and maintaining order within can be realised. The news that his proposals had been accepted and that troops were on the way was a great relief. On 8 February Tyrwhitt was given full authority to dispose of them as he thought fit and told to ask for any further help he needed. "Complete responsibility for the whole show . . ." he told his wife. "I have not to ask or consult anyone and I feel from the bottom of my tummy that I have done the right thing."

He wanted to get the troops ashore as soon as possible, fearful that some compromise might be reached by O'Malley which even now would interfere with his plans. Action not talk was necessary at this stage if the situation was to be retrieved without bloodshed. The Foreign Office were too inclined to chatter and compromise. "Their telegrams are much larger than our letters and d——d hard to understand. "

His troubles, of course, might be said only to be beginning, but Tyrwhitt was calmly confident. Given a free hand and reasonably adequate means he had no doubt that he could do what was needed.

Now, having cast the die, I feel quite happy and am no longer worried. Nothing worries me so much as waiting for other people (wives sometimes) to make up their minds.

On 14 February the troops began landing at Shanghai. They were only just in time. The beaten Northern armies were close to the city, pillaging the country as they retreated. Shanghai would have been a splendid place to fill their pockets. Hot on their heels came the victorious Cantonese and both armies must be diverted from the city. But with the troops ashore confidence was returning.

I only hope [he wrote to Lady Tyrwhitt on 16 February] I shall finish in as good order and *odour* as I have begun. I expect people will start slinging ink about if nothing happens, but I warned them that probably nothing would happen if they sent out the troops.

As Tyrwhitt had prophesied the clear lead of the British was now being followed by the other nations with a stake in China —France, the U.S.A., Japan, Italy, Spain. Warships and transports were arriving daily. Tyrwhitt's own command had been swollen to seventy-nine men-of-war of various sorts and nearly thirty transports and others. Very considerable tact and diplomacy was needed in dealing with the other powers— qualities which he never claimed to possess, but which were amply proved by the comparative smoothness with which something like a common front was presented to the advancing Cantonese.

There are so many side issues to everything . . . I not only have to tell my own people what to do but to tell the Admiralty what is the right thing to do. I pray every night that I shall do the right thing and not make an ass of myself.

His path was not smoothed by the arrival of the British Commanding General, "quite a nice person, but not a general." Luckily he had a very efficient Chief of Staff, later Viscount

Gort, and Tyrwhitt, firm but kindly, managed to impose his will without an explosion.

It was all done very nicely and I think he was really pleased to have someone make up his mind for him . . . he is totally unsuited for the job . . . whoever selected him for it ought to be shot. I am very sorry as he is perfectly charming and would be magnificent in a drawing room at home.

With the arrival of the troops life at Shanghai tended to return to its former gaiety and social invitations came pouring in. Tyrwhitt himself avoided any unnecessary engagements but found it expedient to weld his very diverse flock together by a good many lunches and dinners.

I am afraid this is going to be a bad place for dinners . . . it would suit you as they are all abnormally unpunctual.

By the end of March the crisis was approaching. The Cantonese, prevented by the troops from a direct assault, now planned to reduce Shanghai by disorganising its life with strikes and intimidation by gunmen who had dribbled into the city in large numbers. Shooting episodes were an almost hourly occurrence, but with a second Brigade of British troops now on the spot and with most of the other foreign nationals strongly reinforced the situation remained in hand.

On 24 March the temperature again rose to boiling point when foreigners in Nanking were attacked by Cantonese troops and warships were forced to evacuate their nationals under cover of a short bombardment.

The Nanking outrages in which foreigners were murdered and great damage done to property were engineered by left-wing Cantonese to widen the gulf between General Chiang Kai-Shek and the Foreign Powers and discredit his attempts to follow a more moderate policy. In this they were almost successful. The situation was extremely tense and a definite break with the Nationalists seemed imminent. The General himself, realising that large-scale foreign intervention would jeopardise the entire Nationalist plan, hastened to Shanghai, called a press conference and promised to pay compensation and protect foreign interests in Nanking. But many foreigners were unconvinced, loudly calling for immediate retribution even if it led to war. Tyrwhitt had to restrain the Allied warships at Nanking from taking drastic action. The first short bombardment had been forced upon them, but he was strongly opposed "to any more of that sort of punishment as I did not think it would have met the bill."

I had to be very firm with my man [on the spot] . . . I expect I shall be severely criticized by the fire eaters but I am quite certain I am right.

It was again most fortunate that the principal military adviser in Shanghai was a man of such outstandingly good judgment. Rapid and forceful action two months earlier had averted serious bloodshed. The policy of restraint upon which he now insisted was equally well-timed.

For several weeks the position remained extremely tense. "I am very much afraid we are in for war," wrote Tyrwhitt on 31 March," we are living . . . on a volcano which threatens to go off on 3 April." Fortunately Chiang Kai-Shek's power was growing and that of the communists being reduced by firm action on his behalf.

By early May the immediate crisis had passed. Shanghai was safe, though chaos still reigned inland. Chiang Kai-Shek, rallying moderate opinion behind him, had set up his own government at Nanking, suppressing communist risings and dismissing Soviet advisers. The danger point had swung further north where some of the Cantonese troops had come to terms with the Peking government. Sir Miles Lampson, supported by his military adviser and by the Foreign Office, was in favour of evacuating the Legation to Wei Hai Wei. Tyrwhitt was strongly opposed to action which he felt was unnecessary and would result in serious loss of "face." "If I never do anything else I have done one thing and persuaded them to hang on." His telegram to the Admiralty on the subject beginning "The idea of evacuating Peking Legation fills me with horror and consternation" was typical of his uncompromising style. He carried his point.

Lampson bore him no ill-will and their relations remained good.

A very charming man, [wrote Tyrwhitt] talks like a machine gun. . . . He's huge in person but I'm afraid he's filled with gas but is a delightful man to meet. I have long since got over my reverence if I ever had any for the Diplomatic Service.

As he had prophesied, with the immediate danger over there was a tendency in some quarters at home to describe the Shanghai Defence Force as a "panic measure" and a very expensive one at that.

"With only the slightest imagination," wrote his Flag Lieutenant Kit Caslon to Lady Tyrwhitt on 6 May, "one can imagine the next telegram from home containing instructions to apologize for our very existence."

It was in some ways the most difficult time of all, but Tyrwhitt went calmly on, dealing wisely but firmly with minor crises as they arose. The situation gradually eased, though the first year of his appointment had passed before life had reverted to something like normal. Early in 1929 he returned home. Visiting Shanghai to say goodbye in November 1928 he was given a reception which could have left no doubt in the mind of even this modest man of how he was regarded. The sober jargon of the letter he received from the Admiralty when he returned home in March 1929 contained Their Lordships' approbation.

The tenure of your command coincided with a continuation of the period of chaos in China and presented situations full of uncertainty and difficulty . . . H.M. Government have regarded you as their principal Military Adviser upon broad questions of policy . . . a heavy responsibility in respect of both Naval and Military forces involving the exhibition of qualities of judgment, tact and decision in a high degree.

Their Lordships have pleasure in placing on record their entire approval of the manner in which you handled this difficult situation, thereby performing a service which in their opinion has been universally appreciated . . .

Only once again was Tyrwhitt to emerge from the comparative obscurity in which he preferred to remain. He was at Chatham, as C.-in-C. the Nore, during the financial crisis of 1931 when the sudden announcement of cuts in naval pay, introduced without warning or proper preparation, led to the Invergordon mutiny—men in six ships of the Atlantic Fleet refusing duty.

The various Commanders-in-Chief received a memorandum written by a member of the Board which appeared to give the views of Their Lordships on the causes of the mutiny. It seemed to Tyrwhitt from this memo that the Admiralty was trying to explain away a most lamentable occurrence (he never quite got over the shame of it). He was disgusted by efforts to transfer the blame to the officers of the Fleet when the major part of it rested quite squarely on their own shoulders. Mutiny was inexcusable, but it was ignoble of the Admiralty to suggest that they had never been warned that the reduced rates would cause great hardship—information which if not already in their records could easily have been obtained in advance. To Tyrwhitt's forthright mind the Admiralty's overriding responsibility for the welfare of the Navy was clear; they had not shouldered it.

He made a formal application for leave to state his opinion to the Board, went to London and did so. It is said that after he had left the room those present breathed a sigh of relief, relief which was short-lived when someone reported that he was still walking up and down outside, presumably preparing for a second assault. Those who knew Tyrwhitt will have no hesitation in believing that had he been a member of the Board at the time the cuts would either have been applied in a different form or he himself would have resigned. It is a great pity that he never occupied any of the top posts of the Navy where his good judgment, fearlessly applied, would have been of great and lasting value. The fact that he did not do so was more than a little his own fault. But his only real ambition, fully achieved, was to be *trusted* by his Service.

Trusted and loved. "The two best-loved leaders of my

generation," wrote Admiral Sir John Kelly after Tyrwhitt died in 1951, were "Jellicoe and Reggie Tyrwhitt." Right up to his death at the age of 81 the officers and men of the Harwich Force continued to meet for their annual dinners, bound together by the extraordinary personality of the man under whom they had served over thirty years before. To those who remain "Com. T" is still a name to conjure with.

KEYES
1872-1945
Sword in Hand

HARRY KEPPEL went to sea in 1824 and was still very much alive when Roger Keyes was appointed to his first ship in 1887.

In 1940 Keyes, aged sixty-eight and three years over the retiring age for Admirals of the Fleet, managed to get himself actively employed as Director of Combined Operations. The Royal Navy had changed materially almost beyond recognition in a hundred years, but spiritually the two men had much in common.

Roger John Brownlow Keyes was born in 1872 at Tundiani in the North-West Frontier Province of India. His father served nearly all his life in the Indian Army and his mother was a soldier's sister. John Keyes was commanding the Guides, as fine a body of fighting men as military history has ever known. For years he had been engaged in operations against the fierce, warlike tribes which made the Frontier a very active post. Twice he had been recommended for the V.C. Roger was born into a warriors' world where courage was the highest virtue. It remained his guiding star.

At the age of five he was sent home. None of his ancestors had been sailors, but he seems already to have wished to join the Navy. His father wanted him to be a soldier, but young Roger was born with a gift of persuasion which was often to stand him in good stead. When the time came to offer himself for a cadetship there were other obstacles. He was a puny little boy, only four feet ten inches tall, and his left arm, badly set after being broken at school, was crooked. The good luck which was rarely to desert him ordained that the doctor who examined him should have served under his father, whom he greatly admired. Scholastically it was also a near thing, but with the help of a good crammer Roger passed into the *Britannia* in 1885.

His early days in the training ship and at sea were unremarkable. He was a quick and lively lad with plenty of guts and he did quite well. The life suited him and he was particularly happy when serving in the sailing brig *Martin*, a little vessel of 508 tons almost indistinguishable from the ships of Nelson's day. He saw some active service chasing slavers on the east coast of Africa and in a punitive expedition against the Sultan of Witu in the British Protectorate of Zanzibar. In 1891 he underwent the usual courses for Lieutenant at the R.N. College, Greenwich, and in the Gunnery, Torpedo and Navigation schools at Portsmouth, obtaining second-class certificates in all subjects except pilotage, where he scraped through with a "third." He was a gay young man frequently in trouble for various youthful pranks and not very keen on his books. Riding was a ruling passion. His parents had settled down near Sandwich and on one of his leaves Roger went right through the training course for recruits at the 17th Lancers' riding school at Shorncliffe Camp, proving such a fearless and skilful horseman that he was allowed to work with the rough-riders.

His next few years in the Channel Fleet were again unremarkable. He must have been well thought of, for in 1893 he was selected to join the Royal Yacht *Victoria and Albert* for her summer cruise. "A most alarming old lady," was his comment on Queen Victoria. After a commission in South America and a spell in an ancient corvette he was appointed to his first command, a small destroyer. In 1899 he was sent to China to another destroyer.

With the large Allied fleet which assembled off Taku at the mouth of the Pei Ho River in May 1900 was the little destroyer *Fame*, Lieutenant R. Keyes. Early in June the Legations in Peking appealed urgently for help and the C.-in-C., Admiral

Admiral of the Fleet Lord Keyes of Zeebrugge and Dover,
GCB, KCVO, CMG, DSO, from the painting by Philip de Laszlo (1923)

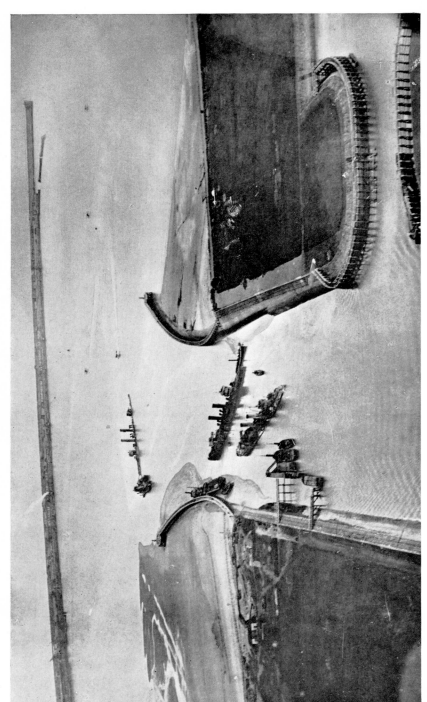

Zeebrugge: Blockships in the canal

Sir Edward Seymour, set off on his ill-starred attempt to reach the capital.[1]

The railhead for the hundred miles of line to Peking was at Tongku, four miles up the Pei Ho from Taku, where three large forts armed with modern guns commanded the mouth of the river. Shallow water kept the heavy ships eleven miles off-shore and the bar at the river's mouth could only be crossed around high water by vessels of light draught. Water traffic to Tongku had to pass within two hundred yards of the forts, which were out of range of the battleships' guns. The soldiers manning the forts, though in an excited state, had not so far joined the rebels.

Tientsin was also gravely threatened. Rear-Admiral Bruce, now the senior British Naval Officer at Taku, had sent a small naval detachment under Commander David Beatty to reinforce the Allied garrison (see page 216).

Fame, drawing only eight feet, had been constantly on the run ferrying troops ashore from the Fleet and acting as a despatch vessel. On 15 June Bruce ordered Keyes to leave his ship at Tongku, take the train to Tientsin and return as soon as possible with first-hand news. Communications with Peking had been cut; nothing had been heard of Seymour for two days and there were rumours of alarming developments. At Tientsin Keyes learnt that Seymour was beleaguered some thirty miles from Peking with the railway cut before and be-hind him. Three columns of Imperial troops, which were now joining the Boxers in large numbers, were advancing on Tien-tsin, Taku and the railway between Tientsin and Tongu. If communications with the sea were cut Seymour was doomed and Tientsin also, unless the river line could be kept open. With the Taku forts in hostile hands all the foreign troops ashore would be completely isolated from their only source of help.

Keyes, after an exciting journey back to Tongku in a com-mandeered locomotive (the line was cut immediately after-wards), rejoined the *Fame* and hurried out to report to Admiral

[1] The events which followed have already been described on pages 175-7.

T

Bruce. The Taku forts trained their guns on *Fame* as she passed, but did not open fire.

From the *Barfleur* nothing could be seen but the distant coastline, and it says a great deal for Keyes' powers of persuasion that this young officer was able to convince the Admiral quietly sitting in his orderly, peaceful cabin, that immediate and urgent action to keep open the lines of communication with Tientsin must be taken without waiting for approval from home. Next morning the Allied admirals met in the Russian flagship and decided to deliver an ultimatum that night announcing their intention of occupying the forts, by force if they were not handed over. The Allied ships had already been denuded of many of their men for Peking and Tientsin, but a scratch body of 900 men was hurriedly assembled.

Four modern Chinese destroyers were lying alongside the Dockyard between Taku and Tongku. These ships must also be put out of action, a task assigned to Keyes in the *Fame* with another destroyer, the *Whiting*, under his command. Keyes had already considered what he would do. He intended to capture them by boarding in the good old-fashioned way.

The ultimatum was delivered at 10 p.m. It would expire at 2 a.m. At 4 a.m. the attack on the forts would begin, preceded by the attack on the Chinese destroyers.

Keyes assembled his small ships' company and told them his plan. *Fame* and *Whiting* would steam up-river at the same distance apart as the first and third Chinese destroyers, each towing a boat with a boarding party for destroyers two and four. The little flotilla would keep in midstream as though making for Tongku. At the last possible moment they would sheer in alongside the Chinese ships, hoping to take them by surprise. Guns would be manned, but not used unless absolutely necessary. As each of the four Chinese destroyers carried nearly twice as many men as *Fame* or *Whiting* it was a sufficiently daring plan. Fortunately, both British destroyers were manned by crews many of whom had already seen active service with the Naval Brigade in South Africa, but it says a lot for Keyes' gift of leadership and ability to inspire others with his own enthusiasm that the men were by now feeling every bit as pugnacious as their young commandant. All the seamen would be needed for the boarding parties and the stokers, armed with bars of iron, were ready to repel a counter-attack.

It was unlikely that the Chinese would accept the ultimatum, but everyone was taken by surprise when the forts suddenly opened fire an hour before it had expired.

This unexpected bombardment caused damage and casualties in several of the Allied ships assembled in the river for the assault, but luckily neither *Fame* nor *Whiting* was hit. Keyes hurriedly got under way and steamed up-river. It was a tense moment as the four Chinese destroyers came in sight and the boarding parties, clutching their weapons, waited as *Fame* and *Whiting* edged across the river. But everything went according to plan.

The Chinamen were taken completely by surprise at such an unexpected form of attack, [wrote Keyes a few days later] and after the exchange of a few shots and a hand-to-hand scuffle we had the whole crew overboard, or shoved down below with the hatches closed over them . . . the whole thing was over in about five minutes.

The attack on the forts was equally successful; by 8 a.m., after some sharp fighting by the mixed force of Japanese, Russians, Italians, Germans, Austrians and British, the mouth of the river and its lower reaches were safely in Allied hands.

It was now learnt that there was a further fort about twelve miles upstream at Hsi-Cheng which must be immobilised before the river route to Tientsin was clear. Keyes, fired by his recent success, asked Admiral Bruce if he could reconnoitre it in *Fame*, but the Admiral, who seems to have treated Keyes a little like an over-indulged and precocious child, put his foot down at this point and refused permission. Keyes now tried to interest a Russian General in the project, only to be told that there were 5,000 Cantonese cavalrymen camped near Hsi-Cheng and that though the Russians now had a considerable force at their disposal an attack was out of the question. But five days later Keyes managed to obtain qualified permission to see if the river was obstructed and the fort occupied; by stretching these instructions he found himself soon after dawn in the reach four hundred yards from the fort. Modern guns could be discerned on the ramparts, but *Fame* was not fired upon. Local rumour had it that the garrison had fled, but as the fort could easily be re-occupied Keyes was determined to put it out of action. Collecting the strongest party he could muster, twenty-two men armed with rifles and thirteen others with pistols and cutlasses carrying demolition charges, he landed and doubled up to the walls. The fort, a huge place like a small walled town, was deserted. Charges were hurriedly placed under the six modern guns which commanded the river. The magazine was full of all sorts of ammunition. Piling explosives in the centre of the chamber Keyes ordered a train of gunpowder to be laid through the door. Telling his men to take cover he remained behind to light the fuse. It was only fifteen feet long and he had barely got away and was standing in the open when there was a tremendous explosion which knocked him off his feet.

I was much shaken, but just managed to crawl under the arch of the great structure of the cavalier . . . I was in a blue funk; it became dark, and the air was suffocating with dust . . . there was an appalling crash as masonry fell from the sky. I never dreamt that anything so tremendous and terrifying could happen when I light-heartedly lit the fuse.

Twenty miles away the windows of the Admiral's cabin of the *Barfleur* rattled and shook. From his stern-walk Bruce saw a great column of smoke rising up far inland. "I am sure that is Master Keyes," he remarked to his Secretary. "I only hope he is not on top of it!"

Nothing succeeds like success and "Master Keyes" was given a quart of champagne and a badly needed bath when, blackened and covered with filth, he returned to the *Barfleur* to report.

Early in July Keyes managed to persuade the Admiral to grant him a few days' leave to visit Tientsin where hard fighting was now going on. Beatty asked him to come as his A.D.C. for an attack on some gun positions; "A very successful little enterprise." Admiral Seymour's battered column had struggled back to Tientsin and Keyes lightheartedly suggested to Sir Edward that he should attach himself to Beatty's naval brigade. The proposal was not a success. "The Admiral was most chilling and unkind, and told me I ought to be in my ship."

With the arrival of Allied reinforcements the situation at Tientsin was brought under control, but the Legations in Peking were still beleagured. On 26 July General Sir Alfred Gaselee arrived at Taku to take command of a relieving force. Gaselee, who had served under Keyes' father on the N.W. Frontier, asked Roger to join his staff. Admiral Seymour was absent and Bruce, as ever clay in Keyes' hands, gave provisional permission. Off went Keyes with General Gaselee, wisely keeping out of sight until the expedition was under way lest he should be recalled. He had taken one of *Fame*'s white ensigns with him, and when the Allied Force eventually arrived before Peking on 14 August he had the felicity of planting it on the wall by the Sha K'au Men gate. A few days later Keyes caught diphtheria and almost died, and it was nearly two months before an emaciated young officer reported back on board the *Barfleur*.

He found himself extremely unpopular. Admiral Sir Edward Seymour had been furious when he heard of his doings and even Admiral Bruce received him coolly. An officer was on his way from England to take over the *Fame* and Keyes was to be sent home. One can but sympathise with Sir Edward's feelings, but Keyes though daunted was still not quite defeated. He told Admiral Bruce that he intended to beard the Commander-in-Chief himself.

"I had no idea what I was going to say when I went up to the Admiral," Keyes confessed later. Sir Edward was walking up and down the poop of the *Alacrity* which he used as a yacht. When Keyes came aboard he stopped.

"What can I do for you, Mr. Keyes," he asked sternly. I blurted out, "I think you have treated me very badly, sir." He looked very much astonished at my temerity, and very coldly asked me what I meant. I said, "If you had been in my place I am sure you would have done exactly as I did." He thought for a moment, and then with a charming smile said, "Perhaps I should; it certainly would have been a great temptation."

Keyes was reprieved, and returned to the *Fame*. Evidently Sir Edward's bark had been a good deal worse than his bite, for in November Keyes was specially promoted to Commander at the very early age of twenty-eight.

The events in China in 1900 have been recounted at some length, for they give an excellent insight into Keyes' character: his courage and pertinacity, his grasp of military essentials, his belief in the value of the offensive either in battle or when dealing with his superiors. Behind all this was an unusually large dose of the strange magnetism which gives one man the power of filling others with his own enthusiasm and willingly placing their lives in his hands. On the debit side it is fairly clear that Roger Keyes was motivated by an intense desire for personal distinction, to be himself in the forefront of the battle. Sometimes he seemed oblivious of the more pedestrian calls of duty. It was not enough to be just one of the team helping someone else to score. But he had proved himself to possess admirable and unusual qualities; how they might be employed in the future was less clear.

There was nothing unusual about his career during the next decade. He commanded a flotilla of destroyers, served in the Naval Intelligence Division at the Admiralty and was Naval Attaché in Rome. In 1905 he was promoted Captain and early next year he married Miss Eva Bowlby of Gilston Park, Herts, and Knoydart, Inverness-shire, an excellent match in every way.

But in 1907, due to an unfortunate mistake, he was very nearly relegated to the disappointed ranks of the has-beens. The Fisher–Beresford dispute, in which he had taken no part, was at its height. It came to the ears of Sir John Fisher that a certain "Keyes" had been trying to get a pro-Beresford article published in *The Times*. It was enough: "their wives shall be widows; their houses a dunghill." Captain Roger Keyes could expect no further appointments whilst Fisher was First Sea

Lord. Characteristically Keyes wished to have it out either with Fisher himself or with *The Times*. Under pressure the matter was thoroughly investigated. Lord Charles Beresford had a secretary named Keys and an approach had been indeed made to *The Times* by someone using that name. Keyes got the cruiser he was waiting for. The incident was closed, but it gives a nasty glimpse of the state of affairs in the Royal Navy in 1907.

In 1910 Keyes was appointed as Inspecting Captain of Submarines. After being looked on as toys or as weapons of limited usefulness submarines were developing fast. Sir Arthur Wilson, who had relieved Lord Fisher at the Admiralty, selected Keyes for what had become a very important post. Wilson had recognised the potentialities of the submarine, but the Navy as a whole was still suspicious or indifferent. The first submariners were a wonderful body of able and courageous young men, but many of their brother officers looked on them as cranks and there was a tendency for the Submarine Service to become a little navy on its own. Keyes, already well-known, a "salt-horse," a fine seaman and free of any suspicion of being tainted by specialisation, was a man who could "sell" submarines to the Fleet as a whole. On his part Keyes had the good sense to realise that he would need the very best possible advice from those who thoroughly understood the complicated submarine weapon and who knew what was technically possible. Not long after taking up his new appointment he detailed a "submarine advisory committee" to assist him. That he was a good picker is proved by following the future careers of the men he selected. Commander P. Addison, later a brilliant Director of Dockyards. Commander C. Little, a most distinguished submarine officer and later a member of the Board of Admiralty. Lieutenant-Commanders Lawrence and Nasmith, both of whom commanded submarines during the war with unusual distinction, Nasmith being awarded the V.C. and later becoming a Lord of the Admiralty. Lieutenant-Commander Charles Craven who as Sir Charles Craven and Managing Director of Vickers-Armstrongs Ltd. was to make a unique name for himself in industry. Engineer-Commander Skelton, a future Engineer-in-Chief of the Fleet. Working closely with his advisory committee was Mr A. Johns, a future Director of Naval Construction. Few could have selected seven young and still unproved men with quite such an unerring eye.

These years, immediately before the First War, were fruitful ones for the Submarine Service. Manoeuvres, carried out under realistic conditions, frequently demonstrated that submaries could be used offensively as well as defensively. As the quite unnecessary loss of some of our surface ships in late 1914 was to prove, the lessons were not always well absorbed, though, luckily for us, the Germans were equally slow in realising the full possibilities.

Lord Fisher, though no longer on active duty, was in continuous touch with Churchill, the First Lord. In July 1914 they were together in the Admiralty yacht at Portsmouth when Fisher expressed a wish to visit Fort Blockhouse to see D 1, the very latest thing in submarines. "He arrived in a very aggressive mood," says Keyes, "showed no interest in the submarine I took him to, but looking at me very sourly asked me why we had not built more submarines." Keyes had been struggling for years to get more of the larger "overseas" type of submarines built, backed by Churchill, but meeting a good deal of indifference at the Admiralty where the battle fleet took priority. He replied hotly that Fisher's own policy of concentrating on the smaller type of purely defensive craft, which would be of very limited value in war, was largely to blame and went on to criticise the monopoly in submarine building given by Fisher to Vickers, Ltd. The visit ended abruptly with Lord Fisher turning on his heel and stalking away. Keyes had made a formidable foe.

When war came Britain had seventy-four submarines built, thirty-one building and fourteen ordered or projected, but only eighteen were "D" and "E" class "overseas" boats, all the others being small craft of limited endurance only suitable for coast defence.

The overseas submarines were based on Harwich with Keyes in charge. Their radio sets were of limited range, and two fast destroyers, *Lurcher* and *Firedrake*, were attached to the flotilla to try and keep in touch with the submarines when on distant patrol in the Heligoland Bight—a difficult task, for the submarines could not be reached by wireless when submerged. Also, having much better weather-keeping qualities, they could remain at sea when the destroyers were forced to seek shelter in harbour. However Keyes, flying his broad pennant in the *Lurcher*, greatly welcomed this opportunity of transforming what might have been a purely administrative post into an active command.

It was Keyes who persuaded the Admiralty to adopt the plan which led to the Battle of the Heligoland Bight on 28 August—a plan based on the reports of German movements made by his submarines earlier in the month. In retrospect it is clear that too little attention had been paid to the difficulty of extricating badly damaged ships from the Bight in the face of superior enemy forces. But Beatty's timely intervention with the battle-cruisers saved the day and gave us a very satisfactory little victory whose moral effects were considerable, as already explained. Keyes, who loved a fight, enjoyed himself. His laying of the *Lurcher* alongside the blazing and sinking German cruiser *Mainz* from which he rescued over two hundred survivors at considerable risk to his own ship was typical of his chivalrous nature and fine seamanlike qualities. Unwounded Germans, who considerably outnumbered the *Lurcher*'s men, were crowded on to her forecastle where they might be better kept under control, but with sixty seriously wounded men cumbering her decks abaft the bridge *Lurcher* was in no condition to fight a further action had she been called upon to do so. "The situation for the next few hours," admitted Keyes, "was not without its anxieties."

On patrol individual submarines did very well, though frequently frustrated by the erratic running of their torpedoes. Using them as a sort of mobile minefield to intercept enemy forces was less fruitful. The difficulty of re-disposing the submarines at sea has already been referred to. As a result they failed to intercept the German heavy ships as they returned to harbour after bombarding the Yorkshire coast on 16 December 1914 and again after the Battle of the Dogger Bank in January 1915. In neither case can the blame be attributed to Keyes who did all he could, sometimes considerably hampered by the attempts of the Admiralty to exercise tactical control.

Lord Fisher's return to the Admiralty as First Sea Lord in November 1914 made Keyes' position very difficult. He knew that Fisher was highly critical of the policy he had pursued before the war and of his handling of the overseas submarines since the outbreak of hostilities. Fisher's tremendous drive would be a great help on the material side—large numbers of new submarines were immediately laid down—but Keyes felt that his own days as Commodore (Submarines) were numbered. He was surprised when Fisher added a P.S. to a letter about new construction.

On no account think I have any designs on you! If I had any such designs you would certainly have been told—but, like many other things, I have not yet mastered on what basis our submarines harm the enemy more than themselves! . . . "Now we shan't be long!"

His reply was characteristically courageous.

Dear Lord Fisher,
I am delighted to hear you have no designs on me, for I have no illusions as to the result if you had. I must confess that I thought your advent would mean my eclipse, but like others who may have had personal misgivings, I was glad because I felt it meant that—"we shan't be long"—in making war, which is the only thing that matters—besides, if I am to be transfered to another sphere, I shall only regard it as Kismet and trust to my luck to give me opportunities of engaging the enemy and proving you were right in promoting me nine years ago.

Fisher was delighted at this riposte. "I got your lovely letter," he told Keyes a few days later when they met in the Admiralty. But after the events of 16 December he was not so sure. Keyes had a powerful friend in the First Lord. "Keyes is a brilliant officer," wrote Churchill to Fisher on 21 December, "with more knowledge and feeling for *war* than almost any naval officer I have met. I think the work and efficiency of our submarines are wonderful." Yet after the Dogger Bank we find Fisher writing to Beatty: "Keyes is *a fancy man*! Why, I don't know. He has made a d—d mess of the submarines in the last 3 years."

Three weeks later he wrote to Jellicoe: "There never was such a mistake as putting Keyes in charge of the submarines, who had not the faintest idea how to employ them!"

But Keyes had already made up his mind that Lord Fisher's hostility was an insuperable obstacle to his continuing as Commodore (Submarines). The First Lord had reached the same conclusion. He still believed in Keyes; the Dardanelles operation was about to begin; here was just the man for the job. Keyes was appointed as Chief of Staff to Vice-Admiral Sir S. H. Carden the C.-in-C. Mediterranean. He arrived at Malta on 4 February.

Turkey had entered the war against the Allies on 30 October 1914. In January 1915 Russia, heavily engaged with Germany and Austria on the Eastern front, was being hard-pressed by the Turks in the Caucasus. They needed help, and uncommitted Balkan countries must be influenced to remain neutral or come in with the Allies. Churchill had for some time believed that we should strike at Constantinople, and now both the Prime Minister and Lord Kitchener shared this view.

I do not see we can do anything which will very seriously help the Russians in the Caucasus, [wrote Kitchener to Churchill on 2 January] the only place that a demonstration might have some effect . . . would be the Dardanelles.

But it had long been regarded as axiomatic that the use of ships against forts was unlikely to be decisive without troops attacking simultaneously on shore. Lord Fisher from the first suggested a combined operation. Still there was no recent experience to show how modern ships would fare and a short bombardment of the Outer Forts defending the Dardanelles on 3 November had proved that the Turkish artillery was outranged by ships' guns (and had thoroughly alerted the enemy).

Early in January Carden was asked if the forcing of the Dardanelles by ships alone was a practicable proposition. The importance of the result would justify severe losses and plenty of old battleships of no use in the North Sea were available. Carden replied that it was impracticable to rush the Straits, but that an operation taking about a month should be able systematically to reduce the defences and, when the channel had been swept clear of mines, break through the Narrows into the Sea of Marmara. The political advantages of a purely naval attack were considerable. If unsuccessful it could be broken off without much loss of prestige. When Keyes arrived in the Mediterranean the War Council had decided that "The Admiralty should prepare for a naval expedition in February to bombard and take the Gallipoli Peninsula with Constantinople as its objective."[1] Military aid on a large scale was not contemplated, but Kitchener ordered a force to assemble in case the Navy needed help at a later stage.

On 19 February the Fleet began the first stage of Carden's plan, the battleships bombarding the outer forts from beyond the range of the guns on shore and later closing to moderate ranges when the enemy fire had been much reduced. Bad weather caused the action to be broken off after a few hours, but on 25 and 26 February the Fleet returned, silenced the entrance forts, entered the mouth of the Straits and sent the sweepers in to begin clearing mines below Kephez Bay. Next day small parties of marines and bluejackets landed to complete the work of destruction of certain forts with demolition charges. They found much damage to communications, ammunition supply and other works, but most of the guns still serviceable—a fact which raised some doubt as to whether a purely naval venture could succeed. It was said later that a few thousand men could easily have occupied the lower peninsula at that time if the operation had from the first been a combined one.

Carden's plan of systematically reducing the defences continued its cautious way. Bad weather interrupted the bom-

[1] *Dardanelles Commission. First Report.*

bardment until 1 March, but that night, after the ships operating inside the Straits had silenced many of the guns on shore, the minesweepers, covered by destroyers, got within one and a half miles of Kephez Point before being driven off by gunfire.

The Turks had certainly been very impressed. There was something approaching panic in Constantinople where women and children were leaving the capital; gold was being sent by the banks to Asia Minor and arrangements had been made to evacuate the Sultan.

The naval bombardment continued every day with short breaks caused by bad weather until 8 March. At night the sweepers attempted to clear the Kephez minefields, but with very little success. The strong current down the Straits hindered them; they were lit up by searchlights on shore which the escorting destroyers were unable to put out and the mine-sweeping trawlers proved almost useless under fire. Small landing parties endeavouring to destroy the guns in silenced forts met with increasing resistance.

The Turks had hurried to strengthen their defences, bringing up field artillery to cover the minefields. The Turkish fire was far from deadly, but the minesweepers with their fisherman crews were ineffective. No doubt their men were individually brave enough, but they were undisciplined and facing strange dangers.

For twelve days the operation dribbled on, the ships bombarding by day whenever the weather was suitable and the minesweepers attempting to sweep up to Kephez Point at night. Battleships endeavoured to put out the powerful searchlights, but without success. The sweepers were heavily fired upon, but the aim was bad; casualties in ships and men were negligible. Keyes described what he saw on the night of 10 March.

The sweepers . . . were so agitated that four out of six . . . did not get their kites down, and so swept the surface . . . a tremendous fire was opened on them as they came down, and they and some of the destroyers in support were hit; but our only casualties were one trawler sunk by a mine and two men wounded.

Next night,

To put it briefly, the sweepers turned tail and fled directly they were fired upon. I was furious and told the officers in charge that . . . it did not matter if we lost all seven sweepers; there were twenty-eight more and the mines had got to be swept up. How could they talk of being stopped by heavy fire if they were not hit?

Rather belatedly as it seems steps were now taken to stiffen the crews of the sweepers with volunteers from the Fleet. Sweeping was now more effective and the area in which the battleships would have to operate when attacking the Narrows forts was believed to have been cleared of mines.

The Admiralty were becoming impatient. To spur Carden on they had told him on 11 March that they were not unappreciative of the results so far obtained, but that the gains were so important that the loss of ships and men was fully justified. Time was precious. The enemy was harried and anxious and the forts were running short of ammunition, but the possibility of U-boats arriving off the Straits must be considered. Carden replied that he fully appreciated the situation and intended to clear the minefields by day under cover of a really vigorous attack on the forts at the Narrows.

Poor Carden had never been really equal to the task imposed upon him. His health was rapidly failing. "He worried terribly," wrote Keyes in his diary, "everything he ate gave him a severe pain, and he was not eating enough to keep him going in such strenuous times." After seeing a Harley Street physician who was serving in the Fleet he was put on the sick list, handing over to his second-in-command Rear-Admiral John de Robeck. In one of his final telegrams he asked that military operations on a large scale should be commenced immediately to ensure his lines of communication after the fleet had entered the Sea of Marmara. General Sir Ian Hamilton had been appointed to command the Army, but the troops had not yet sailed. However Carden had agreed that the moment had come "for vigorous and sustained action" by the Fleet.

His successor fully concurred. De Robeck, an officer with a great reputation as a peace-time admiral, was junior to the other flag officer on the spot Rear-Admiral Wemyss, but Wemyss agreed to serve under de Robeck who was much more in touch with the details of the operation about to begin.

"Thus carefully," wrote Winston Churchill, "did Destiny pick her footsteps at the Dardanelles." But at the moment everyone was satisfied. With de Robeck in command and Keyes as his Chief of Staff the Navy seemed to have strong, able leaders for the big attack planned for 18 March. Hope was high. The events of the next few days were to prove decisive for the whole Dardanelles campaign.

The Turks had never had much faith in the strength of the outer forts and had concentrated their efforts on the defences of the Narrows. Field artillery and howitzers had been disposed below the Narrows forts on both European and Asiatic shores to cover the area below Kephez Point. Nine lines of mines, all of them under the guns ashore, had been laid across the channel from Kephez Bay to just above the Narrows. Ships engaging the forts at Chanak and Kephez would be below this minefield in an area roughly opposite Eren Keui. No fresh mines had been swept up in this area for some time and reports from aircraft, which seemed to be able to see the mines through the clear water and on which considerable reliance had come to be placed, were negative. In February and early March ships had often manoeuvred in Eren Keui Bay, a fact which had not escaped the notice of the enemy. Unobserved by the Allies on 9 March a small mine-layer with a Turco-German crew carefully laid a single line of twenty-six mines, not across the channel like the other minefields, but parallel to the Asiatic shore in Eren Keui Bay. This handful of mines was to influence the course of the whole war.

The morning of 18 March was fine and still. At 8.45 the minesweepers had reported "all clear" up to White Cliffs. The battle fleet moved in to the attack.

The heavy ships were divided into three lines, "A," "B" and "C." Line "A," the modern battleship *Queen Elizabeth* flying de Robeck's flag, four old battleships and the battle-cruiser *Inflexible* would lead the attack and endeavour to silence

the forts and guns by long-range bombardment. When this
was accomplished Line "B," four old French battleships,
would pass through Line "A" and engage the forts at close
range. Line "C," six old British battleships, was held in reserve. The Fleet, preceded by minesweeping destroyers,
steamed into the Straits. At 11 a.m. Line "A" was in action.
It was a splendid sight—pale blue sky, dark blue sea and the
brown shores of Gallipoli and Asia Minor. The great ships,
stabs of flame darting from their guns, vomited cordite fumes
which temporarily hid them from view. Clouds of smoke and
dust rose from the distant forts. Columns of white water
sprang up around the battleships. Soon after noon fire from
the shore had slackened and Line "B" was ordered forward.
Keyes watched Contre-Amiral Guépratte's ships passing
through Line "A," the old battleships "a brave show." As
they steamed into action and began a furious bombardment at
closer range, "their approach woke up the enemy . . . and a
tremendous cannonade ensued." The French fire was effective,
but Guépratte's ships received heavy punishment in return.
Gradually the fire of the forts in the Narrows slackened, but
the intermediate batteries which had been withholding their
fire now roared into action. French and British ships were frequently hit, but their armour effectively protected them from
serious damage or casualties. As the forts at the Narrows
seemed to have been mastered de Robeck ordered the minesweepers to clear the way ahead into Sari Siglar Bay. The old
British battleships of Line "C," fresh and full of ammunition,
were sent in to relieve the French battleships. It was 1.45 p.m.

The position was by no means unsatisfactory. Fire from the
forts had practically ceased. The French battleships which
had borne the brunt of the engagement were somewhat battered, but only the *Gaulois*, struck below the waterline by a
heavy shell, was seriously damaged. Casualties had been extremely light and only one of the ten big ships so far engaged
had had her fighting efficiency impaired.

The French ships turned outwards in pairs to close the
European and Asiatic shores and make way for Line "C."

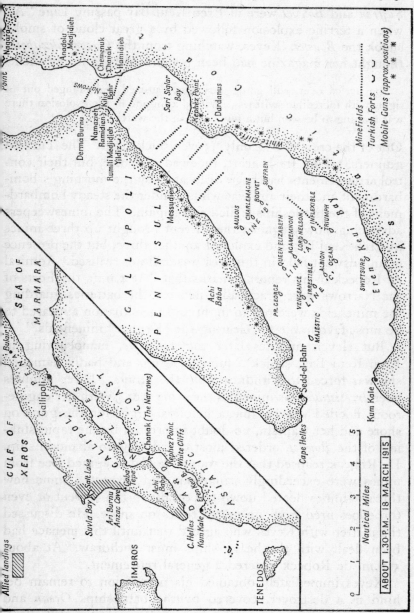

U

Suffren and *Bouvet* were in Eren Keui Bay passing Line "A" when a terrific explosion followed by a great cloud of smoke shook the *Bouvet*. Keyes, watching from the *Queen Elizabeth*, thought her magazine had been penetrated by a heavy shell.

She heeled over, still going very fast, capsized and plunged out of sight, with incredible swiftness. Within a minute of the explosion there was nothing to be seen but a few heads in the water.

Out of the crew of 674 only 35 were picked up. The Turkish gunners, taking fresh heart, renewed their fire, but their control arrangements had been dislocated by the morning's bombardment and their aim was wild. Under the steady bombardment of the battleships it died away again. The minesweepers advancing slowly against the current brought up three mines in Eren Keui Bay and exploded another three, but the presence of an unswept field in this area was still not realised. Admiral de Robeck in his report remarks that "At 4 p.m. the Forts of the Narrows were practically silenced; the batteries guarding the minefields were put to flight and the situation appeared to be most favourable for clearing the [Kephez] minefields."

But eleven minutes later the *Inflexible*, manoeuvring in Eren Keui Bay, struck a mine. Listing and badly damaged she was forced to withdraw from the Straits. Three minutes later *Irresistible* was mined in the same area. With her engine-room flooded she became a helpless target for the guns on shore and her Captain, no doubt impressed by the rapid sinking of the *Bouvet*, ordered most of his crew to abandon ship. De Robeck realised that the waters he had imagined free from mines were exceedingly dangerous and suspected some new threat—mines floated down the Straits in the current or even torpedoes fired from unlocated tubes on shore. He discussed the matter with Keyes who agreed that until this menace had been dealt with the heavy ships must withdraw. At about 5 p.m. de Robeck ordered a general retirement.

Keyes immediately obtained his permission to remain behind in a destroyer, covered by the battleships *Ocean* and *Swiftsure*, to try and save the *Irresistible* which was still afloat.

Delighted to be able to take a personal part in the battle he set off, found *Irresistible* under heavy fire, but on an even keel and in no immediate danger of sinking and endeavoured to persuade *Ocean* to take her in tow. *Ocean* procrastinated (her Captain was senior to Keyes). She was

steaming about blazing away at the forts, much to my anxiety, as it was obvious that the enemy had some unpleasant form of mine about, and it seemed only a question of time before she hit one.

At 6.5 p.m. there was another shattering explosion, *Ocean* took a heavy list and was also abandoned by her crew.

Keyes returned to the *Queen Elizabeth* where he told de Robeck "exactly what I thought of the proceedings of the last two hours and our failure to salve *Irresistible*."

Both she and *Ocean* were still afloat, so he returned after nightfall to try and tow them into the current or destroy them if they looked like drifting ashore and falling into enemy hands. After a thorough search he came to the conclusion that both ships had sunk.

The . . . four hours which I spent in the Dardanelles were intensely interesting and made a lasting impression on me. Indeed, I think they were to a great extent responsible for my feeling of absolute certainty— which has never wavered—that our Fleet, with efficient minesweepers, would have no difficulty in forcing a passage into the Marmara.

Except for the searchlights there seemed to be no sign of life, and I had the most indelible impression that we were in the presence of a beaten foe. I thought he was beaten at 2 p.m. I knew he was beaten at 4 p.m.—and at midnight I knew with still greater certainty that he was absolutely beaten; and it only remained for us to organise a proper sweeping force and devise some means to deal with drifting mines to reap the fruits of our efforts.

In Constantinople the general feeling was exactly as Keyes had guessed. Henry Morgenthau, the American Ambassador, was to write later.

It seems so strange now, this conviction in the minds of everyone then —that the success of the Allied Fleets against the Dardanelles was in-evitable, and that the capture of Constantinople was a matter of only a few days.[1]

[1] *Secrets of the Bosphorus* by Henry Morgenthau, Hutchinson, 1918.

True the morale of the stubborn Turkish and German troops in the forts was unshaken. Casualties had been low and the damage, though extensive, was largely confined to works and communications. Most of the guns were still serviceable, but they had fired away half their ammunition. It could not be replaced without considerable delay and less than twenty of the only shells effective against armoured ships remained. The lighter guns which had kept the minesweepers from the Kephez minefields had ammunition for not more than two or three days and the mines themselves once swept could not be replaced (total reserves amounted to thirty-six). Beyond the Narrows the old forts with their obsolete guns would present no obstacle. The instinct which is such an essential attribute of any successful military commander which made Keyes think the enemy was beaten was not at fault. Except for the men of the *Bouvet* casualties on the Allied side had been negligible. Three old battleships, which could quickly be replaced, had been sunk and three other ships were out of action, but these material losses could easily be sustained. Next day de Robeck seemed quite clearly to believe that the operations should continue after a short delay whilst the minesweeping force was reorganised, by fitting destroyers for sweeping and replacing the civilian crews of the trawlers with volunteers from the crews of *Ocean* and *Irresistible*.

The Admiralty signalled their approval and said that four battleships would be sent at once to replace losses. "Thus everything," wrote Churchill, "was so far steady and resolved."

But de Robeck had been profoundly disturbed by the losses of 18 March. He had been reared in the material school; the school which for years had believed that numbers and size were all-important. Great ships to him were an end in themselves, not just the means to an end. At the height of the battle he had insisted on giving Keyes *written* instructions to torpedo the helpless *Irresistible* if he could not prevent her falling into enemy hands. "Saying I had no idea what a fuss the Admiralty would make about the torpedoing of one of His

Majesty's ships." He knew that his ultimate superior, the First Sea Lord, had always been lukewarm about a purely naval effort. De Robeck had risen to high command in Fisher's Navy and the terrible old man in Whitehall represented everything he had worked for. It was true that the Admiralty at the moment seemed quite undismayed, condoling with his misfortunes and promising reinforcements. To Keyes de Robeck seemed quite "steady and resolved," but his first reactions—on the evening of 18 March—"After losing so many ships I shall obviously find myself superseded tomorrow morning" is the clue to his real feelings. On 21 March he sailed for Lemnos in the *Queen Elizabeth* for a high level conference with General Sir Ian Hamilton.

Hamilton had arrived on the spot just in time to be an eyewitness of the events of 18 March. They made a profound impression on his mind. On 19 March he sent a message to Kitchener which began

I am most reluctantly driven to the conclusion that the Straits are not likely to be forced by battleships. . . . The army's part will be . . . a deliberate and prepared military operation carried out at full strength . . .

Hamilton had strong views, never subsequently departed from, on not interfering in naval affairs, but at the conference next day he found that the Admiral was of the same mind. "The moment we sat down de Robeck told us that he was now quite clear he could not get through without the help of all my troops."[1]

Even after all these years there is no available record of exactly what took place on this momentous occasion. Keyes, busy with the work of re-organisation, unfortunately was not present and de Robeck had given him no inkling of his intention of abandoning the purely naval attack.

Faced with this unanimous opinion of their naval and military commanders the War Council somewhat reluctantly agreed to abandon the attempt to force the Straits with ships alone.

Unfortunately there was considerable delay before the Army

[1] *Gallipoli Diary* by Ian Hamilton.

was ready. "The English allowed me four whole weeks before
their great landings," wrote General Liman von Sanders the
supreme commander of the Turkish and German forces, . . .
"This space of time just about sufficed to carry out the necessary measures." The Army landed in force on 25 April. In
spite of very hard fighting in which the utmost heroism was
time and again displayed, and heavy casualties, they were held
up within a short distance of the beaches early in May.

To watch the troops going ashore to endure all whilst he
remained in safety and comfort in the Fleet was agony to
Keyes, especially as he was convinced that the Navy could do
so much more to help.

Since the 21 March there had been increasing divergence
between his views and those of his C.-in-C. De Robeck was a
man of great personal charm. Ellis Ashmead Bartlett describes
him as

a most delightful man, a perfect replica of the courteous type of the old
English sportsman and country gentleman of bygone days before they
were harassed from their lairs by the super tax and the decline in agri-
culture.

The Admiral and his Chief of Staff remained friends, but with
Keyes continually pressing for strong, offensive action and de
Robeck at the most lukewarm, content for his powerful force
to fill an important but subsidiary role.

In May Keyes managed to persuade de Robeck to try
again.

De Robeck thought as I thought [wrote Hamilton in his diary on
10 May] that the Army would save his ships, but our last battle has
shown him that the Army would only open the Straits at a cost greater
than the loss of some ships and that the time has come to strike home
with the tremendous mechanism of the Fleet.

But the costly initial failure of the Gallipoli landings had
led to Lord Fisher's resignation which in its turn sparked off a
political storm in London from which a Coalition Government
emerged. Winston Churchill was superseded at the Admiralty, leaving Asquith, the Prime Minister, without his

mainspring.[1] The French Government, obsessed by other dangers, were anxious to reduce their commitments at the Dardanelles. They proposed to replace the excellent Admiral Guépratte by a more cautious man. (Luckily this step was delayed). As if all this was not enough U 21 arrived off the Dardanelles on 25 May and sank the battleships *Triumph* and *Majestic*, causing the heavy ships to withdraw to Mudros and other harbours. The small ships of the Navy, destroyers, landing craft and above all submarines, continued to give splendid and devoted assistance, but when the Army, without the support of naval heavy gunfire, attempted to break out of the beachheads in June they were unsuccessful.

The "Keyesites," as they were now openly called, never wavered from their belief that the Fleet could still force the Straits at a cost in casualties only a fraction of those being endured by the Army. In August 16 battleships, 15 cruisers, 16 monitors, 37 destroyers, 18 submarines and 125 trawlers were available; all the larger ships "expendable" without altering the vital balance of power in the North Sea. But, writes Hamilton,

the Navy (was) still divided. Some there are who would wish me to urge the Admiral to play first fiddle in the coming attack. This *I will not do*. I have neither the data nor the technical knowledge which would justify me in my conscience for doing so.

Admiral Wemyss, the second-in-command, had come round to Keyes' view but de Robeck remained inflexible. Great responsibility prolonged over several months is a terrible test. It had been too much for de Robeck. Failing health added to his pessimism; magnifying every difficulty, but blinding him to the possibilities of success.

Keyes continued to press his views and to try and urge him on. "I had it out with the Admiral on Friday and again on Saturday. He can only see disaster, and paints pictures—which one ought not to do in war."

1 "Asquith for sure, chucks away the mainspring if he parts with Winston." Ian Hamilton's Diary.

During the night of 6–7 August a force of 16,000 men
began new landings at Suvla. The project was well conceived
and could have succeeded, but the evil genius of Gallipoli de-
creed that the commanding general should be unequal to his
task. Whilst he was virtually unopposed he wavered. When
reinforcements had been hurried to strengthen the defence he
attacked without vigour or skill. Poor Hamilton had all too
often

to fight with one of the worst combinations of World War 1; raw and
young and perhaps high-spirited troops and superannuated and inefficient
generals, to tackle the most complicated tasks.[1]

The last real chance had gone. How good a chance it was
is proved by the records of the enemy C.-in-C. General Liman
von Sanders.

The Anafarta (Suvla) landing was . . . intended to open the Dardanelles to the Allies by land action while at the same time cutting [my]
Fifth Army from its communications . . . [If successful], the batteries of
the fortress on the Straits would have been quickly silenced as they had
little ammunition. The minefields in the Straits could then be removed
and no further difficulties lay in the way of the victorious British Army
and the Allied fleet . . .
Secure communications between the Western Powers and Russia
would have been established and Turkey would have been split off from
the Central Powers. In that case it is more than improbable that Bulgaria
would have relinquished her neutrality . . .
Thus the Anafarta landing, which in point of time lies approximately
in the middle of the Dardanelles Campaign of eight and a half months,
was its political military summit . . .

Keyes still refused to accept defeat. Wemyss and the
younger officers of de Robeck's staff agreed that the chances
of a break-through by the Fleet were better now than they had
been on 18 March, but de Robeck was adamant, wearily refusing to put forward a plan for a naval attack even when the
Admiralty promised their support for any use he cared to
make of his old battleships.

I am torn to know what to do, [wrote Keyes in his diary]. I can do
nothing while I am on the Admiral's staff. I ought to resign; but if I do

[1] *Naval Operations in the Mediterranean.* Crisman.

so and go home, it will be very difficult to persuade the Admiralty to listen to me.

Resignation might achieve nothing, except the ruin of his own career. Nevertheless, with the full support of his wife whom he felt must be told of a step in which she and his family were involved, he asked de Robeck's permission to go to London and lay his plan before the Board, and offered to resign his appointment. De Robeck, a great gentleman if not a great admiral, allowed him to go, still as his Chief of Staff though hardly with his blessing.

Keyes was so convincing that he succeeded in winning over both the Admiralty and Lord Kitchener to what even Churchill described as a plan "remarkable for its audacity." (Rushing the Straits with old battleships preceded by very old battleships as mine-clearers filled with wood to make them virtually unsinkable.) He asked to command part of the force himself and no doubt would have done so with ardour and skill.

But second thoughts prevailed. Hamilton had been relieved in command by General Monro, who had arrived off Gallipoli already more than half convinced that "we must put a stop to this damned side-show," as his Chief of Staff told Keyes. "He came, he saw, he capitulated," wrote Churchill. Kitchener, after visiting Monro and de Robeck on the spot, decided to recommend evacuation.

In late November de Robeck, a sick man, went home on leave, his place being taken by Wemyss who put through yet another plan for rushing the Narrows (Keyes was nothing if not persistent) only to be informed that evacuation had been decided upon. With the excellent co-operation between the Forces which had survived all vicissitudes this difficult operation was carried out without loss.

Keyes never altered his opinion that the Fleet could have forced the Straits. This is what he wrote in 1943, with all the information from our own and enemy sources available.

I was present when the first shot of the campaign was fired in February 1915, and the last in January 1916, and during all the intermediate fighting . . . I spent many hours in the Dardanelles under fire from the forts and concealed howitzers—a greatly exaggerated menace. I saw ships sunk by mine and torpedo, watched the Homeric fighting on the beaches, and the great battles which followed, in the course of which thousands of soldiers perished.

I lived in close association with the administrative officers at the advanced bases, and the fighting soldiers in Gallipoli . . .

I wish to place on record that I had no doubt then, and have none now —and nothing will ever shake my opinion—that from 4 April 1915 onwards, the Fleet could have forced the Straits, and with losses trifling in comparison with those the Army suffered; could have entered the Marmara with sufficient force to destroy the Turko-German Fleet.

This operation would have cut the communications—which were seaborne—of any Turkish armies, either in Gallipoli or on the Asiatic side, and would have led immediately to a victory, decisive upon the whole course of the war.

From mid-1916 Keyes served in the Grand Fleet, in command of the battleship *Centurion*, and, on promotion to Rear-Admiral, as second-in-command of the Fourth Battle Squadron. In 1917 Wemyss had left the Mediterranean and was serving at the Admiralty as Deputy First Sea Lord. The battle against the U-boats was at its height and both he and the First Lord, Sir Eric Geddes, were convinced that new blood was needed at Whitehall to promote much more vigorous action against the submarines whose success might still be decisive. Wemyss persuaded Keyes to accept the post of Director of the newly formed Plans Division.

Asdic (sonar) for locating submerged submarines was not available in 1917 and destruction of the U-boats preying on the trade routes was difficult. Fortunately their numbers were reduced by comparatively low endurance which limited the time they could spend at sea. But by passing through the Channel to their patrol areas in the Western Approaches U-boats based on Germany and Flanders were able to add several days to the length of their effective patrols.

Admiral R. H. Bacon commanding the Dover Patrol obstinately clung to the belief that the barrage of nets and mines he had laid across the straits of Dover had effectually prevented submarines passing in any numbers, but a few days after Keyes arrived at the Admiralty documents seized in a captured U-boat proved that some thirty submarines a month were safely negotiating the minefield by remaining on the surface at night or by diving underneath it. Bacon now agreed to a deep minefield being laid, but was stubbornly averse to the Admiralty's other proposal to illuminate the Straits at night, forcing the submarines to dive. Geddes decided that a change of command at Dover was essential. Admiral Sir John Jellicoe, the First Sea Lord, disagreed. The dispute between them was a contributory factor to the "sacking" of Jellicoe from the Admiralty and his replacement by Admiral Wemyss. Keyes, who had been on a visit to the Grand Fleet, was sent for by Wemyss on his return and offered the Dover Command.

Well, Roger, you have talked a hell of a lot about what ought to be done in the Dover area. Now you must go down there and do it yourself.

The first reaction of the Dover Patrol to the sudden replacement of Bacon was one of resentment. But the influence of the Commander of a large force on each one of his many subordinates is a strange thing. There were some three hundred ships large and small and a great many men in the Dover Command. Most of them rarely saw their Admiral and few were in direct contact, even with his written orders. Yet after a very few days a new spirit was abroad, offensive rather than defensive.

The essence of Keyes' plan was to make the Straits as bright as Piccadilly and to concentrate every available vessel above the deep minefield, forcing the submarines to dive.

There would be no shallow mines near the deep minefield and nothing to prevent the free passage of patrol vessels above the whole mined area. The patrol would be maintained as densely as possible, both night and day, and brilliantly illuminated with flares and searchlights throughout the night.

The patrols being clearly visible might be torpedoed by submarines and the enemy would certainly be forced to attack them with surface ships. The risks were accepted, welcomed indeed, as they would give a chance of striking back.

These measures were expected to reduce the numbers of
U-boats passing the Straits, forcing them to take the much
longer route around the North of Scotland, but there was a
further plan—to immobilise the base at Bruges in Belgium
from which many of them came.

Bruges, though eight miles from the sea, is a considerable
port. The Germans held the Belgian coast from near Nieuport
to the Dutch frontier. It was very strongly fortified with a
great number of guns, under cover of which defensive minefields were maintained. The coast, low-lying, almost straight,
swept by strong tidal streams, was further protected by shoal
water and numerous sandbanks. Channels, some of which
have to be kept open by dredging, are constantly changing.
There are no natural seaports, but artificial harbours had been
constructed at Zeebrugge, Blankenberge and Ostend. Blankenberge, almost dry at low tide, could only be used by light
craft. Ostend was suitable for submarines and destroyers, but
was under the guns of Allied artillery. By far the most important was Zeebrugge, joined to Bruges by a modern ship
canal. It was the main outlet to the sea for the large number
of U-boats and destroyers based on Bruges, with its dockyard
and bomb-proof submarine shelters.

As early as 1915 Tyrwhitt had proposed the blocking of
Zeebrugge, an idea mooted on a number of occasions but never
translated into a concrete plan until Keyes went to the Admiralty in late 1917. Keyes, with his experience of sea-land
operations in China and the Dardanelles, threw himself heart
and soul into the idea. A plan to block both Zeebrugge and
Ostend was produced to which Bacon agreed, making some
early moves to put it into practice. Now Keyes had a free hand
to carry on with the operation in any way he thought fit. As
Director of Plans he had already obtained Admiral Beatty's
agreement to a picked force of officers and men being drawn
from the Grand Fleet. These men, supplemented by a force
of Royal Marines, were now given intensive training. The
essence of the plan was to block the sea-exits of the small canal
from Bruges to Ostend and the much more important canal

from Bruges to Zeebrugge with sunken ships specially prepared for the purpose. Ostend was always a subsidiary objective. The really important nut to crack was Zeebrugge.

The Belgians had constructed a very large mole at Zeebrugge. Like a great scimitar with its handle touching the shore it swept north and east for one and a half miles, forming a harbour outside the locks through which the Bruges–Zeebrugge canal joins the sea. These locks were about half a mile inland, joined to the coastline by a very narrow "cut," from the end of which a dredged channel continued across the harbour for about a mile to the lighthouse at the end of the mole. There was sufficient water beside the mole for destroyers and other small war vessels. As the whole harbour would soon have silted up if the stone and concrete mole had been continuous its shoreward end was formed by an iron viaduct through which the tide raced, its scour helping to keep the anchorage clear. The rest of the mole was an immensely strong structure over eighty yards wide for most of its length on which was built the railway station, sheds, cranes and other appurtenances of a busy seaport. The eastern extremity was narrow; a long prong ending at the lighthouse. The top of the mole was only nine feet above high water, but along its seaward side was a great wall twenty feet high, its top cut away to make a pathway running the whole length of the mole and protected by a stout parapet. At infrequent intervals flights of steps joined this pathway to the broad surface of the mole proper, sixteen feet below.

The Germans made good use of the mole, inside which vessels were berthed. At the shoreward end was a seaplane base and the various sheds were used as stores and as accommodation for a garrison of about a thousand men. Six guns were mounted on the lighthouse "prong" pointing to seaward and three large guns on the end of the mole proper covered the mouth of the channel from the lighthouse to the canal at point-blank range. On the coast were more guns, commanding the sea approaches, with batteries near the locks pointing directly down the channel.

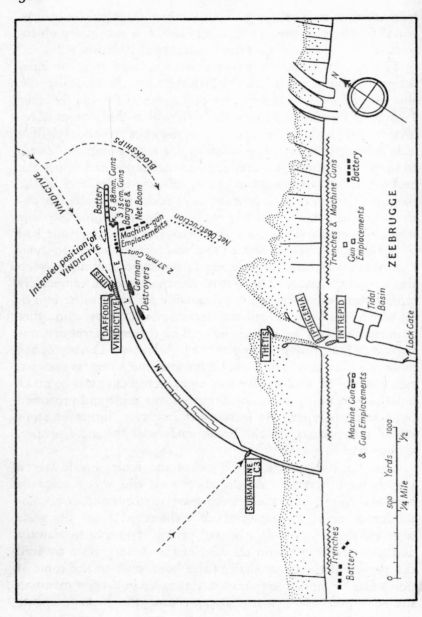

For blockships to reach the vital "cut" between the locks and the sea—the only place narrow enough to be effectively obstructed—was clearly a most difficult proposition. Even if they could get as far as the lighthouse unseen they still had nearly a mile to go, under the guns on the mole, of ships berthed alongside it and of the batteries on shore.

With an onshore wind the approach to the lighthouse, though fraught with many difficulties, might be accomplished under cover of an artificial smoke-screen laid by small vessels creeping in under cover of darkness. There was no radar in those days and given absolute secrecy it was reasonable to assume that such an enterprise by its very daring would take the enemy by surprise. But to allow the blockships to cover the last mile of their journey it was essential to confuse the defence by a diversionary attack. Keyes planned to lay assault ships alongside the mole before the blockships arrived, capture the guns on the spur, attack the battery at the end of the mole proper and generally to create such a disturbance that the enemy would believe that a landing on the mole was the real objective. To prevent reinforcements reaching the mole the viaduct must somehow be breached.

Even on paper it was a complex plan, calling for minute preparation and split-second timing. Special ships must be prepared and every detail worked out in advance. In the turmoil of the attack, which had to be made at night to stand any chance of success, direction would be almost impossible. All would depend on the soundness of the plan and the valour and initiative of the men, carefully rehearsed against dummy objectives, but certain to meet with all sorts of unexpected difficulties.

By early April all was ready. On the eleventh Keyes, flying his flag in the destroyer *Warwick*, sailed from the lonely anchorage off the mouth of the Thames where his force had been assembled. He arrived off the Belgian coast, only to be thwarted by a change of wind from north to south just before he gave the order for the final advance. Two days later he tried again, but was frustrated by a freshening wind and a rising sea which would make it impossible to berth the assault ships on the weather side of the mole. The Admiralty now decided that these delays must have allowed the secret to leak out and were within an ace of cancelling the operation altogether, but Keyes begged to be allowed to try once again ten days later when there would be the necessary high tide around midnight, though with a full moon. On the eve of St George's Day 1918 the expedition sailed for the third time.

The ships crept shoreward through the darkness. Except for a slight swell the sea was calm. The wind was favourable. But soon after 11 p.m. it began to rain; the onshore breeze became fitful, and fell calm. But the die was cast. The motor boats laying the smoke-screen had gone ahead. Clouds of acrid smoke blanketed out the moon, reducing visibility to a couple of hundred yards. At ten minutes to midnight the old cruiser *Vindictive*, assaulting gangways triced up along her port side, towing the converted Mersey ferry steamers *Iris* and *Daffodil*, was within a mile of the lighthouse. Men fingered their weapons as they waited in the darkness. There was no sight or sound of the enemy.

The wind had died away, but now it blew gently, from the land. The smoke which had hidden the shore began to roll away. *Vindictive* passed through thinning clouds into the moonlight, dead on course for the mole, but still about half a mile away. Within a few seconds the guns on shore opened up. The ships replied and the *Vindictive*, at her full speed of 16 knots, surged forward, parting the tow to *Daffodil* and *Iris*. It took her five minutes to reach the mole, five minutes during which the German guns could hardly miss. In their excitement the enemy aimed at her upper works, ignoring the fact that a few shells in her vitals would have brought her to a standstill. But the upper works were crowded with men manning guns, searchlights and flame throwers, waiting to secure the ship to the mole with special grapnels and to pilot her alongside. Casualties were heavy, including many of the leaders of the assault forces waiting nearest to the boarding ladders. *Vindictive* forged along, gaining some shelter as she got close in under the mole. At 0001, just a minute after the scheduled time, she was alongside, but in the confusion she came to rest, not abreast the spur battery, but three hundred yards to the westward. The surge of the swell against the towering face of the mole was making *Vindictive* roll, and the securing grapnels were ineffective, but *Daffodil* now arrived, appreciated the position at a glance and pushed her bow against *Vindictive*, holding her in position. Over the swaying gangways not already smashed by shell-fire seamen and marines swarmed on to the mole.

The scene was indescribable, even by those who lived through it. Starshells and searchlights made it almost as light as day. Continuous gunfire from the ships, the mole and the shore made such an appalling din that it was difficult to pass an order. Through this inferno the assault force clambered over the swaying gangways, suffering heavy casualties, but effectually engaging the attention of the enemy. Coastal Motor Boats sweeping round the lighthouse were now engaging ships alongside the mole, diverting their attention from *Vindictive* at whom they had been firing at eighty yards range.

Suddenly there was a tremendous explosion from the shore end of the mole. The old submarine C3, crammed with explosives, had been run right in under the viaduct—her crew of two officers and four men disdaining to use the gyro-steering provided. Jammed amongst the piers and girders she had blown up, tearing a gap 100 feet wide and cutting off communications with the shore. The gallant crew miraculously escaped alive under a hail of machine-gun fire from a few yards range.

At 12.15 a.m., punctual to the minute, *Thetis*, *Intrepid* and *Iphigenia*, old cruisers converted to blockships and loaded with cement, sighted the mole dead ahead and made for the entrance to the channel. *Thetis* leading the line fouled a wire net which jammed her propellers. As she came to rest near the piers at the mouth of the "cut" the Germans seemed suddenly to become aware of the real object of the attack. Under heavy fire *Thetis* ran aground and had to be sunk where she was, but

Intrepid and *Iphigenia* forged on past her into the narrow channel below the locks, turned across it in spite of a murderous fusillade at very short range and sank themselves right across the "cut."

The job was done. It remained to rescue the brave men who were still alive. Not least of the gallant exploits of an epic act of war was the work of the motor launches; frail, unprotected craft which managed to bring away the living of the crews of *Intrepid*, *Iphigenia* and *Thetis*. *Vindictive* recalled her decimated assault parties and drew away to sea with the gallant *Daffodil*, which had kept her in position for more than an hour. Gradually the firing died away as the ships faded into the darkness. Amongst the very last to go was the *Warwick* with Vice-Admiral Keyes aboard. Searching in the neighbourhood of the lighthouse for damaged ships he came across an M.L. crammed with blockship survivors. The men cheered wildly as they saw the huge Vice-Admiral's flag which *Warwick* was wearing. Amongst them were the captains of *Intrepid* and *Iphigenia*, Lieutenants Billyard Leake and Bonham Carter. The success of the whole operation had hinged on their efforts. They had done what had been entrusted to them, but Zeebrugge was in the best sense a combined operation. Every ship and man who was at Zeebrugge on St George's Day had played their part.

There was no doubt in anybody's mind to whom the victory was largely due. Though forced to remain comparatively inactive whilst the fight was actually in progress it was Roger Keyes who had gauged, and rightly gauged, what was materially and humanly possible; his ardent spirit which had sustained his force during the long weeks of preparation; confidence in his ability which had inspired them in the hour of battle. Keyes and Zeebrugge will always be spoken of together.

Four weeks later aerial photographs showed twelve submarines and twenty-three destroyers still apparently immobilised at Bruges and in the canals "lying like salmon waiting for a spate." These material factors could not be permanent, but the epic of Zeebrugge, coming at one of the critical moments of the war, put new heart into the Allies. On the Western Front they had their backs to the wall. The U-boats were still taking a serious toll. At this, the darkest hour before the dawn of victory, Zeebrugge was a bright flash of inspiration.

In his command of the Dover Patrol Roger Keyes reached the apex of his career. His courage, his burning desire to get at the enemy, his gift of inspiring others, his humanity, his genius for a certain type of war—all had full scope. The proof of his success is in cold figures. U-boats had been passing through the Straits at the rate of twenty-four a month. In April boats based on Germany were no longer attempting the passage. After Zeebrugge the Flanders-based submarines, when they could again negotiate the still partly-blocked canal, were mostly forced to go round the north of Scotland. Only two U-boats passed Dover in September and one of these was destroyed in attempting to return through the Straits, bringing the total score of the Dover Patrol to thirteen for the year. Allied shipping losses in the Channel fell from around twenty to half a dozen ships a month. Minelaying submarines had been putting down over thirty fields a month; the average for 1918 was six.

When the war ended Vice-Admiral Sir Roger Keyes was forty-six. He was actively employed for a further fifteen years, filling some of the highest posts in the Navy. Kindly, considerate and blessed with considerable personal charm he was popular with his subordinates: his tremendous reputation lent him considerable weight. But peace time gave him less scope for his gift for courageous leadership and he had neither the intellectual capacity nor the broad appreciation of technical requirements to make a great administrator. (The Trenchard–Keyes Agreement which governed the maintenance and provision of ship-borne aircraft from 1924 to 1937 had disastrous consequences for naval aviation.) The instinctive good judgment which made men gladly follow him in battle did not develop into the even rarer quality of wisdom.

Somehow his very real accomplishments became obscured, most unjustly as it seems, by trivialities.

He had always been fond of polo and as C.in-C. Mediterranean encouraged young officers to take up what was then an inexpensive game, rightly considering that it developed quick thinking and a willingness to take risks. Naturally enough a good many of those around him were polo players and somehow it came to be more than half believed that the "galloping game" was a swift road to promotion. During combined manoeuvres by the Mediterranean and Atlantic Fleets Keyes' battleships were reputed to have gained an unfair advantage by passing unscathed through a dummy minefield. Some wag drew a cartoon showing the officers of the *Queen Elizabeth* mounted on the lower booms, clearing the way with their polo sticks. Keyes thought it an excellent joke, but the theme probed a tender spot and some of his staff were furious, suggesting that the cartoon was in such bad taste that official action was called for. These were small enough matters, but just before he left the station came the *Royal Oak* affair.

Life in the narrow confines of a ship can be trying, though good sense and the strong stream of tradition can usually be trusted to rub away the jagged edges of conflicting temperaments, as a river rounds off pebbles forced to lie together in its bed. But there can be exceptions, and when the Admiral, Captain and Commander of a flagship are concerned there can be trouble. Keyes had noticed that the Rear-Admiral of his battle-squadron and his Flag-captain were on prickly terms, but after some investigation decided that no action was necessary. But a storm was brewing. Bandmaster Barnacles' melancholy playing at a quarter-deck dance was the primer which set off such an explosion that the C.-in-C. felt compelled to remove the three most senior officers from the *Royal Oak* at spectacularly short notice. The press yelped into full cry. Words like "mutiny" were bandied about; there were questions in the House and all the trappings of a first-class scandal. What Keyes had done *after* the trouble started was supported by such very experienced commanders as Beatty, but his handling of the whole regrettable affair raised dormant doubts in very high quarters as to his suitability for the post which it had generally been assumed he was about to fill—First Sea Lord. It is a post where naval qualifications must be allied to political acumen. The appointment is made by the Government, represented by the First Lord, after consulting naval opinion in the person of the outgoing First Sea Lord. Keyes had had a meteoric career and was not without his enemies, but a great many officers and men were bitterly disappointed when he did not go from Malta to Whitehall. Instead he was offered and accepted the Portsmouth command. When in 1934 it became clear that he would never be called upon to fill the Navy's highest post he accepted nomination as Conservative candidate for Portsmouth North. In February 1934 he entered the House of Commons.

In Parliament he fought hard for the Navy, opposing anything he thought was to its detriment with his usual moral courage. Though a bad speaker he could, on occasions, carry conviction by his sincerity and honesty of purpose, but the causes which he supported were not always wisely chosen.

When war came in 1939 he was sixty-six, still physically very fit and still young at heart. During the unsuccessful Norwegian campaign in the spring of 1940 he put forward a plan for an assault on Trondheim using old battleships of little fighting value, begging to be allowed to organise and lead the attack himself. That he would have done so with dash and courage is indisputable; whether the plan itself stood much chance of success is doubtful. He did, however, manage to get into the thick of things as liaison officer to the King of the Belgians whose friend he had become when in command at Dover. In May 1940, he was with the Army fighting the Germans, only leaving the country when Belgium capitulated.

After Dunkirk when the Commandos were being formed Keyes' great wish of filling an active command was satisfied when he was appointed the first Chief of Combined Operations. It was a post in which his past experience could clearly be of great value, but he was a very famous, very senior officer; it

was difficult for his present superiors (and for him) to forge
it. Keyes was constantly trying not only to carry out policy
but to make it. Churchill had been largely responsible fo
the appointment, but before many months were past h
was forced kindly but firmly to get rid of his old friend
Keyes had frequently been at loggerheads with the Board o
Admiralty, the Chiefs of Staff and the Prime Minister him
self, but he had also succeeded in passing on a good deal o
his fiery offensive spirit and unquenchable optimism to th
young men of his command. His departure was genuinel'
regretted.

Shortly afterwards Keyes suffered a much more grievou
blow. Both his sons were serving, Geoffrey with the Com
mandos and young Roger as a Lieutenant R.N. Geoffrey, wh
had been awarded the M.C. and promoted acting Lieut.
Colonel at the age of twenty-four, was killed in an extremely
gallant attempt to kill or capture Rommel by raiding his Africar
headquarters. He was posthumously awarded the V.C., deniec
to his grandfather, and which his father, given the opportunity
might well have earned.

In 1943 Keyes was raised to the peerage as Baron Keyes o
Zeebrugge and Dover, a very fitting title. In 1944 he went of
on a goodwill mission to Australia and New Zealand on behal
of the Ministry of Information and managed, soon after his
seventy-second birthday, to be present at the American assaul
on Leyte in the Philippines as a guest of General Dougla:
MacArthur, watching from the bridge of a U.S. warship the
highly successful amphibious operation in which 60,000 mer
were landed on a single day. A neighbouring cruiser wa:
torpedoed and Keyes was "gassed" by the chemical smoke
screen laid down to cover her. He returned to England just
before V.E. Day, with his health seriously affected. For some
weeks his heart had been troublesome. He should have given
in, but had refused to do so. Now he was forced to take to
his bed. He died just after Christmas, full of courage to the
last.

On the thirty-second anniversary of Zeebrugge a tablet in

is memory and that of his gallant son was unveiled in Westminster Abbey. "In many ways," said Sir Winston Churchill
s he performed the ceremony, "Roger Keyes's spirit and
xample seem to revive in our stern and tragic age the vivid
personality and unconquerable dauntless soul of Nelson
himself."

BIBLIOGRAPHY

GENERAL

BARNABY, NATHANIEL: *Naval Development in the Century* (W. & R. Chambers, 1904).

BARTLETT, ELLIS ASHMEAD: *The Uncensored Dardanelles* (Hutchinson, 1928).

BEAVERBROOK, LORD: *Men and Power* (Hutchinson, 1956).

BELLAIRS, COMMANDER CARLYON, M.P.: *The Battle of Jutland* (Hodder & Stoughton, *circa* 1919).

BLAKE, ROBERT (editor): *The Private Papers of Douglas Haig* (Eyre & Spottiswoode, 1952).

BRIDGE, ADMIRAL SIR CYPRIAN: *Some Recollections* (John Murray, 1918).

CARR, WILLIAM GUY: *Brass Hats and Bell-Bottomed Trousers* (Hutchinson, 1939).

CHATFIELD, ADMIRAL OF THE FLEET LORD, P.C., G.C.B., O.M.: *The Navy and Defence* (Heinemann, 1942).

CHURCHILL, WINSTON S.: *The World Crisis* (Thornton Butterworth, 1923, 1927).

CLOWES, SIR WILLIAM LAIRD: *The Royal Navy, a History* (Sampson Low, 1897–1903).

CORBETT, SIR JULIAN S.: *Naval Operations* (Longmans Green, 1923).

Dardanelles Commission, First and Final Reports (H.M.S.O., 1917).

DAWSON, LIONEL: *Flotillas* (Rich & Cowan, 1933).

DEWAR, VICE-ADMIRAL, K.G.B., C.B.E.: *The Navy from Within* (Victor Gollancz, 1939).

DIVINE, DAVID: *Six Great Sailors* (Hamish Hamilton, 1955).

DOMVILLE, ADMIRAL SIR BARRY: *By and Large* (Hutchinson, 1936).

DORLING, CAPTAIN TAPRELL, D.S.O., R.N. ("Taffrail"): *Men o'War* (Phillip Allan, 1929).

DREYER, ADMIRAL SIR FREDERICK C.: *The Sea Heritage* (Museum Press, 1955).

"EXCUBITOR": *The Truth about the Navy* (Chapman & Hall, 1906).

FLEMING, PETER: *The Siege at Peking* (Rupert Hart-Davis, 1959).

FREMANTLE, ADMIRAL SIR SYDNEY ROBERT, G.C.B., M.V.O.: *My Naval Career, 1880–1928* (Hutchinson, 1949).

FROST, HOLLOWAY H.: *The Battle of Jutland* (United States Naval Institute, 1936).

FROTHINGHAM, THOMAS G.: *The Naval History of the World War 1914–15* (Harvard University Press, 1924).

——: *The Battle of Jutland* (Bacon & Brown, 1920).

GARBETT, CAPTAIN H., R.N.: *Naval Gunnery* (George Bell, 1897).

GRENFELL, CAPTAIN R. ("T 124"): *Sea Power* (Jonathan Cape, 1940).

GIBSON, LANGHORNE, AND HARPER, J. E. T.: *The Riddle of Jutland* (Cassell, 1934).

HARPER, REAR-ADMIRAL J. E. T.: *The Truth about Jutland* (John Murray, 1927).

HARRIS, ADMIRAL SIR ROBERT: *From Naval Cadet to Admiral* (Cassell, 1913).

JELLICOE, ADMIRAL OF THE FLEET LORD: *The Submarine Peril* (Cassell, 1934).

Jutland (Maps and Diagrams), Fifth War College Edition: September 1906 (Government Printing Office, Washington, 1927).

KERR, ADMIRAL MARK: *The Navy in my Time* (Rich & Cowan, 1933).

LEE, SIR SIDNEY: *King Edward VII. A Biography* (Macmillan, 1925).

LIPSCOMB, COMMANDER F. W.: *The British Submarine* (Adam & Charles Black, 1954).

LLOYD GEORGE, DAVID: *War Memoirs* (Ivor Nicholson & Watson, 1933).

London Gazette, supplement to, Tuesday, 20 October, 1914. Number 28948.

MANNING, FREDERICK: *The Life of Sir William White* (John Murray, 1923).

MARDER, ARTHUR J.: *Portrait of an Admiral* (Jonathan Cape, 1952).

Naval Review. Vol. XII. February, May, August and November 1924.

PARKES, OSCAR: *British Battleships* (Seeley Service, 1959).

PEARS, COMMANDER RANDOLPH: *British Battleships, 1892–1957* (Putnam, 1957).

ROYLE, CHARLES: *The Egyptian Campaigns, 1882–1899* (Hurst & Blackett, 1900).

SEYMOUR, ADMIRAL OF THE FLEET THE RT. HON. SIR EDWARD H.: *My Naval Career and Travels* (Smith & Elder, 1911).

"TAFFRAIL": *Endless Story* (Hodder & Stoughton, 1931).

VAGTS, DR ALFRED: *Landing Operations* (Military Publishing Co, Washington, 1946).

WEMYSS, LADY WESTER: *The Life and Letters of Lord Wester Wemyss* (Eyre & Spottiswoode, 1935).

YOUNG, COMMANDER R. TRAVERS, O.B.E.: *The House that Jack Built* (Gale & Polden, 1955).

CHAPTER ONE

KEPPEL, ADMIRAL OF THE FLEET SIR HENRY (the diaries in the National Maritime Museum).

——: *A Sailor's Life under Four Sovereigns* (Macmillan, 1899).

BROOKE, SIR JAMES, *The Private Letters of* (Richard Bentley, 1853).

JACOB, GERTRUDE L.: *The Raja of Sarawak* (Macmillan, 1876).

MONTAGU, REAR ADMIRAL THE HON. V. A.: *A Middy's Recollections, 1853–60* (A. & C. Black, 1898).

WEST, THE RT HON. SIR ALGERNON, G.C.B.: *Memoirs of Sir Henry Keppel* (Smith & Elder, 1905).

CHAPTER TWO

BRADFORD, ADMIRAL SIR EDWARD E., K.C.B., C.V.O.: *Life of Admiral of the Fleet Sir Arthur Knyvet Wilson* (John Murray, 1923).

CHAPTER THREE

BERESFORD, ADMIRAL LORD CHARLES: *The Memoirs* (Methuen, 1914).

——: "Autobiography" in *Nash's Magazine*.

——: "The Naval Outlook. Mr Churchill's Promises and Performances" in *The Empire Review*, November 1913.

——: *The Betrayal* (P. S. King, 1912).

"EXCUBITOR": "Lord Charles Beresford as a Naval Expert" in *Fortnightly Review*, August 1909.

WILSON, COLONEL SIR CHARLES: *Korti to Khartum* (William Blackwood, 1835).

CHAPTER FOUR

FISHER, ADMIRAL OF THE FLEET LORD: *Memories* (Hodder & Stoughton, 1919).

——: *Lord Fisher on the Navy.* A series of articles reprinted from *The Times* of September 1919. (Hodder & Stoughton, 1919.)

BACON, ADMIRAL SIR R. H.: *Life of Lord Fisher of Kilverstone* (Hodder & Stoughton, 1929).

MARDER, ARTHUR J.: *Fear God and Dread Nought* (Jonathan Cape, 1956)

CHAPTER FIVE

SCOTT, ADMIRAL SIR PERCY: *Fifty Years in the Royal Navy* (John Murray, 1919).

CHAPTER SIX

JELLICOE, ADMIRAL VISCOUNT, OF SCAPA: *The Grand Fleet* (Cassell 1919).

ALTHAM, CAPTAIN E., C.B., R.N.: *Jellicoe* (Blackie, 1938).

APPLIN, ARTHUR: *Admiral Jellicoe* (C. Arthur Pearson, 1915).

BACON, ADMIRAL SIR REGINALD: *The Life of John Rushworth Ear Jellicoe* (Cassell, 1936).

CHAPTER SEVEN

CHALMERS, REAR-ADMIRAL E. S., C.B.E., D.S.C.: *David, Earl Beatt* (Hodder & Stoughton, 1951).

RAWSON, GEOFFREY: *Earl Beatty* (Jarrolds, 1930).

SEYMOUR, LADY: *Life and Letters of Commander Ralph Seymour, R.N* (University Press, Glasgow, 1926).

YOUNG, FILSON: *With the Battle Cruisers* (Cassell, 1921).

CHAPTER EIGHT

GWYNN, MAJOR-GENERAL SIR CHARLES W., K.C.B., C.M.G., D.S.O.: *Imperial Policing* (Macmillan, 1934).

KNIGHT, E. F.: *Harwich Naval Forces* (Hodder & Stoughton, 1919).

LAVERTON, RONALD H.: *General Gort* (Pilot Press, 1939).

LIU, F. F.: *A Military History of Modern China* (Princeton University Press, 1956).

O'MALLEY, SIR OWEN, K.C.M.G.: *The Phantom Caravan* (John Murray 1954).

TONG, HOLLINGTON K.: *Chiang Kai-Shek* (Hurst & Blackett, 1938).

VAN FOREEST, JHR H. A., Royal Netherlands Navy: *Commodore Tyr whitt*, translated by the Admiralty and reprinted from Marineblad Part 5 1937 and Parts 1 & 2, 1938.

WOOLLARD, COMMANDER CLAUDE L. A., R.N., F.R.G.S.: *With Harwic. Naval Forces 1914–1918 or under Commodore Tyrwhitt in the Nort. Sea* (Geo. Kohler, Antwerp).

CHAPTER NINE

KEYES, ADMIRAL OF THE FLEET LORD: *Adventures Ashore and Afloat* (Harrap, 1939).

——: *The Naval Memoirs.* Vol. I, 1910–1915, Vol. II, 1916–1918 (Thornton Butterworth, 1934).

——: *Amphibious Warfare and Combined Operations* (Cambridge University Press, 1943).

ASPINALL-OGLANDER, BRIGADIER C.: *Roger Keyes* (The Hogarth Press, 1951).

CARPENTER, CAPTAIN A. F. B., V.C., R.N.: *The Blocking of Zeebrugge* (Herbert Jenkins, 1922).

CRISMAN, HERMAN HENRY: *Naval Operations in the Mediterranean during the Great War 1914–1918* (Dissertation for Ph.D. at Stanford University, May 1931).

HAMILTON, GENERAL SIR IAN: *Gallipoli Diary* (Doran Company, 1920).

MOOREHEAD, ALAN: *Gallipoli* (Hamish Hamilton, 1956).

NORTH, JOHN: *Gallipoli, The Fading Vision* (Faber & Faber, 1936).

PULESTON, CAPTAIN W. D., U.S.N.: *The Dardanelles Expedition* (United States Naval Institute, 1926).

SANDERS, GENERAL LIMAN VON: *Five Years in Turkey* (United States Naval Institute, 1927).

TERRY, C. SANDFORD (Ed.): *Zeebrugge and Ostend Despatches* (Oxford University Press, 1919).

INDEX

Abu Klea, H.M.S., 212
Addison, Commander P., 295
Admiralty, the, and iron-clad ships, 40; and water-tube boilers, 49–50; the First Sea Lord and, 57–60; and the War Office, 58, 96; and Beresford, 66–7, 79–80, 89, 129; its new Intelligence Department, 80; under Fisher, 110, 111 ff.; lacks a War Staff, 130; and gunnery developments, 144, 156–7, 161; approves Jellicoe's tactics, 185; and the Battle of Jutland, 187, 189; Lloyd George and, 202; and the shelling of Lowestoft, 187, 263–4; and the Dardanelles operation, 300, 302, 308, 313
Aerial warfare, Scott and, 162, 164; Tyrwhitt and, 258–60
Agadir, 58
Alacrity, H.M.S., 293
Alexandria, bombardment of, 68, 69–70, 99–100, 146
Alexandra, H.M.S., 210, 245–6
Alison, Major-General Sir Archibald, 146, 147
Allen Mr, M.P., and the water-tube boiler, 49
Anson, Lord, 19
Arabi Pasha, 43, 67–70, 99, 146
Arbuthnot, Rear-Admiral Sir Robert, 167
Arethusa, H.M.S., 225, 256–8, 262
Argyle, H.M.S., 125, 158
Armstrong, Whitworth and Co., 101
Army, the, and the Dardanelles operation, 299, 300, 302, 309–13
Arrogant, H.M.S., 219

Asquith, H. H., 55–6, 58, 128, 138–9, 299, 310–11 and n.
Astrea, H.M.S., 144
Atbara, Battle of, 214
Attentive, H.M.S., 254
Audacious, H.M.S., 182

Bacon, Admiral Sir R. H., and the effect of Fisher's reforms, 118, 131; on Fisher, 132; commands the Dover Patrol, 314–15, 316
Balfour, A. J., 163, 200
Barfleur, H.M.S., in China, 215, 216, 290, 292, 293
Barham, H.M.S., at Jutland, 187, 190
Bartlett, Ellis Ashmead, on de Robeck, 310
Barton, Sir Sidney, 277
Battenberg, Admiral Prince Louis of, 113, 131; and the threat of war, 169
Bayley, Captain E. H., 216
Beatty, Admiral of the Fleet, Lord, xiii, 185, 244, 245, 247, 316; on the need for bases, 182; and the Battle of Jutland, 187–95, 234–7, 270; Fisher and, 199–200, 232; his battle-cruisers, 207; succeeds Jellicoe as C.-in-C., Grand Fleet, 208, 237; his early life, 208–11; in the Sudan and Egypt, 212–15; and the Boxer Rising, 215–18, 289, 292–3; his marriage, 218, 220–2, 224, 233, 241–2; and the study of war, 219, 220, 224; Rear-Admiral, 222; Commander of the Battle-Cruisers, 223 ff.; at the Battle of Heligoland, 225–7, 257; at the Battle of Dogger

334

El Teb, Battle of, 46–7

Enchantress, H.M.S., 134, 135

Esdaile, Midshipman, 217

Esher, Lord, 131

Excellent, H.M.S., Gunnery School, Wilson and, 41, 42; Fisher and, 94, 96, 97, 100–1; Scott and, 143–4, 147–8, 149, 156–7; Jellicoe and, 172

Falkland Islands, Battle of, 228

Fame, H.M.S., 288–94

Fateh, H.M.S., 214

Firedrake, H.M.S., 297

Fisher, Admiral of the Fleet Lord, xiii, 34, 60, 81; early years, 41, 90–5; Captain of *Vernon*, 41–3, 97; in Egypt, 43, 44, 69, 99–100, 146; Director of Naval Ordnance, 48, 96, 101; his dispute with Beresford, 55–6, 83–6, 88–9, 111, 119 ff., 128–31; Second Sea Lord, 86, 106; his Selborne Scheme, 86, 106–7, 109; First Sea Lord, 87, 108 ff., 177–8, 298; Admiral of the Fleet, 88; on the China station, 92–3; his character, 92–5, 96, 98–9, 103–4, 112, 117, 126; appointed to *Excellent*, 94, 96, 97, 100–1, 148, 172; his marriage, 95; his work for the Navy, 95–6, 102–3, 104, 116–17, 134–5, 167; Admiral Superintendent H.M. Dockyard, 101–2; Third Sea Lord, 102–3; at the Hague Naval Conference, 104; C.-in-C., Mediterranean, 104, 106, 117, 251; C.-in-C., Portsmouth, 107, 113; his redistribution of the Fleet, 109–10, 120; and the building of *Dreadnought*, 112–15; and *Invincible*, 115–16; his lack of discretion, 117–19, 126, 130–2; and the Navy Scare, 127; and a Naval War Staff, 130; created a Baron, 132–3; his influence

on Churchill, 134–5, 170; recalled as First Sea Lord, 1914, 136; and the Dardanelles, 137–9, 299, 309, 310; his resignation and last days, 139–41, 310; Scott and, 156–60, 163; and Jellicoe, 170, 172, 173, 174, 200; and the Battle of Jutland, 199; and the Battle of Dogger Bank, 232; and Keyes, 296, 298–9

Foley, Captain, 171

Forte, H.M.S., 142

Frauenlob, S.M.S., 256

French Navy, xi, 110; introduces armour-plating, 39; her Dreadnoughts, 116; at the Dardanelles operation, 304–5, 311

Fripp, Sir Alfred, 274

Frost, H. H., on Jellicoe, 198–9

Froude, R. E., 114 n.

Furious, H.M.S., 94

Galatea, H.M.S., 65; at Jutland, 189

Gallipoli, 300; landings in, 310–11, 312, 314

Gard, W. H., 114 n.

Gaselee, General Sir Alfred, 293

Gaulois, the, 304

Geddes, Sir Eric, supersedes Carson, 203; and the U-boat menace, 314, 315

George V, 168, 205, 243; and Keppel, 33–4; and Fisher's reforms, 118, 131; and Tyrwhitt, 273, 275–6

German Navy, expansion of, 50, 58, 111; her Dreadnoughts, 116; the Navy Scare and, 127; in World War I, 136, 181, 185–6, 187, 257; adopts director firing, 161; at the Kiel Canal opening, 168; bombards Lowestoft, 187, 263–8; at Jutland, 187–98, 234–6; attacks merchant shipping, 201; at Heligoland, 225–7, 256–7; at Dogger Bank, 228–

Torpedo, the, invention of, 42; Wilson and, 48; Fisher and, 97
Trafalgar, H.M.S., 211
Tree, Ethel, Beatty and, 215, 218, 220–2; *see also under* Beatty
Trenchard–Keyes Agreement, 323
Tribune, H.M.S., 65
Trinkitat, 44–7
Triumph, H.M.S., 311
"Truth about the Navy," xii, 81
Tryon, Admiral Sir George, 173
Turkey, enters the war, 299; and the Dardanelles operation, 301, 303, 304, 307–8, 310, 312
Tweed, H.M.S., 19, 22, 27
Tweedmouth, Lord, 120–1
Tyrwhitt, Admiral of the Fleet Sir Reginald Yorke, xiii, 187; at the Battle of Heligoland, 225–6, 256–7; at the Battle of Dogger Bank, 228, 258; early life, 244–7; commands T.B. No. 78 in Newfoundland, 247–9; in Central America, 249–50; in Martinique, 251–2; his engagement and marriage, 252–4, 262–3, 273–4, 275–6; appointed Commodore Torpedo-Craft, 254; and the Harwich Force, 254, 255–72, 286; his character and appearance, 254–5, 261, 273, 276; and aerial warfare, 258–60; and Churchill, 260–2, 280; and the bombardment of Lowestoft, 262–9; misses the Battle of Jutland, 270; promoted Admiral, 272–3; and George V, 275–6; C.-in-C., China Station, 276–84; protects Shanghai, 278–83; C.-in-C., the Nore, 285; and the Invergordon Mutiny, 285; and Zeebrugge, 316

U-boats, 227; at Jutland, 187–8; and British merchant shipping, 201 and n.; in the Dardanelles, 311; their North Sea bases, 314, 323; Keyes and the battle against, 315 ff.
Undaunted, H.M.S., 82
United States, 279; her Dreadnoughts, 116; her entry into World War I, 202; her battle-squadron, 238

Von der Tann, S.M.S., 234
Vavasseur, Josiah, 101
Vernon, H.M.S., Wilson and, 41–2, 48; Fisher and, 97
Victoria, Queen, 99, 100, 288
Victoria, H.M.S., 17; rammed by *Camperdown*, 124, 173–4, 196, 211
Victoria and Albert, H.M.S. (Royal Yacht), 211, 247, 288
Victory, H.M.S., 17, 91, 107
Vindictive, H.M.S., at Zeebrugge, 320–2
von Sanders, General Liman, and the Gallipoli landings, 310, 312
von Spee, Admiral, 136, 228

Walcott, Captain C. C., 217
Wales, Prince of, *see* Edward VII *and* George V
War Cabinet, Jellicoe and, 200, 201
War Office, and the Admiralty, 58, 96; Fisher and, 107–8; and anti-aircraft, 163
Warden, Mrs Edmund, 92
Warrender, Admiral Sir George, 228
Warrior, H.M.S., 40, 95
Warwick, H.M.S., 319, 322
Washington Conference, 1921, 240
Watts, Philip, 114 n.
Wemyss, Rear-Admiral, and the Dardanelles operation, 303, 311, 313, 314
Westmacott, Lieutenant, 256
Whale Island, converted into a Gunnery School, 148, 149–50
Whitehead, Robert, 42, 97
Whiting, H.M.S., in China, 290–1